SHŌWA

An Inside History of Hirohito's Japan

SHŌWA.

An Inside History of Hirohito's Japan.

Tessa Morris-Suzuki

THE ATHLONE PRESS
London

First published 1984 by The Athlone Press Ltd
44 Bedford Row, London WC1R 4LY

© Tessa Morris-Suzuki, 1984

British Library Cataloguing in Publication Data
Morris-Suzuki, T.
    Shōwa: An Inside History of Hirohito's Japan
    1. Japan – History – Shōwa period, 1926–
    I. Title   II. Saitō, Mutsuo
    III. Tsutsumi, Ayako
    IV. Iida, Momo
    ISBN 0-485-11246-9

Printed in Great Britain by
St Edmundsbury Press, Bury St Edmunds

Contents

Acknowledgements

The writing of this book would not have been possible without the generous help of many people. Thanks must go first and foremost to Saitō Mutsuo, Tsutsumi Ayako and Iida Momo for their patient and illuminating responses to lengthy interviews which at times touched on deeply personal subjects. The three people around whose lives this book is constructed were selected after preliminary interviews with twenty-four people born at the beginning of the Shōwa age. These other interviews, although not quoted here, provided many vital insights into events described in the book, and I should like to give my thanks to all the interviewees involved.

The friends of Japan, Britain and Australia who have assisted in the genesis of the book are so many that it is impossible to name them all here, but my special thanks go to Shimamoto Shuji of Shōgakkan Publishing Co., Ogawa Taku of Eva Press International, and Toshikawa Takao of the *Weekly Post*; also to Jenny Weissel and Barbara Marshall for typing and to Hiroshi for proof-reading the manuscript.

Note on Japanese Names and Spelling

In this book names are presented in the normal Japanese fashion, i.e., surname first and given name second. The only exception to this rule are in the cases of English-language quotations or bibliographical references where the order is reversed in the original.

Macrons have been placed to indicate all long vowels, except in the case of geographical names which are well known to the Western reader: e.g. Tokyo has been left in the normal Western spelling rather than being written in the linguistically correct but visualy disturbing form Tōkyō.

Chronology of the Shōwa Age

1926 25 December Death of Emperor Taishō and succession of Hirohito. Beginning of the Shōwa Age.

1931 18 September Japanese Kwantung Army seizes control of Manchuria.

1932 1 March Creation of 'Manchukuo'.

15 May Attempted *coup d'état* by junior military officers ('May 15th Incident').

1933 27 March Japan withdraws from League of Nations.

23 December Birth of Crown Prince Akihito.

1936 26 February Attempted *coup d'état* by right-wing military elements ('February 26th Incident').

1937 7 July Outbreak of war between Japan and China ('Marco Polo Bridge Incident').

13 December Japanese capture of Nanking.

1939 1 September Outbreak of war in Europe.

1940 27 September Japan signs Axis Treaty with Germany and Italy.

1941 8 December Outbreak of Pacific War.

1942 2 January Japan occupies Manila.

15 January Japan occupies Singapore.

30 April Japanese general election.

5 June Battle of Midway.

1943 1–8 February Japanese withdrawal from Guadalcanal.

1944 8 March Beginning of Imphal Campaign.

20 October US landing on Leyte.

25 October First attack by Japanese naval suicide squadron.

1 November First attack by US B-29 bomber on Tokyo.

1945 1 April US landing on Okinawa.
      26 July Potsdam Declaration issued.
      6 August Atomic bombing of Hiroshima.
      8 August Soviet Union declares war on Japan.
      9 August Atomic bombing of Nagasaki.
      15 August Japanese surrender announced.

1946 30 August Arrival of General Douglas MacArthur at Atsugi Naval Air Base.

1946 15 January Emperor's 'Human Being Declaration' (*Ningen Sengen*).
      10 April First election under post-war electoral system.
      3 November New Japanese constitution promulgated.

1947 31 January GHQ bars General Strike planned for 1 February (*2.1 Zenesto*).

1948 23 December Tōjō Hideki and six other prominent wartime figures executed for war crimes.

1949 7 March American economic adviser Joseph Dodge announces new stringent fiscal guidelines for Japan.

1950 February Beginning of purge of suspected communist sympathizers from public service positions (the 'Red Purge').
      25 June Outbreak of Korean War.
      8 October National Police Reserve (*Keisatsu Yobitai*) established.

1951 8 September San Francisco Peace Treaty signed, ending US occupation of Japan.

1953 27 July Korean armistice signed.

1956 18 December Japan admitted to United Nations.

1959 11 December Beginning of Mitsui Miike miners' strike.

1960 19–20 May Ratification of Mutual Security Treaty with the United States.
      5 September Prime Minister Ikeda announces national 'Income Doubling Plan'.

1964 10 October Tokyo Olympic Games opened.

1967 8 October Mass demonstration at Haneda Airport against Japan's support for US involvement in Vietnam.

1968 June–January 18th 1969 Occupation of Tokyo University campus by protesting students.

1969 10 June Japan's Economic Planning Agency announces that in
previous year Japan's GNP was second largest in the 'free
world'.

1970 4 March Opening of international Expo in Osaka.

22 June Mutual Security Treaty with USA automatically
renewed.

25 November Attempted coup and suicide of Mishima Yukio.

1971 16 August Nixon announces suspension of US dollar's convertibility to gold ('Nixon Shock').

1972 15 May Formal return of Okinawa to Japanese control.

1973 October Beginning of first oil crisis.

1975 2 April Investigation of Lockheed bribery case in Japan
begins.

1978 12 August Japan–China Peace and Friendship Treaty signed.

1983 10 December Ex-Prime Minister Tanaka found guilty by
lower court on charges arising from the Lockheed Affair.

Preface

In Japan years are traditionally numbered, not from a fixed religious or historical event, but from the beginning of each emperor's reign. Each reign in turn has its own name: a name expressing the hopes of a new era. The reign of the Emperor Hirohito, which began in December 1926, was given the title Shōwa – Radiant Peace.

The Shōwa Age has spanned a whole generation. Not only that, it has also spanned a period of momentous upheaval in Japanese history. For many outside observers, the developments of the period have been perplexing, contradictory and often alarming.

In the West, the popular image of Japan which has developed over the past fifty-five years seems to consist of three layers. The oldest and most deeply buried stratum is the image of 'traditional Japan' – country of cherry-blossom and snow-capped mountains, of paper fans and miniature trees and Madam Butterflies. The image which was superimposed upon this by the first twenty years of the Shōwa period is in savage contrast. It is a picture of militarism, fanaticism and brutality – of prison camps and *kamikaze* pilots and death for the emperor. The third image is that created by Japan's post-war economic success. Although less negative than the wartime picture, it is still a slightly disturbing one. It is an image of affluence and conformity, of electronic gadgets and bespectacled businessmen, of robot-like efficiency and overcrowded trains.

Of course, there are many books which penetrate beyond these caricature images – which analyse the workings of various aspects of Japanese society, or which explore the social and economic forces underlying Japan's modern history. The gap in understanding between Japan and the West is not the result of any lack of such political, historical or sociological studies. But what is perhaps lacking is a feeling of the way in which the historical events, the patterns of social relationship, the conflicting images, are strung together into the complex but coherent entities of human lives. There is a form of understanding which we subconsciously bring with us when we study recent European or American history. That is, the understanding of history as it has been experienced by ordinary people, which we absorb through our own memories, or from photograph albums and family legends, from novels and biographies, from film and television. It is this knowledge which fills in the human faces behind the social trends. And it was this knowledge that I was looking for – partly for my own interest, although I hope that it will also be of interest and use to other Western readers – when I set out to write a book about the Shōwa Age in Japan.

The book examines Japan's modern history as seen from within, through the eyes of the 'Shōwa generation'. It is based on the statements of three Japanese people whose memories begin from the early years of Shōwa. All three grew up during the decade when militarism and nationalism were strengthening their hold on Japan. They came of age during the Pacific War; their twenties were spent during the humiliating period of occupation and poverty which followed Japan's defeat, and as adults they have participated in the post-war 'economic miracle'. They are now approaching the peaks of their various and very different careers.

All the people and events in this book are real. The three central figures are of dissimilar backgrounds and characters, and so indicate some of the diversity of experiences contained by the Shōwa period, but none of the three is intended to be 'typical' of his or her nation, social position or generation. They are all individuals, and the interest of their stories lies largely in their individual and distinct personalities.

In recording their memories, I do not expect to prove any theories or provide any simple explanation of the nature of Japanese society. But by letting the three lives speak for themselves, I hope to cut through some of the Western stereotypes of Japan, and to show how the dreams of leaders, the wars, the treaties, the pronouncements and the power-struggle are converted into the common currency of daily life.

1

Shōwa

During the course of 7 February 1927, a huge crowd began to assemble in central Tokyo. It is estimated that as many as two million people may have lined the streets which led from the gates of the Imperial Palace, past the towering modern parliament building, through the business centre of Toranomon and the fashionable residential areas beyond, to the edge of Shinjuku Gardens. Some had come from remote parts of Japan and its overseas empire. Many stood in the bitter cold from early in the morning until well after dark. They were waiting to see one of the oldest ceremonies in the world.

Not that its ancient origins were immediately apparent. The first sign that anything was happening was the firing of a cannon shortly after sunset. Then, by torchlight, a long procession began to wind its way from the gates of the palace. At the head and rear of the procession marched the police inspectors, smartly uniformed representatives of an increasingly powerful force modelled on the German system. Next to them came contingents from the army and the navy, with their military brass bands performing suitably solemn music. In the centre of the procession came the members of the imperial family, the frock-coated politicians, the court officials and the foreign diplomats – not only from American and Britain, France and Germany, but also from the Soviet Union, Chile, Turkey, Siam – their presence testifying to Japan's growing importance in international affairs.

At the heart of it all was the imperial catafalque, flanked by bearers with chests containing the personal effects of the emperor, furniture, clothes and food. It is the discovery of such items, together with the mirror, sword and jewel – emblems of imperial rule – in grave-mounds dating back to the fourth and fifth centuries AD, which provides the earliest tangible evidence of the rule of emperors in Japan. So, in the midst of that mingling of East and West, that fusion of tradition and modernity which has so bemused and fascinated observers of Japanese culture in the twentieth century, the body of the Emperor Taishō was carried on the first stage of its journey to a mausoleum in the hills outside Tokyo.[1]

The crowds which watched the ceremony reflected, like the procession itself, the cross-currents of tradition and change. In the best positions, on chairs set out for the occasion, sat the representatives of Japan's old and new rich classes: the marquises, viscounts and barons of the new aristocracy (created as a replacement for the old feudal nobility in the 1880s); the landowners and factory owners, the bureaucrats and bankers; and beside them those members of the foreign community who were not exalted enough to walk in the procession. Behind them swarmed the masses of factory workers enjoying a day off work; family groups of farmers up from the country; orderly ranks of *yakuza* (gangsters), noted for their nationalist fervour, and recognizable by their loose *happi* jackets emblazoned with the gang's insignia; and among them, the urban employed and semi-employed for whom an occasion like this provided a chance to earn a little money selling mourning badges or commemorative pamphlets. More than five hundred people were injured in the crush, and one elderly peasant fell into a drain and froze to death.

One might have imagined, from the throngs of mourners, that this was the funeral of a great charismatic leader, a military hero, a popular reformer or a builder of empires. In fact, the Emperor Yoshihito, who is better known by his reign-name of Taishō or Great Righteousness, was an obscure and somewhat pathetic figure. The son of one of the Emperor Meiji's many court concubines (for the sons of imperial mistresses were eligible to succeed to the title, although daughters, legitimate or otherwise, were not), he seemed to have inherited none of his father's considerable political acumen. Behind the strained phrases of their formal eulogies, it is possible to detect the fact that the obituary writers could find very little to say about him at all. One recalled that the late emperor had once addressed some kind words to two common soldiers on a military manoeuvre which he was inspecting. Another described how a former army minister had been astonished and overwhelmed when he awoke from a nap on a summer's afternoon to find that the emperor had dropped in for tea. All slid gently and gracefully over

the fact that in 1919, at the age of forty, the emperor had suffered a
mental breakdown from which he never recovered, and his official
functions had been taken over by his eldest son, Crown Prince
Hirohito.

Yet in some senses the lack of personal achievements was unim-
portant. The historical function of the Japanese *Tennō*, to use the
correct word, was not strictly analogous to that of Western, or even
of Chinese, emperors, and strong personalities or great deeds were
the exception rather than the rule. Indeed it seems probable that the
earliest *Tennō* were chosen from a family whose relative unassertive-
ness, combined with the control of certain religious rituals, enabled
it to be accepted as a symbol of unity by other more powerful and
warlike clans. Although from time to time aristocratic factions had
tried to increase the *Tennō*'s political powers in order to advance
their own interests, the role had continued to be essentially a ritual
and a symbolic one. It was because the sacred authority of the *Tennō*
was from the very beginning separate from the intrigue and excitement of actual power that Japan was the only country in which a
single family had reigned in unbroken succession for more than
fifteen hundred years.

With the influx of Western ideas into Japan from the late 1860s
onwards, the concept of *Tennō* had undergone certain changes. In
part, Japan's rulers reacted against the threat of foreign physical and
spiritual domination by reasserting the power of their unique
national symbol, the *Tennō*. In part, the concept of *Tennō* became
fused with the Western concept of emperor, with all its associations
of Caesar and Frederick the Great, Napoleon and Kaiser Wilhelm.
These new trends had affected the role of Taishō *Tennō*'s father, the
Emperor Meiji, and were to affect those of his son, Hirohito, but in
the ailing and simple-minded Emperor Taishō one can see a
temporary reversion to an older tradition, in which the *Tennō*'s title
was everything, and his personality nothing.

The crowds who gathered on 7 February 1927 were therefore
commemorating, not the death of a man, but the passing of an era.
Japanese emperors are not crowned or enthroned in public: the only
formal mark of Hirohito's accession was a religious ritual of purifica-
tion which would not take place until two years of mourning for his
father were complete. The death of the Emperor Taishō and his
succession by Emperor Hirohito, which had occurred quietly in the
early hours of Christmas Day 1926, had been so long expected that it

had been greeted in the end with a sense of resignation, almost of anticlimax. For most people, therefore, the state funeral, with its ancient associations and torchlit pageantry, provided the best occasion to mark the end of the Taishō age and the beginning of the new reign, which was to receive the official title of Shōwa – Radiant Peace.

The Taishō Era, although it had not seen such dramatic and rapid changes as the preceding Meiji Era, had none the less been an important phase in Japan's modernization and development. Later it was to be seen retrospectively as an age of comparative peace and prosperity, and 'Taishō democracy' was to be remembered in nostalgic contrast to what followed. But it requires a certain distance to lend such enchantment to the view, and it is unlikely that many of those who, in 1927, cast their minds back to the previous imperial funeral, that of the Emperor Meiji in 1912, saw the intervening years in quite such a rosy light.

The most fundamentally important development of the past fifteen years had been the continuing rapid growth of Japanese industry. During the Taishō Era the output of Japan's manufacturing industry increased about two-and-a-half fold – this in spite of the terrible Kantō earthquake of 1923, which had destroyed most of the industrial areas of Tokyo and Yokohama and left about 150,000 people dead. There can be little doubt that industrial development had brought very real benefits to many people, although not on an equal scale to all. Wages had been rising faster than prices – more than half as fast again during the past ten years – and one foreign journalist, summing up the achievements of the reign, wrote: 'Japan is no longer a country where labour is cheap'. Factory workers and coal miners could now afford to set aside a share of their wages for *sake* (rice wine) and cigarettes, although the cost of the police presence at the imperial funeral alone, put at over ¥305,000, would have fed and clothed five hundred miners' families for a year. Even in the countryside, although incomes were lagging behind industrial wages, a gradual increase in prosperity was altering tastes and customs. As one observer wrote, in somewhat shocked tones:

Mere tenant-farmers . . . will drink beer and smoke *Shikishima* (a brand of cigarette) and some of them will even go round the fields on bicycles . . . According to the proprietor of a certain big firm in Tokyo, when he was a boy, the bicycle was an article of luxury

4

reserved for the exlusive use of the master, and if an errand boy should be so indiscreet as to use it, he was sure to catch it badly. But things have so changed that errand boys now would get a scolding if they do their round on foot instead of on a bicycle. So cheap have bicycles become and so dear has labour become.[2]

Some side-effects of industrialization were even more shocking, at least to Japan's growing middle classes. In a country where nearly three hundred daily newspapers reached a total readership of six million people, and where foreign news received comprehensive coverage, the British General Strike of 1926 had caused ripples of concern. Could similar events happen in Japan, and if they did, what would their outcome be? Japan's first trade-union federation, founded in 1919, was still a comparatively weak body, but fears of growing radicalism among the workforce were very real. The bitterness of industrial conflict in circumstances where traditions of unionism and negotiation were not well established can be seen in the events which took place at the Toyoda weaving mill in Osaka during the final year of the Taishō Era. In the autumn of 1925, workers at the mill had gone on strike to demand the institution of a pension scheme by the company. The management agreed to set up the scheme within three months, and the strikers went back to work. But when the three months were up the company, far from announcing the promised pension scheme, closed the factory and dismissed the entire workforce. Resentment at this action came to a head in November 1926, when three of the sacked workers broke into the home of the mill's president and, finding him absent, assaulted his son and another mill manager, leaving both seriously injured. All three workers were sent to prison.

These troubling undercurrents in Japanese society were reflected in a strange, intangible malaise which infected political affairs. The great achievement of 'Taishō democracy' had been the institution of universal manhood suffrage in 1925. But although this produced a proliferation of new liberal and left-wing parties, power remained in the hands of the two conservative groupings which had emerged as slightly degenerate heirs to the great political reformers of the Meiji Era. Riven by factionalism, and increasingly enmeshed in accusations and counter-accusations of corruption and scandal, neither of these parties seemed able to come to terms with the real political issues of the day: the worsening international economic situation, demands for land reforms in the country and for social reforms in the cities.

Fears of radicalism produced sinister manifestations. The Taishō Era, which saw the introduction of the principle of One Man (but not One Woman) One Vote, also saw the introduction of measures designed to prevent the dissemination of 'dangerous thoughts' in Japanese schools and colleges. These were intended to control the teaching of the unproductive and pernicious social sciences, and particularly the ideas of Karl Marx and his followers. The police who were responsible for enforcing these measures, however, had little understanding of the niceties of academic debate, and caused a good deal of hostility by their haphazard harassment of anyone using what appeared to be radical terminology. As often happens in societies where established values are threatened, the power of the police was becoming greater and more obtrusive. The newspapers of the period carried a growing number of reports of unexplained deaths in police custody, and within two years of Hirohito's succession, the powers to suppress 'dangerous thoughts' were to be put to a new and more significant use: after the elections of 1928 many Japanese left-wingers, including most members of the small but expanding Japanese Communist Party, were rounded up and imprisoned.

In international as well as domestic affairs the reign of the Emperor Taishō had brought rapid advances, but also new and intractable problems. Through its support for the Allies in the First World War, Japan had extended its overseas empire. Now, as well as its first colonies – Taiwan and Korea – Japan held mandates over the Caroline, Mariana and Marshall Islands in the Pacific, and over the Shantung Peninsula in China. But each expansion brought widening areas of vulnerability: new economic interests to be protected, new borders to defend. Already there were many forces within Japan pressing for a more 'active' policy on the Asian mainland, and sections of the army were even arguing the need to separate Manchuria, where Japanese interests were heavily concentrated, from the rest of civil-war-torn China. But the old colonial nations were not entirely happy at Japan's new status in Asia. In Britain, Viscount Grey had chosen Armistice Day 1926 as the occasion for a widely publicized speech lamenting Europe's loss of military and moral superiority in the East, and arguing that Western nations should unite to reassert their power in Asia. Although its own empire was growing, Japan, as the first non-white nation to challenge the might of the West, could still serve as an inspiration to nationalist movements elsewhere in Asia in their struggle against Western colonialism. The first Pan-Asiatic Conference, opened in Nagasaki in the summer of 1926, brought delegates from India, China, the Philippines and even Turkey and Persia to hear the Japanese organizers call for the establishment of 'a real and permanent peace in the world based on the principle of equality and justice for all'. But none of this was taken too seriously by Western experts, who recognized that such woolly idealism bore little relation to Japan's real economic and military status in the region. And when, six months before the beginning of the Shōwa Era, a disgruntled right-wing American general warned that Japan had plans to attack the United States and invade the Philippines, his claims were, quite rightly, greeted with ridicule.

The mixture of hopes and fears which surrounded the beginning of the new era was expressed with surprising clarity in the Imperial Rescript issued to mark the accession of the Emperor Hirohito. Although this was a ceremonial occasion when very little of real political import was expected, the emperor referred in only slightly veiled terms to the current social problems besetting Japan. He mentioned the emergence of 'conflicting ideas' which resulted from recent changes in world affairs, and noted that 'the economic interests of the people are not always identical.' Speaking of the future, however, the emperor adopted a tone of cautious optimism. He hoped that all people would work together to promote the common interests and prosperity of the nation. Flippancy and levity were to be avoided, as was the slavish imitation of others (a reference to the haphazard borrowing of Western habits and fashions). Simplicity and originality were to be encouraged. On the other hand, the emperor spoke with some emphasis of the need to cultivate the spirit of universal brotherhood.

This theme was taken up by the press at home and abroad as they greeted the Shōwa Age. The Tokyo *Asahi Shimbun* saw the name as prophetic of brightness and serenity. It recalled Shintō mythology, comparing the succession of the new emperor in a time of trouble and national mourning to the moment when the Sun Goddess Amaterasu Ōmikami emerged from her cave to brighten the world. The *New York Times* noted that the new emperor, during his years as prince regent, had travelled abroad and mixed more freely with the people than any of his ancestors, and hoped that, in due course, he might create a system more nearly approaching the constitutional monarchy of England. In London, the *Oberserver* paid tribute to the late emperor, and concluded by offering good wishes to his successor. 'May his reign be long, pacific and prosperous!' Few platitudes could have provided such a striking combination of the inappropriate and the prophetic.

History books and biographies of the famous often begin with descriptions of great state occasions: royal funerals, coronations, weddings, anniversaries. These are the moments which bring together those in power, providing a fleeting snapshot image of a certain society at a certain time. The newspapers leave us ample documents of the occasions, while the events themselves tend to prompt reflections on the state of the nation, retrospective summaries of recent history and predictions for the future.

But always among these documents what captures the imagination is not the detail of the ceremonies and processions, but the curious, irrelevant items which fill the corners of the pages and which, more than anything else, convey the feeling of the age and the reality of forgotten existences. In the end, the descriptions of Emperor Taishō's funeral and the loyal greetings to the new era are less moving than the reports in the same newspaper of 'the arrival by the Korea-Maru, on her way to Manila, of a young woman weighing 783 pounds, and with a waist measurement considerably in excess of her height . . .';[3] or the news that 'Urawa police arrested Tange Motomaro, aged 20, on the 19th instant on a charge of having written on the wall of the Hikawa Shrine in that locality some treasonous remarks . . .'.[4] What did he write, and what became of him? But that is something which escaped the written record.

The purpose of this book is to recapture some of that other, unofficial history of the Shōwa Age. And for that it is necessary to go back, not to the formal inauguration of the era on 25 December 1926, but to another beginning; or rather to three separate beginnings on three historically insignificant dates.

Saitō Mutsuo was born on 21 March 1923, in the year of the Great Kantō Earthquake; Iida Momo on 10 January 1926, in the last year of the Taishō Age, the first of Shōwa. Tsutsumi Ayako was born on 20 April 1928, two months after the first general elections under the new franchise, but also at a time when hundreds of left-wing figures were being arrested for 'dangerous thoughts', and only weeks before the Manchurian war-lord Chang Tso-Lin was blown apart by a bomb planted on the orders of Japanese army officers.

Those years in themselves provide as good an introduction as any to the direction of the first decades of Shōwa.

In some respects the three lives described here are sharply contrasted: one began in the extreme poverty of rural Shikoku; one in a household just beginning to rise from poverty to prosperity in the back streets of Tokyo; one in the comfort of a provincial middle-class environment. But the accident of birth in 1920s Japan imposed on all three some kind of common pattern. First came the all-important progress up the ladder of the Japanese school system; then the wartime labour service; later the post-war hunger when every grain of rice was carefully counted, the shock of reversed values and discredited ideals, and the new prosperity of the 1960s and 1970s. Within this pattern the special interest lies in examining and understanding the ways in which three very different individuals have come to terms with the shared experience of life in a particularly critical phase of history: how children perceived life as members of the ruling race in Japan's colonial empire; how, in wartime, one chose to resist conscription, another faced the prospect of certain death as a suicide pilot; how as adults in the post-war world they have reconciled themselves to the overthrow of all that they had been brought up to believe in; how each chose between duties to family and the demands of political conscience or the desire for individual self-expression.

The Japanese historian Ienaga Saburō has written of the war period:

> Unless we look back at the decisions we made and consider whether we acted properly or not, we cannot lead a serious existence in the post-war world. In other words, I agree that the unexamined life is not worth living.[5]

The normal function of history is to analyse and divide the human experience, to render it into segments from which we can build a comprehensible total picture of societies and civilizations, of causes and effects. In this book I should like momentarily to reverse this process: to reconstitute the parts into the mysterious whole of human lives. By examining these lives it becomes possible, I believe, to comprehend the diverse ways in which crucial choices are made, opportunities accepted or disasters overcome; and in doing this, we may come to a better understanding, not only of the experience of life in Shōwa Japan, but also perhaps of our own position as individuals in the midst of history.

PART I

Growing Up – 1926 – 41

The Way here set forth is indeed the teaching bequeathed by Our Imperial Ancestors, to be observed alike by Their Descendants and the subjects, infallible for all ages and true in all places. (*Imperial Rescript on Education*)

2

Saitō Mutsuo

His first memory is of the wake. Suddenly, and for no apparent reason, the house was filled with guests. There were friends, relatives and strangers; people dressed in their smartest suits or in sombre, formal kimonos; people eating and drinking, and talking, as grown-ups do, in hushed and mystifying tones. To a small child it was a new and delightful experience. Never before had the house been so full of visitors, so full of kind faces bending down to smile at him, hands patting his head. He ran from group to group and from room to room until, in his excitement, he tripped and tumbled down the stairs, and his delight dissolved in bruises and tears.

Now, looking back, Saitō Mutsuo – a successful businessman nearing retiring age – can perceive this childhood image with an outsider's eye. He is a tall thin man, bespectacled, with thinning hair; a person with an air of dignity but with a face that creases often into a little, faintly self-mocking smile. He recalls his memories calmly, pensively, his voice only becoming slightly lower as he approaches a particularly painful moment. Somewhere in the background, the sliding screens of his small suburban house rattle as his wife comes, bringing cups of green tea, or goes in search of a photograph, a memento or a family document. With these to guide him, Saitō Mutsuo can locate his memories on the map of time and place. Events which, to a child's eye, seemed vast, all-encompassing and incomprehensible become ordered into the pattern of adult rationality. He understands now that this first, hazily recalled scene must have taken place in Maizuru, on the western coast of Japan, that the year must have been 1926, the first year of Shōwa, and that the occasion was the funeral of his mother. The mother whose face he could never afterwards picture had died of tuberculosis at the age of thirty-nine.

After that come the other obscure memories: another house, this time in the big industrial city of Osaka. There was a time of strange, chaotic freedom. Once his father had left for the office each morning the children – four-year-old Mutsuo, his brother Kōichi and his sisters Haruko and Yasuko – were alone with a girl who was scarcely more than a child herself. They were told that she was their nanny, but she seemed more like a big sister than a substitute mother. She joined their wild romps, their make-believe *Samurai* swordfights. Together they waged spinning-top battles, watching to see whose little whirling, wooden top was strong enough to knock the others' down. On fine winter days they went out to fly their kites or to practise their skills at balancing on bamboo stilts. And in the evening their father would return to find the house in chaos and the meals uncooked.

Sometimes Haruko would try to keep us in order. Being the eldest, after mother died, she seemed to feel somehow that she was responsible for the rest of us – almost a substitute mother. She was a strong character. She would only have been in sixth grade of primary school then – about thirteen – but she was a really strong character.

One day, I remember, Yasuko fell in the river. There was a river which flowed near our house in Osaka – well, it was more of a stream really, but it had a very strong, fast-flowing current. We children liked to play on the bank of the stream, and on this occasion Yasuko and I were playing there together, when she slipped into the stream, and the current began to carry her away. I was only about four at the time, so of course all I could do was scream. But Haruko – I think she'd been playing somewhere nearby – she came rushing up and leapt straight into the stream and pulled poor Yasuko out.

About this time, however, the pattern of life changed once more. Mutsuo's father was away from home for several weeks, and when he returned, he brought with him a 'new mother'. The marriage was an arranged one. Mutsuo's father had written to a relative asking him to find a young woman suitable to become his wife and the stepmother of his four children. This was not in itself unusual. *Omiai*, marriage arranged by a trusted friend or relative, was the rule rather than the exception in pre-war Japan, and is still common today.

What was unusual in the Saitōs' case, however, was the speed with which the match was arranged and completed. Their father had had enough of seeing the children run wild and the housework left undone. So instead of having a formal meeting with his prospective bride, and then spending several months becoming acquainted with her as would have been the normal practice, he relied on the good judgement of the go-between, and the photograph he had received in the post, and set off for his home town to meet and marry a woman he had never seen before, and who was just twelve years older than his eldest daughter.

I can't remember precisely when my stepmother arrived, but I do remember being told that a 'new mother' was coming, and being very excited about it. Of course, I think that the older children felt differently. They had a certain sense of resistance to this new-comer – not surprisingly, I suppose. There weren't any particular overt clashes, just a slight sense of tension. But on the whole it worked out well. Our family never had any of that friction that you sometimes get between step-parents and stepchildren. And of course Yasuko and I, who had virtually no memories of our own mother, were delighted at the arrival of the 'new mother'.

Mutsuo's stepmother, too, provided an element of stability in a childhood which was otherwise full of changes. Mutsuo's father, Kōsuke, had a good position in one of the handful of major insurance companies which had been set up in the late nineteenth century and which, since then, had grown with the growth of the Japanese economy. But jobs in such companies usually involved frequent transfers from one branch to another: in Kōsuke's case, from Sendai, where Mutsuo had been born, to Maizuru, from Maizuru to Osaka; and later to Kyoto and then overseas, to Japan's colonial possession of Taiwan.

His job had, incidently, almost cost him his life. For it took him to Tokyo on 1 September 1923, just six months after the birth of Mutsuo, on the day of the Great Kantō Earthquake.

Afterwards, when he recounted the events of that day to the children, what impressed them most was not the earthquake itself, but the horrors which followed. Their father had been unhurt in the 'quake, and his first instinct had been to find a way of getting home to Sendai, some 150 miles away, as quickly as possible. But even before he reached the station, the scale of the disaster became apparent. Not only were there no trains running, there were no railways for them to run on. A bridge near the station had collapsed into the river, and it was only when a temporary pontoon had been erected that Kōsuke could begin the journey on foot through mile after mile of devasted city to a place where normal life still continued.

A foreigner living in Japan at the time has left a vivid picture of the scene which confronted the survivors of the earthquake:

A deathly stillness had fallen, in which the scraping of our own feet sounded ghostly. Shattered fragments of buildings rose like distorted monuments from a sea of devastation beyond belief. Over everything had settled a thick, white dust, giving the ruins the semblance of infinite age; and through the yellow fog of dust, still in the air, a copper-coloured sun shone upon this silent havoc with sickly unreality . . . It was as if life had been blotted out – the end of the world.[1]

In districts where wooden houses were closely clustered together fires spread rapidly, burning to death many of those who had survived the initial disaster.

Through this apocalyptic landscape Kōsuke trudged, with no more than a vague sense of direction to guide him, and nowhere to shelter at night. The only food to be had was *suiton*, flour dumplings in soup, which was dished out to the dazed survivors from hastily-constructed soup-kitchens. From the ruins also there arose an ugly atmosphere of fear. There were rumours that communists were planning to take advantage of the chaos to seize power, that Korean nationalists had put poison in the remaining unpolluted wells. Gangs of young men roamed the streets, stopping passers-by, and on several occasions lynching those whose accents revealed Korean origin. Many notable left-wingers were rounded up by the police, and some were never seen alive again. It was not the end of the world, but it was perhaps the beginning of the end of the comparatively liberal and optimistic environment in which Saitō Kōsuke had come of age. Kōsuke eventually reached home safely, but never again for the rest of his life could he bear to eat *suiton*.

Many years later, when Mutsuo was in Sendai on a business trip, he looked for the house where he had been born, and to which his father had returned after the great earthquake, but found only a forest of office blocks, restaurants and bars, neon lights and department stores. What had once been a quiet residential district had been transformed, swallowed up in the prosperity of post-war Japan.

In April 1930, at the age of seven, Saitō Mutsuo entered primary school. By now the family had moved again, this time to a seaside town on the southern outskirts of Osaka. Japanese children at that time attended primary school for six years, from the age of seven to thirteen, so for the first year the three younger Saitō children went to school together.

Haruko was already at Girls' School, which lasted from the age of thirteen to seventeen or eighteen. For the boys, the six compulsory years of primary school education would be followed by the option of Middle School until eighteen, and then High School (or Preparatory University) until twenty-one. Beyond that, at the pinnacle of the educational pyramid, were the universities – the elite imperial universities, of which the very most prestigious was Tokyo Imperial University, founded in 1870; and the private universities, such as Keio and Waseda, set up by prominent reformers in the late nineteenth century to spread Western learning and the skills of industrial modernization. The universities, which offered three-year undergraduate courses, were open to men only, although there were separate colleges which provided a more restricted higher education for women.

In Japanese society, where the influence of Confucian values has left an enduring respect for education, the beginning of school is an important event in a child's life. For Mutsuo it meant new friends and new experiences, but also an end to the rather carefree and unrestricted life which Japanese infants enjoy at home. He soon discovered a natural aptitude for mathematics. History was enjoyable too – filled with stories of medieval heroes, like the great *Samurai* clans of Minamoto and Taira, and resonant with the names of the one hundred and twenty-four emperors from Jimmu Tennō in the seventh century BC right down to his successor Hirohito in the present day.[2] But most important of all was the beginning of the long process of mastering one of the most complicated writing systems in the world: the endless copying and memorizing, first of the two sets of phonetic characters (*kana*), each with forty-six characters, and then, gradually, of the two-thousand-odd Chinese ideograms (*kanji*) which would be needed to achieve full literacy. Like seven-year-old children all over Japan, Mutsuo and his classmates sat in rows of

17

desks and chanted the first words of their very first reading book: '*hana, hato, mame, masu, minokasa, karakasa*' ('flower, dove, bean, measuring-cup, straw hat, paper umbrella').

At my first school, we used to have assembly every morning out of doors, in front of the school shrine. The school had its own little shrine in the courtyard, and inside it there was a picture of the emperor and a scroll containing the Imperial Rescript on Education [*Kyōiku Chokugo*]. Every morning we had to line up before the shrine, and the headmaster – he was what you might call a fanatical Shintōist – used to come and chant a long litany. I can hear his great booming voice even now. Of course we didn't understand a word he said. It was all full of archaic phrases. But I can still remember parts of it to this day, phrases about the first emperor coming from heaven to govern the nation, and so on.

Ceremonies like this were becoming more and more common in schools throughout Japan during the early 1930s. In Mutsuo's school, because of the headmaster's interest in Shintō, with its emphasis on nationalist mythology, they started particularly early. But stress on the traditional virtues of respect for parents and superiors and loyalty to the emperor was not a new thing in Japanese education. Ever since the introduction of a universal education system in the 1870s there had been those who feared that the spread of learning might encourage individualism and undermine established values. So in 1890 the Emperor Meiji had issued the Imperial Rescript on Education, reminding teachers and pupils that the aim of education was not individual self-betterment but service to the nation. It was a copy of this document which was kept in the shrine at Mutsuo's school, as it was kept in schools throughout Japan, and later Mutsuo, like all Japanese schoolchildren, would be required to memorize its words by heart.

At the age of eight Mutsuo, with his family, moved to Kyoto, the ancient capital of Japan; and at the same time, his childhood began for the first time to be shadowed by an atmosphere of war. For the month in which the Saitōs moved house was also the month in which fighting broke out in Manchuria.

The military crisis in China had been long coming, but still when it arrived, it seemed something sudden, extraordinary. There were many currents which converged in the Manchurian Incident (as it is known in Japanese history). One was the rapid growth of Japanese industry, and the concomitant search for markets and sources of raw material in continental Asia. With this had come a steady expansion in the number of Japanese civilians – bankers, traders, factory managers – resident in China. Meanwhile the Japanese military presence in China was also increasing, with the acquisition first of the colony of Taiwan in 1895, then of rights to control the Liaotung Peninsula and the South Manchurian railway in 1905, and later of a temporary military foothold in Shantung during the First World War. Associated with this was a rising restiveness amongst the Japanese military – an impatience at the apparent ineptitude of domestic politicians, and at the refusal of the Western nations to recognize Japan's rightful status as a major military power. Lastly, there was the political vacuum created by civil war in China. This, since it threatened the lives and property of Japanese residents in China, provided not only the opportunity but also the excuse for military intervention.

On the night of 18 September 1931, Japanese troops guarding the South Manchurian railway heard a series of explosions. Whether or not this was in fact, as was claimed, an attack on the railway by Chinese saboteurs is one of the many unsolved mysteries of a decade of increasingly obscure and convoluted political intrigue. But what is certain is that it provided the Japanese army in Manchuria with a long-awaited chance to seize control of the region. A military officer, sent by the Japanese government to halt the exploits of the army in Manchuria, carefully delayed his arrival until it would be too late to have any effect. In a matter of days, Japan's army had irrefutably demonstrated its ability to outmanoeuvre the country's more cautious political leaders. By January of the following year the whole of Manchuria was controlled by the Japanese military, and the fighting had spread south, to Shanghai. Here, in response to a spontaneous outburst of anti-Japanese sentiments, the Japanese navy launched a bombardment while locally-stationed Japanese troops and newly-arrived reinforcements attacked the surrounding Chinese garrisons in an attempt to secure control of the city. The battle for Shanghai was hard-fought but inconclusive. Japanese troops ultimately withdrew, leaving an estimated 24,000 people – including 1400 Japanese troops – killed, wounded or missing. In Manchuria, however, the Japanese army had achieved its aims and in the autumn of 1932 the Japanese government gave its formal recognition to the independent state of 'Manchukuo', nominally headed by the heir to the Manchu Dynasty, Pu Yi, but in fact firmly under the political control of Japan itself.

Japan's actions, both in Manchuria and Shanghai, met with widespread international condemnation. The Lytton Commission, appointed by the League of Nations to investigate events in Man-churia, concluded unequivocally that

> without a declaration of war a large area of what was indisputably Chinese territory has been forcibly seized and occupied by the armed forces of Japan, and has, in consequence of this operation, been separated from and declared independent from China.[3]

When the Assembly of the League of Nations endorsed this finding, in the spring of 1933, the Japanese government responded by withdrawing from membership of the League.

To the majority of Japanese people of the time, however, the Manchurian Incident was presented in terms very different from those of the Lytton Commission. The picture which they received of events in China was one framed by the impassioned rhetoric and imagery of the popular press of the early 1930s. 'Manchuria State Declared Formed – Its Aim is Peace'; 'Maladministration of Pros-perous Area Deplored – Future is Bright', proclaimed the headlines. What filled the pages of the mass-circulation newspapers was not so much discussion of the long-term impact of the Manchurian crisis on Japan's international diplomacy, as stories like the saga of the Three Bomb Heroes (*Bakudan San-Yūshi*) of Shanghai, who had helped to breach the defences of a Chinese fortress by tying a bomb to their own bodies and running forward into the enemy lines to die in the ensuing explosion.

Not everyone in Japan, of course, accepted this approach to the crisis.

> A group of leading women intellectuals has come together for regular discussion of the Manchurian problem in all its phases, particularly endeavouring to understand the Chinese attitude and interests and to make contact with women leaders in China toward that end . . . University audiences have been known to heckle official and military lecturers who were busily explaining the government position in Manchuria, with cries of 'Why? Why?' . . .[4]

But the cries of protest were easily drowned by the clamour of patriotic passion which swept the country.

The children have not been neglected and the glorious valour of their army is taught to them in school. Military items have been included in journals, magazines and periodicals, lectures have been given in schools and to boy scouts and other similar organisations; special motion pictures for children are being prepared and a special publication by the Army for schoolchildren is planned . . . A glimpse at any toy shop, and they are numerous in Japan, will reveal the military inclinations of the people. There one can find toy soldiers, tanks, helmets, uniforms, rifles, armored motor cars, airplanes, anti-aircraft guns, howitzers, cannons, besides the usual pop guns, bugles and drums. In the fire works stall there are the 'Three Human Bombs', the Japan news of the Shanghai affair, and many other ingenious devices stimulating war. The public is solidly behind the army as is proved by the above and the many contributions of money and weapons made by all sections of the Empire.[5]

In Saitō Mutsuo's memories the Manchurian Incident is inextricably linked with the problems of an eight-year-old newcomer, eager to establish his place in the complex social networks of the local children.

For a child of my age, it was in some ways difficult to have to move houses and schools so often. I went to four primary schools altogether – that gives you some idea of how frequently my father was posted from one place to another.

In Kyoto, because we moved in the middle of the school year, there was no room for me in the boys' section of the school that my father wanted me to attend. So, for one term, I was put into the girls' section – the only boy in a whole class of girls. I loathed that. I felt extremely shy and embarrassed. What made it particularly humiliating was that this was just the time of the beginning of the Manchurian Incident – war fever was raging; all the boys were playing soldiers. It was the worst possible time for being in a class full of girls.

Even at that age, we were greatly interested in what was going on in Manchuria. The boys from my street used to play war games, armed with bamboo poles as rifles. Of course Kyoto was a splendid place for that, because there were so many old shrines and temples with gardens or graveyards where we could play.

There was one big temple just near our house – the Kurodani Temple – it's still there today. I used to go there after school with the neighbours' boys. We pretended it was a Chinese fort. In particular, I remember, we played at being the Three Bomb Heroes of Shanghai. Three of the boys would get a large log of wood and tie it to their backs with string, to be the 'bomb', and the rest of us would be enemy guards and so on.

We were very impressed by the story of the Three Bomb Heroes. We were told that only Japanese soldiers could do something like that.

Saitō Mutsuo gives a wry smile as he remembers that particular incident. It is ironical now to remember how easily war is transformed into a child's game. Yet even for him, an educated and liberal-minded businessman, it is a little hard to find post-war history books suggesting that the story of the Three Bomb Heroes of Shanghai may have been invented by the army for propaganda purposes. He can remember their names, their faces and their life histories from the pages of newspapers and children's comics. They are real to him – almost as real as if he had experienced their exploits himself. It is a shock for him to find those exploits subject to the sceptical scrutiny of contemporary historians.

By 1933 the Manchurian Crisis appeared to have reached some kind of resolution and, although the events of the past two years left a bitter residue of hostility between Japan and China, the fighting at least had come to a halt. But the precarious balance of peace and war on the Asian mainland continued to cast a powerful and inescapable influence over the lives of the Saitō family – all the more so because Mr Saitō's next posting took them to Taiwan, the island which Japan had secured as the prize for its victory over China in the war of 1894–95, and which had therefore become Japan's first true overseas colony.

Taiwan in 1933 was a very different place from the semi-tropical backwater of the Chinese Empire which Japan had acquired in 1895. Since that time, Japanese investment and Japanese migrants had poured into the island – roads and ports and railways had been built, mines had been opened, large sugar plantations developed. Japanese rule had clearly brought some benefits to most of the five million or so Taiwanese: the literacy rate had risen and life expectancy increased. But the type of development pursued by the Japanese authorities in Taiwan served to tie the colony very tightly into the economic structure of the metropolis. Taiwan became the sugar-bowl of Japan, a vast plantation devoted to the produce of those dessert crops too delicate to withstand the cold winters of the main Japanese islands.

By the time the Saitōs went there, there were a quarter of a million Japanese residents in Taiwan, some of them relatively poor migrants, but many occupying those senior posts in the administration, in business, finance or education, which were still reserved for expatriates of the colonial power.

The Saitōs travelled by ship to Taipei in the autumn of 1933. Only Haruko, who was now twenty, stayed behind in Kyoto to complete her college education.

A few weeks after their arrival the island of Taiwan, together with the whole of Japan, was plunged into official rejoicing, for on 23 December 1933, after nine years of marriage and the birth of four baby girls, the Empress Nagako had at last given birth to a son and heir, Akihito. For the time being at least, the unbroken succession of emperors was assured.

The Saitōs lived in a succession of rented houses in Taipei: comfortable, wooden, grey-tiled houses which could have been in Japan proper but for the palm trees and tropical flowers which filled the gardens.

In Taipei we had first a daily help and later a living-in maid to look after the housework. The maids were known as 'chabo', which I think meant something like 'Missy' in Cantonese. It seemed that our maid came to work for us as much because she wanted to learn Japanese language and customs as for the money. At any rate, she came from a quite respectable and well-off family. On Chinese festival days her family would sometimes ask us all round to their house, and they always seemed to produce enormous and delicious meals to celebrate the occasion.

Once again, Mutsuo entered into the rituals of forming friendships, shaping his attitudes and his interests to fit the unfamiliar environment of his new school. Mutsuo and his new classmates talked about the common schoolboy obsessions of sport and war, comparing cut-out pictures of the newest Japanese tanks and fighter planes, and dropping casual remarks to demonstrate their knowledge of the technicalities of horsepower and cruising speeds. At other times they would pore over the latest comics. One of the favourites, which had only recently come out, was *Bōken Dankichi*, the serialized travels of a sort of Japanese Rin Tin Tin, who meets with all kinds of adventures amongst savage Indians and South Sea Islanders, whom he invariably overwhelms with his superior strength and cunning.

The school curriculum was exactly the same in Taiwan as it had been in Kyoto, but the pressures here were greater, for the entrance exams for Middle School were now drawing close. Taipei had only two Japanese Middle Schools, and competition for places in them was fierce. Mr Saitō kept a strict eye on his son's academic work, but even more rigorous supervision came from Mutsuo's elder brother Kōichi. Kōichi was the clever child of the family, the one who came first in class; the eldest son, the bearer of his father's hopes and ambitions.

While they were in Kyoto Kōichi had been seriously ill, suffering from recurrent fevers and fits of coughing. By the time they moved to Taiwan he seemed to be better, but later that year the illness returned, and a diagnosis of tuberculosis was confirmed. Kōichi grew thinner and weaker, and spent more and more time away at hospitals and clinics. He seemed, too, to grow more distant, more serious, as though he were no longer a big brother and playmate but, quite suddenly, an adult, conscious of a weight of responsibilities beyond his years. He began now and again to take his younger brother aside for little, solemn lectures on the importance of working hard at school and of fulfilling his duties to the family – lectures whose significance Mutsuo only dimly comprehended.

On the day of the Crown Prince's first birthday we had a half-holiday. There was a short ceremony at school, and then we were all given rice cakes to eat. After I had eaten my cake and chatted with the other boys for a while, I went home. The house was very quiet. Mother [his stepmother] was not there. That was not unusual, because Kōichi had been in hospital for some time now, and she was away most days, visiting him.

But the afternoon and the evening wore on, and still she wasn't there. It was only the next morning that she came to us and told us

24

that Kōichi was dead. Afterwards, she said that even in the hospital the sounds of the celebrations for the baby prince's birthday had been audible, and Kōichi had remembered to say 'Long Live Prince Akihito'. Then a little later in the day, he died.

After his brother's death Mutsuo, now suddenly the family's only son, began to prepare in earnest for the entrance exam to Taipei No. 2 Middle School. His form master that year was a particularly strict teacher named Mr Takahashi. Mr Takahashi had a little bamboo stick which he used to grip in his hand as he paced up and down the rows in the classroom. The stick was made from the bottom part of a bamboo stem, and at its end there was a hard knot of coiled roots. Boys who could not answer questions received a brisk clip on the side of the head with that end of the stick. If this failed to stimulate their intelligence, they were kept behind after school. There were many days when Mutsuo sat in the darkening, empty classroom, struggling hopelessly with unanswerable questions until at last he despaired, and just counted the minutes until six o'clock, when the school was locked up and, answer or no answer, he would be sent home. In the mornings he woke with a sinking dread of school and Mr Takahashi. He began to invent excuses for staying at home, to suffer from imaginary headaches and fevers. Mr Saitō, with the memories of Kōichi's illness fresh in his mind, was worried. He let Mutsuo stay at home, and ordered rest and nourishing food. But in the end his concern was Mutsuo's undoing, for after the boy had complained of headaches several times in one month, he called in the insurance company's doctor to give him a thorough examination, the doctor reassured him that his son was in perfect health and quite fit to attend school.

Unlike No. 1 Middle School, which was exclusively Japanese, No. 2 School, for which Mutsuo was preparing, was mainly for the children of the Taiwanese elite, and only a small proportion of its intake was Japanese. There was a three-part written examination to be taken first. To pass this was quite an achievement, for usually about seven out of eight children failed. Those who passed then had to face the final selection, which took the form of an interview.

I passed the written exam, but I shall never forget the interview. You had to go in one by one, and stand in front of a table where three teachers were sitting.

25

'Name?' said one of the teachers.

'Saitō Mutsuo,' I replied

'School?'

'Asahi Jinjō Primary School.'

'Recite the Imperial Rescript on Education to us please', he said.

This is easy, I thought, after all, I don't know how many hundred times I've heard the Rescript read. So I started off confidently enough,

'Know Ye, Our subjects: Our Imperial Ancestors have founded Our Empire on a basis broad and everlasting, and have deeply and firmly implanted virtue; . . .' etc., etc.

Well, I got about halfway through, and then I must have lost the thread somewhere, because suddenly I found myself back at the beginning, saying: 'Our Imperial Ancestors have founded our Empire on a basis broad and everlasting . . .'

There was nothing I could do but go on. This time, I thought, I must be very careful and not make the same mistake again. But it was no use. The more I tried, the more I got stuck in this terrible maze of words, going round and round in circles without ever finding the end. My knees started to shake, and I didn't know what to do. I kept looking at the examiners, but none of them would help me out. Finally, after going on like this for what seemed to be hours (though I suppose it was only about ten minutes really) I burst into tears.

Then the teachers started to laugh.

'It's all right', they said, 'You can go now.'

I walked out through the door into the room where all the candidates and their parents sat waiting. I wanted to run off and hide. I felt as though the world had ended. There was no chance to re-sit the examination if you failed. The only thing you could do was go to something called a Higher Primary School for a year and then try again. I thought about how ashamed I would be to have to go to that school, about how I had let everybody down, and about all that wasted work and preparation.

I could hardly believe it when they told me later that I had passed after all.

Mutsuo's father Kōsuke, when he was not at work or spending time with his family, loved to practise *utai* – the slow, tremulous chanting which accompanies *nō* theatre performances. Sometimes when he rehearsed *utai* at home the wooden house would echo with its ancient, haunting sound.

In Taipei, as he had done before in Sendai and in Kyoto, Saitō Kōsuke joined the local *utai* club, which provided a chance not only to immerse himself in traditional Japanese music but also to mingle with other members of the upper echelons of colonial society – businessmen, civil servants, university teachers. Amongst Kōsuke's friends at the *utai* club there was one who particularly attracted the curiosity of the Saitō children. His name was Professor Mikami, and he proved to be none other than the father of the young naval officer Mikami Taku, who soon after the Manchurian crisis had, with a group of associates, staged an attempted *coup d'état* aimed at purging Japan of its 'corrupt' politicians and plutocrats and creating a purified imperial *kokutai* – 'national body' – a phrase which vividly expresses the militarists' vision of the nation as an organically united whole.

In the chaos of the 'May 15th Incident', as the attempted coup of 1932 was called, Prime Minister Inukai was assassinated and unsuccessful attempts were made to blow up banks and power stations, but the plot developed a somewhat farcical dimension when it was discovered that the general whom the young officers had hoped to install at the head of their new government was out of town, and that his deputy flatly refused to co-operate with their schemes. The main conspirators were quickly rounded up by the police, but such was the mood of sympathy to nationalism amongst the judicial authorities that most of them served relatively short sentences. Soon after the Incident, the minister of war said of the May conspirators that 'they had no intention of committing treason. They acted upon the genuine belief that this was for the interest of the Imperial country. Their case should therefore not be dealt with in a narrow-minded way'.[6]

In the Saitō household they sometimes discussed the plight of Professor Mikami, speaking in sympathetic tones of the shame which had been brought to his family by the actions of his wayward son. But there was also a faint aura of dangerous glamour about the name Mikami. It provided a single tenuous link with the distant wave of militarism which was now, little by little, engulfing Japan. For the defeat of the May 15th conspiracy had been no more than a temporary setback to the cause of radical right-wing militarism. The intractable political and social problems of 1930s Japan – the venality and bickering of the established political parties; the hardships of the peasantry (from which much of the junior officer class was drawn); the gulf between the poverty of the urban workers and the growing wealth of the newly-rich capitalist classes; Japan's increasing isolation in international affairs – all provided a fertile soil to nourish such ideologies.

After May 1932 there were many others waiting to carry forward the dream of a 'Shōwa Restoration' in which the emperor, freed from the influence of his 'evil advisers', would take personal control of the nation's destiny. And in 1936, just a couple of months before Mutsuo entered Middle School, the dream was very nearly realized: on 26 February of that year, extremist elements in the army staged a coup which was very much better planned, and on a very much larger scale, than that of Mikami Taku and his friends. Several prominent political figures were assassinated and for days the future of Japan's political system hung in an uneasy balance, as over one thousand rebel troops set up camp in central Tokyo, surrounding the Imperial Palace. During these days the Saitō family, like families throughout the Japanese empire, waited anxiously for each bulletin from the radio or the newspapers, little by little piecing together the confused and bewildering events in the capital. It was not until almost a week after the beginning of the 'February 26th Incident' that they heard at last that the coup had collapsed: the rebel soldiers had surrendered without firing a shot, and life in Tokyo had returned to normal.

Or at least almost to normal; because normality after 26 February 1936 would never again quite be the same as normality before. The rebels had ostensibly failed to gain their objectives. But the events of 1936 had proved the strength of ultra-nationalist feeling in the armed forces, and from then on Japanese governments would find it more than ever necessary to formulate policies with one eye on the interests of the military extremists.

Although of course there had been other assassinations and disturbances before, the February 26th Affair came as a profound shock. I felt somehow that, well, things like that might happen in places such as Europe, where political life was more turbulent. But I had always been taught to think of Japan as being united as a single family under the emperor. It was shocking to discover that even in Japan violent disturbances could take place.

We did not discuss the February 26th Affair in class – in general our curriculum avoided political subjects. But I did talk about it with my school-friends. I remember discussing with them that would happen next. Our main feeling was that the Affair was the result of the military meddling with government. We respected the army as a fighting force, of course, but we felt it wrong that soldiers should become involved in politics.

The entrance to Middle School was an important rite of passage, the admission to a new and more adult world. On the first day there was a special ceremony for the one hundred and fifty thirteen- and fourteen-year-old new boys, at which they were welcomed to the school and given a little moral exhortation by various local dignitaries, who told them to work hard and become a credit to their families, their schools and their country. Academic work at the new school was actually less hard than it had been in the final year of primary school. One examination hurdle was now behind them, and the next was still a long way ahead. But there were many changes to become accustomed to.

One new subject on the curriculum was military training. The school employed an ex-army officer, now on the reserve list, to look after their training programme, and there was also a serving army captain who came in once a week to put the boys through their paces. During the first three years the drill consisted mainly of square-bashing and exercises with wooden model guns, but from the fourth year onwards they were trained in the use of real weapons. For all their love of war games, the boys found that the novelty of military exercises soon wore off. Week after week there were the same repetitive drills to go through, the same dusty parade ground was filled with the same sweaty, reluctant teenagers, while the drill master at the front shouted wearily: 'Shoulders *straight* boy! Hold your head up! No talking at the back there!'

The school exercised quite extensive control over the lives of its pupils. The boys, for example, were not allowed to go to the cinema in their spare time except to see films recommended by their teachers. The recommended films were usually such classics of the Japanese cinema as *Kurama Tengu*, the story of a loyalist outlaw in the days before the Meiji Restoration, but they also included some Hollywood pictures.

There was one American film which I particularly enjoyed, called *The Girl in the Orchestra*.[7] Funnily enough, they showed a re-run of that on one of the late night TV programmes recently. I stayed up specially for it, and was filled with nostalgia for those distant days in Taiwan. In my first year at Middle School I also saw a film of Chaliapin in Massenet's *Don Quixote*. That impressed me immensely, particularly the scene where they burn the books. You could hear Chaliapin's marvellous powerful voice booming out over the crackle of the flames.

That year was Olympics year, and on the hot summer afternoons the boys would sit indoors, crowded around radios listening to the latest reports from Berlin, and trying hard to fill in with their imaginations the scenes described by the sometimes barely comprehensible sports commentaries. When the time came for the women's 200 metres breaststroke, in which the young Japanese swimmer Maehata Hideko was expected to do well, the radio announcer was so overcome with emotion that his commentary on the race consisted of one sentence, repeated again and again: 'Come on, Maehata! Come on, Maehata! Come on, Maehata!', and then, while applause broke out around the pool, his voice cracked with relief as he gasped: 'She's won! She's won!' The newspapers were filled with pictures of the vast Berlin Stadium, and of comments on the disciplined power and splendour of the Olympic ceremonies.

Our geography teacher that year was a great admirer of Germany. After the lesson had finished he often used to stop and talk to us.
    'If only Japan had supported Germany in the Great War, instead of siding with the Anglo-Saxons', he would say, 'We wouldn't have all the problems we have today. If we'd backed the Germans, we could have been in control of half of Asia by now.

Japan's control over Asia, however, was soon to be extended. In China, after the secession of Manchukuo and the brief outbreak of violence around Shanghai five years before, the situation had returned to an uneasy, watchful truce. But on 7 July 1937, as a Japanese infantry company on patrol near Peking passed by the walled town of Wanping where Chinese troops were garrisoned, a volley of shots rang out. The Japanese commander on the spot was quick to blame the Chinese forces for the incident, and demanded

30

entry into the town to punish those responsible. When this was refused, a full-scale battle broke out.

The military faction which now dominated the War Ministry and the army High Command in Tokyo had been waiting for just such an opportunity to expand Japanese involvement in China. In spite of some half-hearted opposition from Prime Minister Konoe they reacted swiftly, pouring 150,000 Japanese troops into the region. Peking and Tientsin were rapidly captured, and in August the fighting spread to Shanghai. The bombing of cities by both sides caused many civilian deaths and provoked considerable international criticism. The Japanese press, naturally, dwelt in particular detail on bombing raids by the Chinese, like the attack on Shanghai on 14 August in which the victims were, ironically, mostly Chinese or foreign.

Mutsuo and his Japanese school-friends followed events in China with avid interest. There was never any doubt in their minds that Japan was entirely in the right, and that it was no more than Japan's duty to punish the ferocious Chinese, first for their unprovoked attack on the Japanese troops at Peking, and later for their barbarous bombing raids. There was one slight difficulty, however. The majority of pupils at Mutsuo's school were, after all, themselves of Chinese origin. Although the Taiwanese boys never openly criticized Japan's activities in China, their enthusiasm at Japanese victories was noticeably more muted, and they seemed to avoid discussions of the war except when these became inescapable.

The relationship between Japanese and Taiwanese pupils in the school was a delicately balanced one. In academic matters, the Japanese boys were mostly at the bottom end of the class. This was because, while the school recruited the very best pupils from Taiwanese primary schools, for the Japanese in Taipei it was only the second-best option.

But the Japanese boys nevertheless had certain advantages, a sort of faint reflection of their elders' political power.

Most of the Taiwanese boys used to have much better packed lunches than we did. Particularly on days when there had been some kind of festival, they would get the leftovers from the previous day's feast in their lunch boxes, all sorts of exciting delicacies. Our packed lunches were nearly always the same: rice with salted fish and pickled plums. So sometimes the bigger

Japanese boys used to commandeer the Taiwanese students' lunch boxes.

They's just walk right up to them and say: 'Here, I'm having that. Hand it over.' It seems rather ridiculous to think of it now, but in fact the victims nearly always did hand their lunches over with hardly a murmur.

All the younger boys in the school, however, shared in the fear of the Big Boys. These eighteen- and nineteen-year-old top formers were not only physically much larger and stronger but were also recognized by staff and students to have awesome, absolute rights to discipline younger pupils. The Big Boys had to be treated with great respect, for those who defied their authority might be captured and marched off behind the gymnasium, where they would be beaten until they apologized abjectly. Mutsuo for the most part managed to escape the attentions of the Big Boys, but having an average teenage propensity for mischief, he did not always keep out of trouble with his teachers.

There was one music teacher whom I particularly disliked. Her name, I remember, was Mrs Miura, and she had apparently been trained at one of the best music academies in Japan. The problem was that my voice was breaking at that time, and, being rather sensitive about it, I hated having to sing in front of the rest of the class. I used to play all kind of tricks on poor Mrs Miura.

One day I balanced the board rubber over the door so that it would drop on Mrs Miura's head as she came into the room. I must have chosen exactly the right spot, for as soon as she came through the door the rubber hit her squarely on the top of her head, covering her hair and shoulders in a cloud of chalk dust. Unfortunately, the reaction was more than I bargained for. Mrs Miura started to cry, and ran off in tears to the staff room. A few minutes later she came back, accompanied by the gym master, who happened to be our form teacher that year.

'Which of you did this?' he demanded. Everyone knew it was me, so I had to own up. I got a good hiding for that, and for the rest of the year we had our music lessons with the gym teacher standing at the back of the class, keeping a stern eye on us.

As the summer of 1937 turned to autumn, the residents of Taipei began more and more frequently to hear at night the drone of planes flying low over the city. The waves of sound would grow, and then rise and fade into the darkness, as the planes banked westward across the China Sea to bomb Nanking. For the war was changing Taipei into a military base. The army camps buzzed with activity and increasing numbers of uniformed men could be seen on the streets of the city.

Even the Saitō household was momentarily caught up in the whirlwind of military activity. The army, which was running out of accommodation for soldiers on their way to fight in China, had started to recruit the help of Japanese civilian families in Taiwan, and four soldiers were billeted with Saitōs. The day before the soldiers arrived Mrs Saitō and the maid bustled about, buying supplies and planning special meals for the uninvited guests. Their presence, for a brief interval, filled the house with the intangible smell of battles and glory and far-off places. Mutsuo gazed with intense curiosity at these strong, laughing young men, already, it seemed, halfway to becoming heroes, and at the clean new kits and the shiny, unused weapons which they laid out on the bedroom floor. In the evening, when family and guests sat down to a special meal of *sukiyaki* which Mrs Saitō had prepared to make the visitors feel at home, he listened to the talk of tactics and strategy, to news of army comrades already in China and to second-hand tales from the battle-front. Sometimes he plucked up the courage to put in a hesitant question.

'We'll write to you from China, and tell you all about it,' they promised him. 'We'll bring you back a Chinese sword as a souvenir.'

After three days, they left. The family turned out to wave them goodbye and wish them good luck. And then they were gone, and the house returned to peace and emptiness. Mutsuo never heard from them again.

It was soon after that – just after the end of the summer holidays – that the Chinese planes bombed Taipei airport. We had heard any number of squadrons of Japanese planes taking off for air-raids on China, but this was the first time that there had been a return raid.

I remember that we were right in the middle of lessons when the planes came roaring over. Our school was quite near to the airport. Of course there was a tremendous uproar. Immediately, lessons were suspended and we were called to an emergency assembly, where we were all issued with rifles and sent out to guard various local buildings in case disturbances broke out.

That was my first experience of actual warfare.

After school, Mutsuo and his friends went to the airport to inspect the damage. There they discovered that the Chinese bombers' aim had not been entirely accurate. All around the wire perimeter fence of the air-strip, the grass was scarred with the raw earth of bomb craters. In a matter of moments the boys were down in the craters, squatting on their heels as they sifted through the crumbly earth, searching, with as much dedication as any prospector seeks the glint of gold, for the gleam of metal which would reveal that greatest of all treasures: a bit of real bomb.

In December the children of Taipei, like children in cities throughout Japan, held a procession through the streets to celebrate the capture of Nanking. The processions were held in the evening, and each child carried a globe-shaped paper lantern hung on a little pole. As the stars began to appear in the sky the procession formed into a great river of bobbing lights flowing down towards the harbour. Later, there would come a time when victory processions were so common that they seemed no more remarkable than the many school half-holidays, and the memory of each procession blurred into the memory of others. But at the time of Nanking the taste of victory was still new, and real excitement was reflected in the faces of the Japanese girls and boys as they moved in waves of flickering light through the darkened streets.

In the newspapers and on the radio the capture of Nanking was hailed as a decisive victory which would turn the tide of war:

> Who would have imagined [exulted the Japanese press] that Nanking would fall within four months of the outbreak of fighting in Shanghai? The fall of Nanking will produce far-reaching effects on the Chinese people in many directions . . . The Chinese casualties up to date are roughly put at a million, and it is believed that the Central Army under General Chiang Kai-Shek's direct command has suffered so crippling a blow that its reconstruction is well-nigh hopeless. Thus, the Chinese troops have been practically deprived of their power of resistance in modern warfare.[8]

All over Japan the Rising Sun flag appeared everywhere in spontaneous outbursts of patriotism, and the authorities were eventually obliged to intervene when over-enthusiastic entrepreneurs began to decorate 'unsuitable' objects, such as matchboxes and handkerchiefs, with the national flag.

What the papers did not report, neither then nor later, were the

34

other, troubling rumours which began to seep out from Nanking: rumours that discipline in the Japanese forces had broken down, stories of civilians murdered in the streets, of houses looted and women raped. The army High Command must have heard some of the rumours, for the commander-in-chief in Central China and two of his divisional commanders were quietly recalled to Japan. But what they heard they immediately suppressed. So the boys and girls who held their lanterns high in triumphal parades throughout the country had no way of imagining that the capture of Nanking would be taught to future generations of school-children, not as a famous victory, but as one of the darkest episodes in the history of modern Japan.

Every year, the boys at No. 1 and No. 2 Middle Schools in Taipei contributed money to their schools' travel club. The money was saved up until the summer of the Fourth Year, when the boys would be taken by their teachers on an educational holiday abroad. The boys of No. 1 school, who were Japanese and were therefore assumed to have seen the sights of Japan, were sent on a trip to Manchuria, but the boys of the No. 2 School, being mostly Taiwanese, were taken to see the great historical and architectural centres of Japan: Kyoto and Nara, Kamakura and Nikkō.

Mutsuo and his classmates were to go on their journey to Japan in the summer of 1939. It was an event which they looked forward to, not only because many of the boys had never been to Japan proper before, but also because they had heard from teachers and older boys about the adventures and misadventures of previous trips: about boys caught smoking, or slipping off in unsupervised moments to explore local attractions which were not on the official itinerary. But as the long-awaited holiday approached, Mutsuo began to be troubled by symptoms of ill-health – small at first, but then growing until they could not be ignored. He became weak and easily tired, and suffered from pains in the chest. The doctor was summoned, and the Saitō parents waited with dread for a diagnosis which they must already have guessed at in their hearts: it was tuberculosis.

In pre-war Japan, where average life expectancy was only 45 years, tuberculosis was the most feared of all killers. It was more than twice as common amongst Japanese as it was amongst Britons or Americans, and every year between 120,000 and 130,000 people died of the disease. The toll was particularly great amongst those between the ages of fifteen and thirty. For Saitō Kōsuke, the battle against tuberculosis had developed a dimension almost of personal enmity. His attitude to the disease was one of simple and grim determination: it had killed his first wife and his eldest son; he was not going to allow it to kill his only surviving boy as well. Mutsuo was immediately sent to a sanatorium at Peito, a spa in the mountains near Taipei. So while his classmates set off on their journey to Japan, Mutsuo's summer turned into a timeless, dream-like blur of days spent lying on a couch to breathe in the mountain air, or soaking in the warm, healing waters of the thermal springs.

His father's swift action saved Mutsuo's life. Because the disease had been caught early he made a good recovery, and soon he was well enough to read books and take an interest in his surroundings. Most of the other patients in the sanatorium were, he discovered, soldiers from the China front. Many of the sick or seriously wounded were sent to hospitals in Taiwan, and then spent a few weeks recuperating in Peito before returning to their regiments. Their presence brought some excitement and variety to the tedium of illness, and many long afternoons were whiled away listening, in the clinical silence of the sanatorium, to their tales of courage and death in the distant war.

Even when he was home, Mutsuo was not yet well enough to go back to school. The rest of the year was spent mostly indoors, listening to records and reading the modern classics of Japanese literature while, slowly and painfully, his strength returned. Each weekend his father would take him out of town, to picnic in the mountain forests and imbibe what was then the only known cure for tuberculosis: fresh air. On the way back from each outing they would stop at Peito and bathe in the spa waters.

While I was still in the sanatorium I had made friends with a young man by the name of Gamō, Flying Officer Gamō. He was, I suppose, about twenty-two or twenty-three, and had gone straight from flying school to piloting bombers in China, where he'd been wounded. He used to tell me all sorts of stories about the war on the continent – about the bombing missions he'd flown and so forth.

After we were both released from the sanatorium, I went to visit him once at the air force base in Taipei. He let me go in his plane – not actually flying, that is, but sitting in the cockpit as the plane stood on the runway. That was the first time I had ever been inside an aeroplane. It was a light bomber – a Type 88, I think – with the bombs slung under its wings.

I can remember the inside of that plane's cockpit quite vividly. But of course I had no idea at that time that I would ever pilot a plane myself.

At the end of 1939 Saitō Kōsuke was posted back to Japan, and the family moved to Tokyo. The atmosphere of war was closing in around them now. In China the fighting dragged on without any end in sight, and for the first time, Mutsuo heard rumours of Japanese defeats. It was whispered that at Nomonhan on the Mongolian border, where Russian and Japanese troops had clashed the year before, a whole regiment of Japanese soldiers had been wiped out.

When the Saitōs arrived in Tokyo, they found the department store restaurants still filled with customers, and the *sushi* bars still displaying their artistic arrangements of delicately sliced fish in rainbow hues of pink and pearly grey. But the shortages of ordinary, essential goods and the queues in the shops were more noticeable than they had been in Taipei.

The Saitōs settled into a house in the residential district of Sendagaya (once again without Haruko, who had married while the family was in Taiwan and was now living there with her husband, a young official in the colonial service). When the family was installed in their new home, Mr Saitō's first concern was to organize his son's education. Mutsuo was now due to take the all-important examinations for High School and Saitō Kōsuke was eager that his son should obtain a place in his own old college, Keio. Soon after their arrival, therefore, he contacted the headmaster of Keio Middle School to enquire whether they had a place for Mutsuo. The Middle School was attached to Keio High School and University, and although graduation from one to the other was not automatic, acceptance at the school would certainly help Mutsuo's prospects. But the headmaster's reply was brisk and to the point: they had no vacancies for the current academic year, and even if a place had been available, it was unlikely that Mutsuo's qualifications would have been considered adequate.

Mr Saitō's parental pride was hurt. In a state of indignation, he went to see the headmaster of Keio's chief rival amongst private schools, Waseda.

The headmaster of Waseda Middle School happened to be an old friend of Father's, so he was quite willing to meet him and discuss my education. But when he saw my reports from school in Taiwan (which were not particularly good) and heard that I'd had to have months off school because of illness, he started to shake his head. In the end, what he said to my Father was this:

'As you are a friend, I'm prepared to give your boy a chance. But I shall have to make it clear that he will be allowed just one term to prove his abilities. If he doesn't make real academic progress by April, then I shall have to ask him to leave.'

With this threat hanging over his head, Mutsuo entered Waseda Middle School in January 1940. Here he found life very different indeed from his schooldays in Taiwan. Not only was the standard of work much higher, but the attitudes of the boys too were somehow more serious and sophisticated. In Taiwan they had talked of battles and aeroplanes, or gossiped about the teachers, mimicking this one's way of walking and that one's funny turns of phrase. But at Waseda the talk was all of study and examinations, full of earnest discussions about mathematical problems or last week's essay subject. Mutsuo was determined to live up to his father's expectations, and to prove that this school was not too good for him. Every afternoon he came home with his satchel filled with books, and shut himself up in his room to study. There he stayed, with only a brief break for the evening meal, until one or two in the morning, when he would drop exhausted onto his *futon* (sleeping mat) to snatch a few hours' rest before it was time to wake and prepare for the next day's lessons. Never in his life had he worked so hard.

Then April came, and Mutsuo waited with fear and anticipation for his fate to be decided. Out of the two hundred-and-fifty boys in the Fourth Year at Waseda, Mutsuo was among the top hundred. His place in the Fifth Form was assured. Now he could relax a little, and found that he had time to turn his attention to other things besides work.

My best friend at Waseda was a boy called Tsuji. I remember vividly the day when Tsuji took me skating for the first time in my life. In Taiwan, of course, there had been no opportunity to skate, but in Tokyo at that time there were three indoor skating rinks, two in the suburbs and one in Isetan department store in central Tokyo. We went to the one in Isetan.

I strapped my skates on and walked rather shakily out on to the ice. At first I clung to the rail at the edge, but quite soon I seemed to get the hang of it, and started to strike out more boldly across the rink. I was beginning to really enjoy the feel of gliding along on the ice. The rink seemed very big, and I sped down towards the far end. But then I saw what seemed to be another skater coming very fast towards me. I moved to avoid him, and at that moment realized that it was my own reflection – one side of the rink was a big glass mirror, which I crashed into at full speed. Luckily (perhaps because other people had made the same mistake before) the mirror must have had some kind of cushioned backing, for I bounced off it quite harmlessly, and suffered nothing worse than shock and a little injured dignity.

Another distraction from academic work was the girl next door. Her name was Miss Ogata; her father was an eminent professor of medicine; and she was very beautiful. As war approached, sexual morality in Japan was imposed with increasing strictness. Any signs of Western decadence, such as dating between schoolgirls and schoolboys, were firmly suppressed and Mutsuo's experience of girls was therefore limited to occasional polite conversations with daughters of his father's business colleagues. To Miss Ogata he never spoke. But in the mornings when he set out for school he would sometimes glimpse her figure framed in the doorway of her house, and would glance up nervously to steal a fleeting glance at her face. Then, on the way home, when he saw her far off down the street walking towards him, his cheeks would begin to flush so furiously that he would dive into the darkness of a side alley to avoid confronting the materialization of his dreams.

As examination time approached it became more and more difficult for the boys at Waseda to pretend that their education could continue normally or that their lives would be untouched by war. On 27 September 1940 the Japanese government signed the Tripartite Pact, allying Japan with Germany and Italy, and it seemed increasingly inevitable that the country would be drawn into the international conflict.

Japan joined the Axis just at the time when we were making our final decisions about the High School exams. A lot of boys decided at that time to specialize in science subjects, because they reckoned that science students would be the last ones to be called up if it came to all-out war. Although I'd admired the soldiers and pilots whom I'd met in Taiwan, I was no more keen on the thought of joining the army than the rest of the boys. But on the other hand I also knew that I was no good at science.

When I was in Taiwan I had had the idea that I might become a judge, but by now I had decided that I would probably go into business. So I planned to specialize in economics. If war came I would just have to hope for the best.

In the spring of 1941 Mutsuo took entrance examinations for Keio and Yamagata High School, and failed. Failure in these rigorous entrance exams was disappointing but not unusual, and so, like many other Japanese students, Mutsuo enrolled at one of the hundreds of *yobikō* (crammers) which flourish on the rejects of the examination system, and prepared to try again the next year. In June 1941 the Yoshizawa mission, which had been sent by Japan to the Dutch East Indies to try to secure vital imports of oil, returned without success. America and Britain had already placed embargoes on the export of aviation fuel and iron and steel to Japan, and the situation was becoming desperate. Already, charcoal-fuelled cars could be seen chugging around the streets of Tokyo. Rationing had been in operation for over a year, and now ration tickets were needed to buy all the most essential goods: rice, soy sauce, salt, sugar, charcoal and even matches. Rations were allotted to the *tonarigumi*, the local neighbourhood councils, which in turn distributed them to each family in the area. Mutsuo and his friends watched events with mounting excitement and concern.

From the summer of 1941 onwards, the fish rations began to get very monotonous. It was squid, squid, every day squid. I didn't think anything about it, except that it would have been nice to have a bit more variety occasionally, but when I was at the crammer one day the teacher said to us: 'Does any one of you know why your rations always consist of squid now?'

None of us knew the answer so the teacher explained to us.

'Squid', he said, 'is caught in coastal waters. Why are we only getting fish from coastal waters? Because the fishing fleets aren't doing deep-sea fishing any more. And why aren't they doing deep-sea fishing any more? For one thing, because they haven't enough fuel – all the fuel is going to the military now – and for another thing because the big boats have been requisitioned by the navy. They're being fitted with weapons and turned into gunboats. So now you know what your squid rations mean – there will be war in the Pacific very soon.'

3

Tsutsumi Ayako

The extraordinary circumstances of the 1920s and the 1930s imprinted on the minds of that generation of Japanese children a mental map of the world totally different from anything imagined by earlier or by subsequent generations. For the children of the Meiji and Taishō periods, as for those of the post-war age, Japan is a small chain of islands poised beyond the rim of a vast yet unfamiliar, uncomprehended continent. But for the children of the early years of Shōwa the circumstances of Japan's imperial expansion opened up quite different visions of continental Asia: Taiwan, Korea, China, Manchuria became momentarily Japan's new frontiers, places of challenge and boundless opportunity where technological skills might be applied, military might vaunted and fortunes made.

Tsutsumi Ayako's consciousness of this world, like Saitō Mutsuo's, was shaped, not in Japan itself, but in the environment of Japanese colonial society abroad. Yet her upbringing differed from his, reflecting not only the differences between the education of boys and girls in pre-war Japan, but also the quite distinct position which her family occupied in the social strata of Japanese colonialism.

As Japan's power in Asia grew, company officials (like Saitō Kōsuke), civil servants, lawyers, doctors and teachers were sent out to look after the nation's expanding interests abroad. Such professional people normally served only limited terms overseas, while remaining on career ladders whose pinnacles pointed to Tokyo. But they were followed by a steady stream of other, more permanent Japanese emigrants. These came mostly from impoverished rural backgrounds – people who in Japan proper formed the lowest level of the social pyramid, but who had discovered that in areas where Japan held political control they became, overnight, members of the ruling class by virtue of race alone. Such families formed a solid stratum of shopkeepers, small businessmen and minor functionaries, bonded together by that heightened sense of national identity which so often exists in expatriate communities.

Thus, after Japan's defeat in the Second World War, there were found to be some three million Japanese civilians awaiting repatriation from various parts of Asia. Among them were Tsutsumi Ayako and her family. Those who returned were the lucky ones, for it is believed that many expatriate Japanese were killed in the upsurge of avenging anger which followed Japan's surrender. A few remained so that, for example, once relations with China were normalized at the beginning of the 1970s, it was discovered that there was still a handful of pre-war Japanese emigrants waiting to come 'home' after perhaps forty or fifty years in China.

Ayako is no longer sure where she was born. It was somewhere on the southern island of Shikoku, that much she knows. But was it the town of Marugame, or maybe Tadotsu? Her life, with its sharp reverses of fortune, its moments of prosperity and dizzying descents into poverty, has not been conducive to the collecting of documents or the writing down of facts and figures.

A quiet-faced woman in her fifties – grey-haired but with a soft and unlined face – she brings her memories of childhood and adolescence to the surface of her mind hesitantly, almost painfully. She remembers the small and the domestic, but sometimes large political events have vanished from her consciousness without trace. Her personality has been shaped by the pre-war education system in which girls were taught self-control rather than self-expression. Her hands make small and nervous movements as she speaks.

We meet her in her house in the pottery village of Kasama – a spacious house on a quiet street. Behind, in the hill-slope garden, the bamboo stems rattle together and the green of the surrounding woods is splashed with autumnal reds and golds. Stacks of firewood lie waiting to fuel the rambling brick-built kilns of her pottery. But the sense of serenity and of solid achievement imparted by these surroundings does not quite dispel a small feeling of tension, an edge of unease in her voice; as though calm and prosperity were still something new, something in whose permanence she does not quite believe.

She thinks (for her mother sometimes spoke of this) that her birth was a hard one. Her family was very poor at the time, living in cheap rented rooms. Her father was away from home, finding work on some construction site, and her mother had no one to help her at the confinement. Afterwards, Ayako would be told that this was the reason why she had always been a sickly child, why she suffered from the poor eyesight which later was to hamper her artistic career, and which now forces her to wear thick, dark-rimmed spectacles.

Ayako knows something of her father's family background, too. This she discovered from subsequent painful experience. Hasebe Ritō, her father, had not always been poor. He was the eldest son of a farmer, moderately well-off by the standards of the rural Japan of that time, his family cultivating their own small plot of land. He was approaching middle age, and was married with four young sons, when he fell in love with the nineteen-year-old daughter of a travelling salesman who used to call at the farm to sell his wares. They had an affair, and when the girl became pregnant Hasebe Ritō abandoned his farm and his family to live with her, supporting himself and his new household by working as a navvy on building sites around Shikoku. Such casual separations were not unusual in Japanese rural life before the war. It is post-war prosperity which has brought a greater middle-class respect for the sanctity of marriage. The attitude to illegitimacy was also a tolerant one. A Western observer noted in the 1930s:

> The Japanese laws and customs governing the legitimating of children born out of wedlock are much more lenient than those in most countries of the world . . . In Japan, a child of unmarried parents at birth is a member of the mother's family; upon recognition by the father, however (whether the father be married or not), the child enters the father's family as a *shoshi*, or legitimated child, and takes the father's name.[1]

This is, apparently, what happened in the case of Ayako's elder brother and sister. Around the time of Ayako's birth, however, her father finally divorced his first wife and made official his relationship with Ayako's mother. This meant that the children of their union acquired the right to inherit property from their father, a right which does not pertain to *shoshi* (and which was later to be a source of controversy and unhappiness).

It was about one year after this that Hasebe Ritō took his family across the Japan Sea to Korea, a country which, since its incorporation into the Japanese empire in 1910, had attracted a particularly large inflow of Japanese migrants.

The Japanese government had presented its role in Korea as a *mission civilatrice*, whose aim was to incorporate the country as closely as possible into Japanese national life. 'Korea is not a vassal state of Japan, nor is it a Japanese colony . . .' wrote the nationalist philosopher Kita Ikki in 1919; 'It is part of the Japanese empire and one of its administrative districts.'[2] For this reason the use of the Japanese language was enforced in Korean schools, place names were changed from the Korean to the Japanese pronunciation and most Koreans were eventually coerced into adopting Japanese-sounding names. At the same time, the Japanese administration pursued an energetic policy of modernizing and reorganizing Korean finances, communications, transport and industry so that the country's economy would fit more closely into the total economic structure of the Japanese empire. In the 1930s this policy included massive schemes such as the construction of the Yalu River dam and power station at Suiho, which was one of the largest projects of its kind in the world. But the domination of the administration and economy by expatriate Japanese, and the suppression of Korean culture, provoked bitter resistance from many people in Korea. In one anti-Japanese rebellion, the Mansei rebellion of 1919, almost 8000 people were killed and over 50,000 were imprisoned by the Japanese authorities.

Ayako has no recollection of the journey to Korea, and only two distant images of the three years which the family spent in the north of the country. One image is of the winters – the indescribably cold winters when the knife-edged winds from Siberia would sweep the snow down the mountain ridges of the Korean peninsula. The other is of the apples. There seemed to be apple trees all around the place where they lived, and the fruit was so abundant and cheap that the children could eat apples whenever they were hungry.

There were other things which I heard about afterwards. My father used to tell me about the bandits. There were Chinese bandits, he said, who came over the border from Manchuria. Sometimes he would see them when he was out working on a remote construction site.

My little sister was born while we were in the north, and I think we must have been very poor at that time, because my mother used to tell me how, in those days, she had never been able to afford enough meat or fish to feed all six of us. Instead, she would buy enough for one helping – for my father. The rest of us just got bowls of rice with soy bean paste.

In 1932 the Hasebes moved south to the city of Kwangju, which the Japanese called Kōshū. Hasebe Ritō had now gained enough experience of construction work to be able to set up his own little company, which acted as a sub-contractor on projects such as dams and bridges. Another of Ayako's early memories is of visits to her father's construction sites, riding piggy-back on the shoulders of one of the workmen. In the middle of the site there would be a banner with the company's name, 'Hasebe-Gumi', written in bold characters. All around it the workers, tens or (on big projects) hundreds of them, swarmed like ants. They were not regular employees, but were recruited from the local labour market for a few weeks' work. In summer they wore only loin-cloths, and their naked torsos glistened with sweat. They carried baskets on their backs, staggering to and fro, to and fro, from one side of the site to the other, filling and emptying basket-loads of sand or cement. For each trip they received one slip of paper, and at the end of the day their pay was calculated according to the number of crumpled scraps of paper which they had collected.

The Hasebes lived in a small house in the south of Kwangju. In this district, the several thousand Japanese residents of the city formed a little world of their own: an entirely self-contained Japanese community. They encountered Koreans almost exclusively in the capacity of employees, servants or tradespeople, and even when they went out in the evenings it was to restaurants serving Japanese food or to cinemas showing Japanese films. In the Hasebe household, the meals were prepared in Japanese style by a Korean maid supervised by Ayako's mother.

My little brother was born the year after we moved to Kwangju. I know that he was born the same year as Crown Prince Akihito although I can't actually remember the celebrations for the Crown Prince's birth.

At that time I had to stay indoors almost all the time, because of my poor health. I liked playing with marbles, and used to make bean bags and teach myself to juggle with them. It was lonely, though. Mother was always very busy looking after my little sister and brother, and the older two were away at school during the day. Even when they were at home they didn't want to stay indoors and play with me.

But there were happy times, too – autumn days when they would go chestnut-hunting on the mountain-slopes outside the city, crunching

46

through piles of brown leaves, and gingerly splitting the spiky green spheres to discover the hoard of ripe nuts inside. In summer the family went to the seaside, and Ayako was carried in her mother's arms and held in the salty waves in the hope that this would make her strong. There were also occasional evenings when her father would bring home colleagues from the construction business, and they would sit about the table in the main room, eating, drinking *sake*, growing red-faced and argumentative, and filling the house with their raucous laughter. On those evenings the children could always steal titbits of the special delicacies which were prepared for the guests: fried beef, chilled carp, steamed wild duck.

The Japanese community in Kwangju had its own primary school, following the same curriculum as schools throughout Japan. Because there was only one school for the Japanese children of Kwangju, however, its classes contained girls and boys from every part of the spectrum of colonial society: from the children of governors and judges to those of travelling fortune-hunters.

All the five Hasebe children attended Kōshū Central School, as it was called. Ayako started in April 1935. In her year there were about one hundred and fifty boys and girls, divided into four mixed classes each named after a colour: Blue Class, Red Class, Yellow Class and White Class. Ayako was in the Blue Class.

There seemed to be ever such a lot of new things to remember at the beginning of school. The older children helped us to learn what we had to do. For example, in each class there was a picture of the Nijūbashi [the bridge over the moat at the entrance to the Imperial Palace in Tokyo]. The picture hung at the front of the class, above the blackboard, and when you went into the classroom you had to bow your head towards it. Then there was the little shrine by the school gate, which contained a portrait of the emperor. Every time you went in and out you had to bow your head to that, too.

The school also had its own special code of behaviour, which had to be memorized. There were three rules. The first was 'respect the Imperial Family and respect your ancestors' and the second was 'do not waste even one drop of water'. We were told that meant that we must always appreciate the value of even the most ordinary everyday things. The third one I have forgotten.

Like schools in Japan, Kōshū Central School held a ceremonial reading of the Imperial Rescript on Education on all national holidays. The pupils would stand in rows with their heads bowed listening as the headmaster read the words which were etched on the memories of generations of pre-war school-children:

Know ye, Our subjects! Our Imperial Ancestors have founded our Empire on a basis broad and everlasting and have deeply and firmly implanted virtue. Our subjects ever united in loyalty and filial piety have from generation to generation illustrated the beauty thereof. This is the glory of the fundamental character of our Empire, and herein also lies the source of our education. Ye, our subjects, be filial to your parents; affectionate to your brothers and sisters; as husbands and wives be harmonious; as friends be true; bear yourselves in modesty and moderation, extend your benevolence to all; pursue learning and cultivate arts; and thereby cultivate intellectual faculties and perfect moral powers; further-more advance public good and promote common interests; always respect the Constitution and observe the laws; should emergency arise offer yourselves courageously to the State; and thus guard and maintain the prosperity of Our Imperial Throne coeval with heaven and earth. So shall ye not only be Our good and faithful subjects, but render illustrious the best traditions of your fore-fathers. The Way here set forth is indeed the teaching bequeathed by Our Imperial Ancestors, to be observed alike by Their Descendants and the subjects, infallible for all ages and true in all places. It is Our wish to lay it to heart in all reverence, in common with you, Our subjects, that we may all thus attain the same virtue.[3]

The reading was followed by a speech from the headmaster. During the summer term the ceremony was held out of doors, and on particularly hot days some of the children would frequently enliven the proceedings by fainting.

On Mondays the headmaster would come to give Blue Class its lesson in Ethics (*Shūshin*), which formed a compulsory part of the curriculum, much as religious lessons do in many other countries. The main emphasis in the Ethics lessons was on respect for parents and teachers, and on the values of loyalty, friendship and social responsibility; but it also served to develop in the children a sense of patriotism for Japan, the leader of Asia (*Ajia no Meishū*), the country of which they were part and yet which many of them had never seen. On special occasions, they were shown films of the 'Mainland' (as

Japan proper was then called, in contradistinction to the outerlying area of the empire): films of places whose names they knew from history lessons, or of the shining, efficient modern factories and the bustling roads, railways and harbours of the richest nation in Asia. In reading lessons they read the story of Kiguchi Kohei, a trumpeter in the Japanese army during one of the ferocious battles of the Russo–Japanese War, who was found, when the fighting was over, still standing with the trumpet pressed to his lips, but stone dead, a bullet through his heart.

In the grounds of our school there was what we called the Animal Corner, where they kept some pets. There was a cage of monkeys there. After lessons had finished, we sometimes used to play around by the Animal Corner for a bit before we went home. One time, I was playing beside the monkey cage. There was one monkey who seemed to be specially friendly. He kept sticking his hand out through the bars. I wanted to play with him, but then suddenly he grabbed hold of a big handful of my hair and started pulling it. He pulled and pulled; he wouldn't let go. I was crying and trying to get away, and at last he pulled the chunk of my hair right out.

I ran off crying to our form teacher. She put some medicine on my head, which was bleeding, and took me home. Even then, I remember, we stopped to bow in front of the school shrine as we passed the gates.

The school was in the centre of Kwangju, about ten minutes' walk from Ayako's home, and in between school and home lay a Korean area of town. During her first year Ayako went to school with her older brother and sister, but later, when she went alone, this was an area to hurry through without stopping. On other occasions, when she went on outings with the family, they would pass through much poorer districts of town, where she would gaze, puzzled and slightly frightened, at the tiny, one-roomed houses, through whose open doors and windows you could see children washing themselves in big metal tubs, or others looking up from their bowls of boiled wheat and rice to stare back at the passers-by with blank inpenetrable eyes.

The Hasebe parents began each day by paying their respects before the *butsudan* and before the portrait of the emperor which hung on a wall in their house. The Hasebes, like most Japanese families, were comprehensive rather than exclusive in their religious observances. Their house contained not only a Buddhist *butsudan* (Buddhist altar) and a picture of the emperor, but also a Shintō shrine (*kamidana*), where the memories of the family ancestors were venerated. The various religious traditions were not in competition but coexisted in harmony, each having a part to play at particular times of year or on particular important occasions in life.

·After the brief morning rituals the family would gather for a breakfast of soup, rice, pickles and dried fish. This was the one meal of the day which Ayako's mother prepared herself. The maid normally arrived just at the time when the children were setting off for school.

Round about my second year at primary school we got a new maid. We used to call her *Omoni* (that's the Korean for 'Mother'). She must have been somewhere in her late thirties, and I suppose that she had some children of her own at home. She was a very good, reliable person, and Mother grew quite fond of her. I remember her often saying, 'We're so lucky to have such a good *omoni*.' She stayed with us for years and years, right until the time when we left Korea.

The children were not expected to join in their parents' religious observances, but during her second year at school Ayako began to spend more and more time each morning standing with her head bowed before the *butsudan*. Her parents, if they noticed, did not ask the reason for her behaviour, but Ayako's sudden attack of piety arose from a fear which began to obsess her more and more as spring approached. At the end of her first year Ayako had received a poor report, with bottom-grade marks for all her subjects except art and composition. Her new form teacher was strict and unsympathetic, and her mother seldom had time to attend parents' meetings. Ayako began to be convinced that she would be kept down at the end of the second year, a punishment which was rarely inflicted and so was all the more to be dreaded. Day after day Ayako prayed with all her might, summoning up the most powerful magic she could think of to work miracles with her next report.

The local shops in Kwangju used to deliver to the house. So in the mornings there would always be a succession of tradesmen coming round – from the greengrocers' and fishmongers' and so on – to

50

take our orders, and in the afternoon they used to come back again
and deliver whatever you'd asked for.

There was one little Korean boy I particularly remember. He
was the errand-boy for the cake shop. In the mornings he used to
come round to see if we wanted anything, and then later in the day
you could see him doing his rounds with his trays of cakes. He
can't have been very much older than me, but there he was, out at
work, not having to worry about marks and reports and getting
into trouble at school. During that year I used to look at the boy
when he called at our house each morning, and there was nothing
in the world that I wouldn't have given to be able to change places
with him.

The outbreak of the war in China was echoed by an intensification of
the pressures of the colonialism in Korea. 1937 saw the introduction
of a new Korea policy, aimed at increasing the incorporation of the
colony into Japanese political and cultural life, and enlarging the
Korean contribution to the wealth and glory of the empire. One face
of this new policy involved some minor measures of liberalization:
Koreans, for the first time, were to be allowed a limited representation in the Japanese Diet. The other face involved the growth of
economic exploitation and cultural suppression. From now on, all
schools were to use the Japanese language only. In 1938 a 'volunteer'
system was created, through which Korean youths were pressed into
the service of Japanese mining and military production, to fill the
growing number of gaps created by wartime military service. The
following year Korean forced labour began to be used. Between then
and 1945 over 700,000 Koreans were sent abroad as involuntary
labourers, mostly to Japan, China and Manchuria. Many never
returned.

But for the children of Kōshū Central Primary School, the
beginning of the war in China was marked only by a speech from the
headmaster. All the children were assembled in the gymnasium, and
were told that, since Japan was now at war, they had a special
responsibility to behave well and work hard.

Ayako and her family were by that time living quite close to the
school, in a big house which they had rented for a year. This house
had once belonged to the governor of Kwangju himself, and it was
surrounded by grounds so large that it took Ayako a couple of
minutes to walk from the gate to the front door.

51

My best friend at school was a girl called Nakanishi-san. Although her house wasn't in the same direction as mine, I used to walk home with her first before going back to our house. But on the way from her house to ours I had to go down a very narrow dark road, which had gardens with thick trees and hedges on either side. Once when I went down there, this boy suddenly leapt out from among the leaves in front of me. He was a Korean boy whom we'd seen before on our way home from school. I think Naka-nishi-san and I had once shouted something rude at him when we passed him in the street. I was very frightened when I saw him. I tried to run past him, but he caught me and pulled my hair and kicked my shins. It happened once again, a few days later. I never told my parents about it, but after that I used to go home a different way.

It had taken Ayako's father less than ten years to rise from being an itinerant building worker to being the managing director of a prospering small business and the resident of a house which had once belonged to the city governor, and he revelled in his success. Ayako, who slept in the bedroom next to her parents', would hear the muffled murmurs of their conversation through the dark wooden walls at night, and often her father would be talking about his business deals, boasting how he had made so much profit on this contract, and so much on that. Sometimes she overheard other things. Once or twice she was startled out of sleep by the sound of raised voices, and from the confusion of angry words she knew that her parents were quarrelling over her father's infidelities. For a part of his new-found wealth was spent in the area of Kwangju to which émigré geishas had transplanted their own corner of Japanese city life.

My father was never physically violent, but he knew how to hurt with words. Sometimes he would get angry about little things. At meal times, if the food wasn't good enough, he would push his bowl away. 'I can't eat this rubbish!' he'd say, and he'd storm out of the house and go off to drink with his friends. He would shout at us children too sometimes – 'You dirty little thing! You *ahoge* child!' ('Ahoge' is Shikoku dialect for 'stupid'.)

He was very strict about our manners. We had to go and greet him politely each morning, and if he had friends in for a meal we were expected to bow to them properly. But most of the time he wasn't there. He rarely took days off work, even at weekends, so we didn't see much of him really. I was rather frightened of him. I played with my mother when I was little, but I never remember my father playing with us or having fun with us.

Ayako was still suffering from the weak health and eye trouble which she had endured since infancy. Her mother took her to one doctor after another, and when each failed to find a cure she sent her for a course of treatment to a clinic run by a Korean doctor whose name was Dr Bin.

I went to the clinic several afternoons a week for almost half a year. After I had eaten my packed lunch at school, I had to go and ask the teacher for permission to go to the doctor's. At the clinic, Dr Bin used to give me injections of something which as far as I can remember was called 'yatogorin' (but I may have got the name wrong). I don't know what it was, but it did actually seem to make me stronger. Also Dr Bin and his nurses were very kind to me. I was fascinated by their medicine bottles. They had lots of different bottles at the clinic, brown glass and green glass and colourless, all different shapes and sizes. I started to collect them. Every time I went to the clinic he would give me one or two empty bottles for my collection, and soon I had scores of them all round my bedroom, gathering dust.

Sometimes I was more seriously ill. I got fevers and swollen tonsils. Then Mother would send for Dr Bin, and he always came right away. He used to come in a rickshaw (they had rickshaws in Kwangju then). He'd come rattling up to the door in the rickshaw, with his black bag in his hands, and one of his nurses from his clinic running along the road behind him.

Until the end of the Third Year classes at Kōshū Central Primary School were mixed, but from the Fourth Year onwards girls and boys were taught separately, and indeed from the age of ten until adulthood they would lead almost entirely separate lives.

This segregation was emphasized by the lay-out of the school: girls' classes and boys' classes were in opposite wings, with the mixed classes of little ones in the middle. In the playground boys and girls played separately, the boys playing *sumō* wrestling or acting out battles from the China War, the girls skipping to the rhythm of age-old rhymes.

We also used to play 'hana-ichi-momme'. That's one of those games which you play in two groups. Each group links arms and then they walk up to each other and the leader of each group says: 'Hana-ichi-momme, I want so-and-so' (naming one of the girls in the other group). Then the two leaders made the shapes of scissors, paper and stone with their hands, and the one who makes the stronger shape wins the girl they have chosen for their team. When I played it, I always seemed to get left over at the end, because no one ever wanted to choose me for their team.

After the brief year of grandeur as tenants of the house which had once belonged to the governor, Ayako's family moved to smaller rented accommodation while their father, who had bought a plot of land in the city, built them a house of their own. When school and homework were finished, Ayako would go out into the street in front of the house to play, or to watch the world passing by. Sometimes the *kamishibai* man would come round and set up his show in their road, and Ayako and the neighbouring children would cluster round to buy a handful of sweets, which were their admission ticket to watch the performance. Then the *kamishibai* man would take out one big coloured picture card after another and deftly slip them into the wooden screen which he carried with him on the back of his bicycle. As picture followed picture a story unfolded before their eyes, while the *kamishibai* man chanted the narrative, provided the sound effects and created the voice of each of his characters. Sometimes he told traditional tales of ogres and goblins, talking foxes and magic crocks of gold, but often his show had an educational message, bringing stories of Japan's recent victories in China, all illustrated in brilliant colour, into the quiet Kwangju street. On other days the Korean candy-man would pass by, dressed in white national costume and carrying strips of sticky sweet-potato candy from which he would cut whatever length you could afford with your sen's[4] pocket money.

But much of the time Ayako spent in the twilit gloom of the outside shed where the family crammed their empty suitcases and unwanted furniture. There she would squeeze into an unoccupied corner and balance herself where a trickle of light came in through the door, reading. In bed she would read too, late into the night, until her sensitive eyes were aching and red with tiredness.

I read all the usual Japanese fairy stories on my own. I don't remember my mother or big sister ever telling me stories.

54

My mother didn't like me reading. That's why I had to do it where she couldn't see me. If she ever caught me reading she used to say: 'If you've got spare time, why don't you do something useful like sewing or cooking?'

I remember she was always telling me that I couldn't just do what I liked with my time. I had to learn to do housework properly.

'Otherwise', she'd warn me, 'you will never be a bride. Or even if you do get married, your husband will soon send you away.'

I used to say to her: 'When I'm grown up, I shall have someone to do the cooking and sewing for me.'

But Mother would reply: 'Even if you do have someone to do it for you, you still have to know how it's done, otherwise, how can you supervise them properly?'

She was always boasting to me how much she enjoyed sewing, and how good she was at it. And it was true. She used to do her needlework with a group of friends, and she always finished what she was making in half the time they took to do theirs.

Now that the children were growing up, Ayako's mother had more time in which to practise the accomplishments of a Japanese housewife. Until the maid arrived in the morning she was always busy: first there was the rice to be washed and cooked; then a little bowl of rice had to be placed as an offering on the *butsudan*; next she had to pay her respects also to the Shintō *kamidana* and the emperor's portrait; the family's breakfast had to be served, her husband seen off to work and the children packed off to school. But when the Korean *omoni* arrived to take over the more mundane tasks of cooking and sweeping and washing dishes she had time, not only for her needlework, but also to take lessons from the flower-arranging teacher who called at the house a couple of days a week. Later, too, an increasing amount of her time was taken up with the meetings and charitable activities of the Patriotic Women's League (*Aikoku Fujinkai*), an organization which had been set up in Japan in 1901, initially to provide assistance to wounded soldiers and bereaved families, but which by the Shōwa period was engaged in all kinds of moral and social activities including running nurseries, providing health education, and discouraging decadent fashions amongst women.

During Ayako's fourth year at primary school, her mother was suddenly taken ill and rushed off to a hospital in the city of Mokpo. Afterwards, Ayako learnt that her mother had suffered an ectopic pregnancy. For almost three months she was away in hospital, while the children were looked after by a nanny who had been hastily brought over from Japan. Each weekend, Ayako and the rest of the family would make the two-hour train journey from Kwangju to Mokpo to visit her mother in the strange antiseptic-smelling ward of the big hospital. Even when she was allowed home, her mother was still weak, and the nanny was kept on for another year to help look after the family.

For a while, therefore, Ayako had more opportunities than usual to slip away in quiet moments and read her books. She developed a love for history, and would spend hour after hour immersed in the lives of the great heroes of medieval Japan.

In the fifth form our teacher set us a history question which I spent days pondering about. The question was: 'Which character in history do you think best represents the virtue of *chū-kō* [loyalty and filial piety]?'

The answer which almost everyone gave was Kusunoki Masashige. That was because in the fourteenth century, after the imperial family had become divided into two rival lines and the Shōgun Hōjō had gained control over the emperors, Kusunoki Masashige helped the Emperor Go-Daigo to regain power, and so he helped to ensure the succession of the imperial line which has lasted right down to today. That was supposed to be the supreme act of loyalty, and that was the answer you were really meant to give. But I thought and thought about it, and in the end I wrote Taira-no-Shigemori. The teacher was very surprised at that. He asked me why I had put Taira-no-Shigemori. I explained that it was because Taira-no-Shigemori's father, Taira-no-Kiyomori, was a very strong person and had gained control over the court and all the rival *Samurai* clans, but Taira-no-Shigemori criticized his father and persuaded him that he should not seize all power for himself, but ought to submit himself to the emperor. So because he had persuaded his father to be loyal, it seemed to me that Taira-no-Shigemori showed the greatest amount of both loyalty and filial piety.

At this time, however, even needlework lessons in school were acquiring a new interest. The girls' task for the year was to make

'Consolation Bags' to be sent to the soldiers fighting in China. Each bag contained several things. First, there was the *sen-nin-bari*, a piece of cloth on which one thousand stitches had been embroidered, each by a different hand. The girls would stand at a street corner stopping lady passers-by to collect a stitch, into which was sewn one person's compassion and concern for the unknown soldier in the far-off war. Then there was a letter to be addressed to the soldier. This consisted of a few, carefully-thought-out sentences of gratitude and encouragement, to be painted in your very best brush writing. After that the bag was filled up with sweets, books and other presents which the girls paid for out of their own pocket money.

Music lessons were changing, too. No longer did they learn songs about the fall of snow or the coming of spring, but rather songs about the feelings of a soldier as he set off to fight for his country in a foreign land:

I see those faces, hear those voices.
My wife and son are waving,
Waving their flags until they break.
Their message to me is to fight well.
I look at the sky, and in the spaces
Between the clouds I see them waving still.
From the deck of the great fleet of battleships
I say goodbye to the land of my birth,
Goodbye to my wife and son.
I look to the place where the sky arches
Above the Imperial Palace
And I swear I will fight well.

Or the more cheerful, marching song of the rising sun flag.

With a tiny hand
I waved the flag
From my mother's back
That far-off day
Still returns to my mind
And patriotism's hot blood
Courses more strongly in my veins.

After the capture of Nanking, the children of Kwangju held a lantern procession which started from the Shintō shrine high on the hillside above the city. The shrine was large and new – new, like

Shintō shrines in every Korean city, each of which was a piece of mosaic of Japanese culture which colonial policy was laying out across the Korean peninsula: one of the measures of 1937 had been the enforcement of compulsory attendance at Shintō shrines, a regulation which evoked intense hostility, particularly from the Christian element of the Korean population.

Ayako regarded the Kwangju shrine with a special, almost proprietary, interest, because it was her father who had been responsible for levelling a terrace on the steep mountain-slope and building the massive, stone-blocked foundations on which the shrine rested. When every school-child in the city had assembled at the shrine, they lined up in groups with their own school and formed into a long procession which wound down the hill and into the town. Children from the three Japanese schools walked at the front of the procession. The Korean schools brought up the rear.

Soon after, Ayako's family acquired their first radio, which enabled them to follow both the fighting in China and events on the 'Mainland' more closely. But for much of the time the radio was monopolized by Ayako's brothers, who used it to listen to sports, particularly to reports of *sumō* contests from Tokyo. Ayako's older sister was now finishing school, and since no higher education for girls was available locally it was decided that she should be sent to a domestic science college in southern Japan.

Ayako, too, was beginning to worry about her own future now. The end of primary school was approaching, and beyond that there were three possibilities. If she did well enough in her exams, she could go on to Kōshū Yamato ('Yamato' being an archaic term for 'Japan') Higher Girls' School, the only school in the city which offered secondary education for Japanese girls. If she failed to be admitted to that school, she would have to go all the way to Mokpo, which had a larger Girls' School with lower entrance requirements. If she could not even get into Mokpo school, then she would have to be sent to a private boarding school in Japan. This would be not only very expensive, but also something of a disgrace. Because of the great emphasis on education in Japan's modernization policies, it is state schools and colleges which have (with a few exceptions) provided the highest level of education, while private education has tended to be seen as a refuge for those with more money but less ability. Ayako therefore set her heart on winning a place at Kōshū Girls' School, and put all her efforts into reading and re-reading her text-books and going over the notes of each lesson in the evenings after school.

In the November of Ayako's last year at primary school, the 2600th anniversary of the creation of the Japanese nation was celebrated throughout the empire. The story of the creation of Japan is derived from two eighth-century chronicles – *Kojiki* and *Nihon Shoki* – which tell how the Japanese islands were born from the union of the primal god and goddess, Izanagi and Izanami:

Izanagi and Izanami (it is written) stood on the floating bridge of Heaven, and held counsel together, saying: 'Is there not a country beneath?' Thereupon they thrust down the jewel-spear of Heaven, and groping about therewith found the ocean.

The brine which dripped from the point of the spear coagulated and became an island which received the name of Ono-goro-jima.

The two Deities thereupon descended and dwelt in this island. Accordingly, they wished to become husband and wife together, and to produce countries.

So they made Ono-goro-jima the pillar of the centre of the land.

Now the male deity turning by the left, and the female deity turning by the right, they went round the pillar of land separately. When they met together on one side, the female deity spoke first and said: 'How delightful! I have met with a lovely youth!' The male deity was displeased and said: 'I am a man, and by right should have spoken first. How is it that on the contrary thou, a woman, shouldst have been the first to speak? This was unlucky. Let us go round again.' Upon this the two deities went back and having met anew, this time the male deity spoke first, and said: 'How delightful! I have met a lovely maiden.'

Then he enquired of the female deity, saying: 'In thy body is there aught formed?' She answered, and said: 'In my body there is a place which is the source of femininity.' The male deity said: 'In my body again there is a place which is the source of masculinity. I wish to unite this source-place of my body to the source-place of thy body.' Hereupon the male and female first become united as husband and wife.

Now then the time of birth arrived, first of all the island of

Ahaji was reckoned as the placenta, and their minds took no pleasure in it. Therefore it received the name of Ahaji-no-Shima [Island of my shame].

Next there was produced the island of O-yamato no tōyō-aki-tsushima [Rich Autumn Island of Yamato, i.e., Honshū].

Next they produced the island of Iyo no futa-na [Shikoku], and next the island of Tsukushi [Kyushu]. Next the islands of Ōki and Sado were born as twins. This is the prototype of twin-births which sometimes take place among mankind.

Next was born the island of Koshi, then the island of O-Shima, then the island of Kibi no Ko.

Hence first arose the designation of the Great Eight-island Country.[5]

The chronicles further tell how Izanagi gave birth to the Storm deity, the Moon deity and the Sun deity, whose name was Amaterasu Ōmikami. The Storm god was very violent, and did many wild things which offended his sister Amaterasu, so she hid herself away in a cave, leaving the world in darkness. Then all the gods and goddesses of heaven gathered before the cave. There they planted a sacred tree on whose branches they hung a mirror and a jewel. One of the goddesses began to dance a comical dance, and Amaterasu, hearing the sound of merriment, was tempted out of the cave, and her light returned to illuminate the world.

Later the Storm god killed a great many-tailed monster, and in one of its tails he found a sword, which he presented to Amaterasu. Amaterasu's grandson, Ninigi-no-Mikoto, was sent down from heaven to rule the land, and when he descended from the clouds on to a mountain in Kyushu, he carried with him the sword, the mirror and the jewel, which became the symbols of Japanese emperors for all time. Ninigi's great-grandson was the first earthly emperor, the Emperor Jimmu, and he extended his empire northwards from Kyushu into the land of Yamato. Here he founded his capital by building a palace of honour in his ancestress Amaterasu. This event, which according to tradition occurred in 660 BC, marked the birth of the nation of Japan.

This mythology had not in fact played a great part in Japanese people's consciousness of their history until the early nineteenth century, when a group of nationalistic thinkers began to revive interest in early historical and legendary writings. But it was after the Meiji restoration, and above all during the 1930s, that a literal interpretation of Shintō myths was used both to reinforce a consciousness of national unity – creating a vision of the imperial line as the origin and head of the family of Japanese people – and to assert the uniqueness and superiority of Japanese culture. The culmination of this process were the 2600th Anniversary celebrations, which were held in 1940.

The central celebration, involving speeches, traditional dances and patriotic songs, was held in an open space close to the Imperial Palace in Tokyo on November 10–11. An observer recorded the scene:

> . . . fortunately the weather smiled on Japan during both days, which were sunny and crisply cold. The first was the day of ceremonial greetings, and the second the day of celebration. For several months squads of men and schoolgirls have been working in the big plaza opposite to the palace, levelling it off, setting up decorative poles, laying out an enormous number of flowers, and finally building a big pavilion and rows of seats in front of it for about 50,000 people. They were the only people, all specially invited, who could witness the ceremonies, because no one was allowed on the roofs or in the windows of the big office buildings in Marunouchi [the business centre of Tokyo], which would have afforded observation spots for many more thousands. No one may look down upon the emperor, and I noticed how completely vacant these roofs and windows were.[6]

In Kwangju they held their celebrations on the mountain-slope before the Shintō shrine. Thousands of Japanese and Korean children spread over the rugged, rocky ground like ants clustered on an anthill. They wriggled their toes and shifted their feet furtively to keep them from going numb as they stood in the cold listening to speech after speech, first from the city governor, then from other municipal dignitaries, headmasters and local business leaders, each reminding them of their nation's long and illustrious history, of the grave situation in China, and of the need to devote themselves more than ever to the national cause. Then, waving their flags like flowers in the wind, the children sang the special song which they had learnt for the occasion, and turning east towards the Imperial Palace in Tokyo, sent up a great many-throated cry of 'Long live the Emperor'.

61

A couple of months later Ayako heard, to her delight and surprise, that she had been accepted by Kōshū Yamato Higher Girls' School. Her new school was a large, modern red-brick building in the centre of Kwangju. There were some four hundred pupils in the school, divided into four years, each of which was subdivided into two classes of fifty girls. The curriculum was identical with that of Girls' Schools throughout Japan, and all the pupils were Japanese, except that two places in each class were reserved for Korean girls of good background and outstanding ability. One of the Korean pupils in Ayako's class, a girl whom they knew by the Japanese name of Kanemoto-san, was to become her close and lifelong friend. Their teacher in the first year was a man named Mr Sugiyama, who came from the island of Okinawa, and was teased by the girls for his regional accent and his dark, un-Japanese appearance. He had a bristly chin which never seemed to have been properly shaved, and Ayako's classmates nicknamed him 'scrubbing brush'.

Admission to Kōshū Girls' School made a great impact on Ayako.

Until I went to secondary school I wasn't really interested in politics and that sort of thing. But after I moved to the Girls' School my attitudes seemed to change. I think it was because I really hadn't been expecting to get into Kōshū Girls' School. It was quite a shock when I was accepted. After that, I sort of felt that I had something to repay. I began to get interested in the war situation. I really believed that Japan was the Land of the Gods [*Shinshū*] and that it was absolutely essential that Japan should win the war, and I believed that I have to sacrifice myself to help Japan's victory.

I also felt – it sounds funny now, but at the time I really did feel – that I was tremendously privileged to be Japanese. I remember being genuinely sorry for people who, through no fault of their own, had been born Taiwanese or Korean.

Much of her free time was now spent at the youth meetings of the local *tonarigumi* (neighbourhood council). The *tonarigumi*, each consisting of five to ten households, had been created by the Japanese government in 1940. They were deliberately modelled on the traditional structure of Japanese village society, in which small groups of families had formed, as it were, the cells of the social organism – providing mutual help to build irrigation channels, harvest rice crops, rebuild houses or put out fires, and carrying ultimate responsibility for the delinquencies of member families or individuals.

The new *tonarigumi*, although artificial creations, were supposed to fulfil similar functions, including the distribution of rations and the raising of contributions towards Japan's war effort. Like their forerunners, they also served the interests of the state by directing the most powerful of all pressures – the opinion of the neighbours – against dissident members of society. The *tonarigumi* formed the basis of a pyramid of local, regional and national organizations whose apex was the *Taisei Yokusankai* – the Imperial Rule Assistance Association – created at the same time and acting as a new, national organization to support the war effort and replace the old and now totally impotent political parties. Together with the Patriotic Women's League, the *tonarigumi* and the *Taisei Yokusankai* were the pillars on which rested the edifice of Japanese wartime social control.

But for teenagers like Ayako, the so-called 'Junior Citizens' section of the *tonarigumi*, which met several times a week, was above all a chance to gather in a friend's house, drink tea and chatter, and perhaps listen to a little talk from your next-door neighbour's mother or a man from the local fire brigade.

By now, Ayako's family had moved into the new house which their father had built for them. It was a typical Japanese one-storey house, with four large matted rooms separated by sliding screens. On three sides the house was surrounded by a range of other, newly-completed buildings which Ayako's father had had put up at the same time. These contained four small sets of rooms which were rented out to tenants.

One of our tenants was a policeman. He was a Japanese policeman who worked in the main police station in Kwangju. We used to see him quite a lot. Sometimes he would stop and chat to us children. Now and then he used to talk about what they did at the police station. He said some strange things which worried me. He wasn't in the military or the political police, just in the ordinary civilian force. But I remember he once told me what they did to political prisoners, communists and people like that. He said they made them drink lots and lots of water, until their stomachs swelled up. I felt peculiar when he told me that. I thought that it was something which I shouldn't ever repeat to other people, and in fact I never did talk about it to anybody else.

By now the suppressive aspects of the cultural assimilation policies had reached their symbolic peak. In 1940 the main Korean language newspapers were closed down, and from 1939 the colonial authorities began to force all Korean families to renounce their surnames and replace them with Japanese-sounding names. One of the genuine similarities between Korean and Japanese culture is the importance which both attach to the preservation and honouring of the family name. This act, therefore, was one which was to leave a particularly deep scar on future relations between Japan and Korea.

Such events, however, hardly impinged on the consciousness of the teenage Ayako, whose horizons were at this time bounded by more intimate family concerns.

I do have some sort of memory of hearing about the order for Koreans to change their name. But I don't think it made any impression on me really. After all, nearly all our friends were Japanese, and as for the Korean girls at school, well, I don't remember ever discussing that kind of thing with them.

In 1941 Ayako reached puberty. With her family, she celebrated the passing from childhood to womanhood in the traditional way, with the ceremonial meal of red snapper mullet and rice prepared with red beans. But almost at the same time, a strange and unexpected thing happened. Her mother informed the children that they were all being removed from her father's family register, and would therefore no longer be able to use the family name, Hasebe.

The register, or *koseki*, into which each child's name had been entered at birth, was the continuation of an administrative system which in Japan goes back many centuries. Every Japanese family has a *koseki* in which birth, marriage and death are recorded. Nowadays, it is usual for a newly-married couple to establish their own, separate *koseki* at the nearest local government office, but in earlier times, when a family would usually remain in one village for centuries, the record was maintained by the community for generation after generation. Before the Meiji period one of the most serious punishments for criminal offences was to be struck off your village's register, a sentence which deprived you of the privileges of the membership of society and rendered you officially an 'unperson': *hi-nin*. (The descendants of these 'un-people' still form part of an oppressed group now known in Japan as *burakumin*.) In modern times the family register is important mainly as an administrative document, a copy of which is needed on all kinds of occasions, from entering school to obtaining a passport. But it also becomes crucial where questions of legitimacy and legacies are at stake.

The relationship between Ayako's parents had been made official simply by the process of entering the names of Ayako's mother, Tsutsumi Yoshino, and each of her children in the Hasebe family register. By 1941, however, the four children of Mr Hasebe's first marriage had reached adulthood, and had become concerned at the prospect of having to share their inheritance with five younger half-brothers and sisters. What kind of legal or moral pressures were put on her mother Ayako never know. All she knew was that, one day, her mother called the children together and told them without emotion that their names were all to be expunged from their father's register. From now on, although her parents continued to live together exactly as before, her mother had officially been demoted from the status of wife to that of mistress. And Ayako would have to face the whispers, the sidelong glances and giggles of the girls at school when they discovered that overnight she had lost her father's name, Hasebe, and acquired her mother's, Tsutsumi.

4

Iida Momo

At the beginning of this century Japanese society was predominantly rural and agricultural. About two-thirds of the working population was engaged in farming, forestry or fishing, and of these the great majority were peasants who were either landless or owned only tiny holdings of one or two acres. Fading images of rural poverty, therefore, provide the background to many family histories in the Shōwa period. Like Tsutsumi Ayako, Iida Momo traces his origins to such a background; though his family's and his own destiny was to be very different from hers.

Life in the Japanese countryside was generally harsh: an unending cycle of back-breaking labour in the rice fields or the mulberry orchards (for silk production supplemented the income of many farm families). There was never more than a small margin between the endemic poverty of rural life and absolute destitution, and the steady flow of labour from the villages, which fed the workshops and factories of Japan's expanding towns would become a flood in periods of natural disaster or economic distress.

It was during one such period, the economic recession which followed the Russo–Japanese War of 1904–05, that the Iida family, overwhelmed by the grinding hopelessness of agricultural labour, fled from the farm where their ancestors had worked for generations to the nearest big city, Nagoya. Like most of the peasant families who migrated to the towns, they found life in the spreading suburban slums little easier than the rural poverty they had left behind. Twenty-five years later, when Iida Momo as a child used to visit his grandparents' house, they were still living in a shanty town environment of squalid makeshift housing and marginal employment.

That part of town was full of people who had drifted in from the countryside. The houses were built like barracks, side by side

66

around courtyards. My grandparents' house was one of nine which were built round three sides of a yard. At one side of the block there was a shared lavatory and at the other there was the water pump. The yard in the middle was used as a sort of communal work space. It was always full of scrap and junk, and when you stood in it you could see everything that was going on in any of the nine households round about. The house was built in the simplest and cheapest way possible: just big posts driven into the ground, and earthen partitions in between, which divided it into four rooms.

When I used to go there, the house was right by a huge wall – the longest wall in Japan, I heard it was – which surrounded the Nagoya works of Mitsubishi Heavy Industry. Most of the children from the neighbourhood, as soon as they were old enough, went straight in through those factory gates to work for Mitsubishi. But that was all comparatively new. The factory had grown up since my grandparents moved there.

In my grandparents' house there were only two big bits of furniture. One was the clock – a great big, rather shoddy-looking clock. My father had saved up for that out of his very first pay packets. My grandparents were like most country people. They were used to living by the sun and the seasons, and when they moved into Nagoya I suppose that it was the first time that my grandfather had had to regulate his life according to mechanical, city time. The other thing I remember in the house was the huge *butsudan*. That was because my grandfather was a devout follower of the Ikkō-Shu sect of Buddhism. Afterwards it seemed to me that that was really all he had left behind him – the only thing he had to show for a whole lifetime of hard work – just one big *butsudan*.

Iida Momo talks with a quiet but intense involvement about his family origins. Much of his life has been a search for an understanding of his own place in the convoluted processes of history. So he sees small memories – the colours, smells and textures of the past – in symbolic terms, as part of a wider reality.

All around him, the walls of his study are lined with row upon row of books: books on politics, history, literature, philosophy; translations of Greek and Roman poetry, Russian novels, works of French and German social thought. Every now and then the telephone rings, and Iida Momo breaks off his discourse to discuss a deadline for an article he is writing or the arrangements for a political meeting. Apart from that the silence of the big room, with its tiers of books and its dark polished grand piano, is broken only by his voice and by a clock – far more elegant than the one which once graced his grandfather's slum tenement – interspersing his conversation with its soft Westminister chimes.

My father didn't complete primary school. He was taken away when the family migrated from their village to Nagoya, and afterwards he never went back to school again. So I think that he only had four full years of education, though whether he left right at the end of the fourth year or in the middle of fifth year I couldn't say for sure.

At any rate, soon after they arrived in Nagoya, my father, who was straight out of primary school himself, got a job as a kind of caretaker-cum-servant in a place called Meirin Primary School. Meirin was a private school – a tremendously elite place. My father used to have to stoke the boilers there and serve tea and things like that.

Now Father, when he was a boy, always wore clothes which were too big for him. You can imagine how it was: my grandparents were poor people, and when they bought him clothes they would buy them several sizes too big so that they would last for years. (It wasn't like nowadays when people buy new clothes virtually with every change of season.) Of course, the problem about this was that by the time Father had grown into the clothes, they were usually worn-out and tattered.

One day the children at the school where he worked started to laugh at him about something. My father was angry, and he ran up and tried to kick one of the boys, but, because his shoes were several sizes too big, they just flew off into the air, and of course that only made the other boys laugh more than ever.

My father told me that story over and over again. I don't know how many times I heard it. Eventually, when I was older, I realized that there must have been a reason why he told it so often. I suppose for him it had a kind of symbolic significance.

When he was about twenty years old, Momo's father Toshifumi fell in love with a young woman from the neighbourhood. She was

68

already engaged to be married to another man, but she did not much care for her prospective husband. So, on the night before the wedding was due to take place, she and Toshifumi eloped together. In the closely-knit community in which they lived, where everyone knew everyone else's business, this caused a terrible scandal. The family of the rejected bridegroom threatened revenge, and Toshifumi's parents refused to support him.

But Iida Toshifumi was a person of unusual determination and resourcefulness. It was clear to him that the only way to win social acceptance was by becoming rich, and so he set out to exploit any available opportunity to do precisely that.

The First World War had recently ended. More and more Japanese troops were being posted to continental Asia to protect the country's growing economic and strategic interests in China and Manchuria. Japan had also just embarked on one of its more disastrous overseas military ventures: the Siberian Expedition. This was an attempt, supported by Western powers, to rally anti-Bolshevik forces in Siberia against the new revolutionary Sovvet government. In all, the expedition lasted for four years (from 1918 to 1922) and involved some 75,000 Japanese troops, but it failed to achieve any of its objectives and brought little credit to those involved.

Wherever Japanese forces were stationed on the Asian mainland, there appeared the inevitable excrescences of garrison life: the little clusters of cheap bars and restaurants selling Japanese food, the cabarets and the brothels. These were filled mostly with the daughters of impoverished farm families who would bind themselves to their employer, sometimes for as long as three or four years, in return for a lump-sum payment and the promise of food and shelter. But the practise of procuring girls by an advance payment laid the brothel-owner open to an old and often-practised trick, which provided Iida Toshifumi with the inspiration for his first business venture. He and his mistress would travel together from one garrison town to another. In each, they would select a suitable brothel or geisha house to which she would 'sell' herself for an agreed sum. Then, at the first opportunity, she would escape with Toshifumi's assistance, and the couple would move on to another town, where they repeated the same trick. In this way they seem to have supported themselves for some time, travelling from Korea to Manchuria and then on to Siberia, and Iida Toshifumi might well have joined the ranks of Japanese settlers seeking to create a new life for themselves on the Asian continent. But the life was hard and the earnings were unreliable, and Iida Toshifumi must eventually have come to the conclusion that this was not the way to make his fortune, for in the 1920s they returned to Japan and soon afterwards Toshifumi settled in Tokyo, where he began to explore other methods of becoming rich.

My father was always a very frank person. He was never ashamed of the things he had done in his past, and he used to speak about them to us quite often. One of his schemes for making money was some kind of exchange fiddle. As far as I can remember, he used to say that it was exchanging Rentenmarks. This would have been at the time when they had that massive inflation in Germany, and people there used to go out shopping with suitcases full of banknotes. I feel sure that I can remember Father saying that he used to go down to the harbour at Yokohama and exchange money with German people coming off the boats. Then he would go to some remote little village, where of course no one knew what was going on in Germany, and sell the virtually useless Mark notes to people who thought they were really valuable.

But after my father's death, when I talked about this to one of his relatives, she said that I had got it all wrong.

'It wasn't Rentenmarks,' she said, 'it was Roubles. Your father collected a whole trunk full of worthless Tsar's Roubles when he was in Siberia, and when he got back to Japan he sold them and made a nice little profit for himself.'

Well, I don't know, Rentenmarks or Roubles, or perhaps it was both. At any rate, that was the sort of thing he did for a living in those days.

In Tokyo, where life was rapidly resuming its normal patterns after the Great Earthquake, Toshifumi became a member of a society of *yakuza* (gangsters). Traditionally, Japanese *yakuza* practised a form of division of labour. There were the *bakuto* gangs, whose main interest was in the control of illegal gambling, and the *tekiya* gangs, who controlled the fairs and street markets, issuing licences to stall-holders, collecting protection money and selling everything from candy-floss to doubtfully-acquired bargain goods and worthless 'miracle cures' for acne or arthritis. Toshifumi's gang was of the second type, and for some time he went the rounds of the markets and festivals, selling anything that the crowds were credulous enough to buy.

But in spite of his lack of formal education, Iida Toshifumi had a natural gift for mechanical things. He could mend all kinds of electrical gadgets, and liked to take things apart and put them together again. At about this time he began to develop his talent, thinking up improvements to the cheap household appliances which he sold, and eventually coming up with his own inventions. One of these was an ultraviolet sun lamp in whose rays the sun-starved city-dwellers could bathe themselves. He called it the 'Radio Rayer' – radios at that time being the last word in technological sophistication – and it was such an instant success that he was able to obtain a patent and set up his own little company manufacturing the lamps.

In 1925 Iida Toshifumi married. He had never formalized his relationship with the girl from Nagoya, and now, with his newly-acquired status as managing director of his own company, he was able to marry into a quite wealthy and well-established family. His bride was the daughter of a rice-merchant, and a graduate of a highly respected women's college. The bride's family, however, had some doubts about this upstart suitor, and her brother in particular tried to persuade her against the match.

On their way home after the marriage ceremony, my parents were met in the street by the assistant manager of my father's lamp-making business.

'You mustn't go home,' he said, 'I've booked a room for you in a hotel.'

Well, my mother thought that this was some kind of surprise which had been arranged for the wedding day, and she was very impressed, because in those days staying in a hotel was an almost unheard-of luxury. It was only afterwards that she discovered the truth: my father's mistress from Nagoya had heard about the wedding, and in a fit of jealousy she had stormed round to the house brandishing a chopping knife and demanding to see the newly-wed pair. Eventually my father's employees managed to get her to go away, but she came back one day later on when my mother was in the house, and that was how my mother found out all about it.

The following year, on 10 January 1926, the Iidas' son was born. He was named Momo (peach), a name reminiscent of the legendary

Momotarō, who was born from a peach stone and grew up to win fame and fortune and to rid the nation of marauding ogres.

But Iida Toshifumi's marriage, having begun so inauspiciously, did not last long. A few months after Iida Momo's birth his parents separated, and soon after Toshifumi remarried, this time to the nineteen-year-old daughter of a Tokyo sweet-shop owner.

Momo, as was normal in such cases, remained with his father and was looked after until the arrival of his stepmother by a woman employee in his father's firm. Toshifumi's business interests were now going from success to success. The company was a typical small business, with workshops, offices and the family's home all housed in the same building. At the time of Momo's birth this was a small wooden bungalow in the middle of a building plot in the Shiba district of central Tokyo. Outside was an iron gate and a brass nameplate with the words 'Radio Rayer Co. Ltd' engraved on it.

But by the time that Momo was three or four the business had expanded so much that his father had been able to build a fine five-storey concrete building, one of the tallest in that part of town. On the ground floor were the company offices. The first and second storeys were occupied by the workshops, where ten to fifteen workers were employed. Above, on the top two floors, lived the Iida family. Immediately below their apartment the condenser coils for the lamps were produced. These were covered with a wax coating, and Momo's early memories of childhood are consequently haunted by the unforgettable smell of molten wax which permeated every corner of the place where he lived.

Soon after Momo's father remarried a stepsister, Noriko, was born. Then in the following year, 1930, Momo's stepmother became pregnant again, and the four-year-old boy was sent to stay with his grandparents in Nagoya during the birth of the new baby. At his grandparents' house, Momo contracted whooping cough. He was not seriously ill, but when he returned to Tokyo he passed the disease on to the newborn baby, Ineko, who died of it.

My father had brought a family grave in the cemetery at Aoyama, and during his funeral last year, when we opened up the grave, we found a small urn with the name 'Iida Ineko' on it. When I saw it the memories suddenly came back.

There was a big hospital near our house, where they took baby Ineko when she became seriously ill. After she died my stepmother was distraught with grief, and she carried the cold body of the baby back to our house in her arms, crying out loud all the way. The strange thing is that although I know I didn't see it myself – it was just something that I was told about afterwards – yet all the same I have this picture in my mind of my stepmother walking through the streets with the dead baby in her arms. It seems as vivid to me as if it were a real memory.

In 1931 Iida Momo was sent to kindergarten. That in itself was a measure of his father's commercial success, for kindergartens were private and fee-paying, and were normally attended only by the children of the well-to-do. Momo's kindergarten was attached to the large and ancient Zōjōji Temple, which was just a few minutes' walk from his house. Most days, however, he did not walk but was given a ride on the back of a bicycle by one of his father's employees. He enjoyed weaving through the busy streets on the bicycle, swinging round corners with the bell tinkling, and listening to the young man on the saddle in front of him whistle a catchy tune. Years later Momo would still have a good repertoire of mid-1920s popular songs remembered from those days. At lunch time in the kindergarten they were given big bread rolls. Momo loved to eat a hole through the middle of his roll and then hold it up to his eye like a telescope, viewing the world through the hollow crust.

The grounds of the Zōjōji Temple were also the scene for some of the many local fairs and festivals, for the Shiba district, which had been one of the main entertainment quarters of Tokyo since the eighteenth century, had a particularly rich tradition of such events. The fairs became a source of endless excitement and fascination for little Momo, who at that time only dimly realized that they had provided the beginnings of his father's business success.

My father had left the *yakuza* when he started his own business, but there is an incident which I clearly remember from when I was young. I was at home one day when a stranger came to the house and asked to see my father. I heard afterwards that he was the son of the man who had led Father's gang.

He came into the room where we were and started talking to my father.

'The old man is dead,' I heard him say, 'what about it? Are you going to send some flowers for the funeral?'

My father offered his condolences, and said that of course he would send some flowers. Then they chatted for a while, and parted with bows and friendly smiles. But later Father explained to me that all the talk about 'flowers for the funeral' had been some sort of euphemism for money. The son was going to inherit the *yakuza* leadership, and he was asking my father to contribute to the expenses of setting himself up as the new boss of the gang.

Fairs at the Zōjōji Temple or the nearby Shinmei Shrine took place several times every month, and on these days Momo would be off down the street, with his five-sen pocket money clutched in his hand, to buy candy-floss or the wonderful edible birds and butterflies which the sweet-sellers would spin from strands of caramel. These were bought not only for the taste but for the delight of watching the sweet-seller's hands as he twirled the sticky thread with almost magical dexterity. Then there were the soft rice-flour sweets which could be bought ready-shaped or taken home to be moulded and remoulded to resemble all kinds of improbable objects before, grey and gritty from the touch of many fingers, they would be popped into the mouth and devoured.

Other stalls attracted Momo's curiosity. There was one little tent with a sign saying 'Arita's Chamber of Horrors'. Here, for a few sen, he was admitted to the smoky, crowded interior, where he could squeeze between the adults' legs to gaze, with fascinated, half-comprehending revulsion, at the pictures and models of freaks and monsters, and the photographs of disfigured bodies illustrating 'the Ravages of Syphilis'.

One man at the fair who particularly intrigued me was the fountain-pen seller. When I first saw him he was sitting by the side of the street with his wares spread out in front of him. On one side was a row of shiny new fountain-pens, and on the other side a little pile of similar pens which were twisted and blackened by fire. He was calling out to the passers-by in a loud, mournful voice, saying something like this:

'Ladies and gentlemen, last night I suffered a terrible misfortune. My pen factory was burnt to the ground. What you see before you is all that I could rescue from the flames. I have lost everything. I am forced to sell these last few pens for just a fraction of their real value so that I can at least buy a little food to feed my unhappy family. But my bad fortune is your good fortune. You will never get another opportunity like this one. Come and buy these last few pens while you have the chance.'

The first time I saw him, I fell for it. I spent my pocket money on one of his pens and hurried home feeling very pleased with my purchase. But of course it was a complete dud. It worked for about half-an-hour, and then it would do nothing but scratch holes in the paper.

A few weeks later I went to the fair again, and there was the fountain-pen seller, sitting by the road with the same little pile of burnt pens.

'Ladies and gentlemen,' he was saying, 'last night I suffered a terrible tragedy . . .'

Momo started primary school in 1933, attending the local state-run Sakuragawa School. Like most city primary schools, it was large: each year was divided into five classes of thirty-five to forty children. There were two classes for girls, two classes for boys, and one mixed class.

In the year that Momo started school a brand-new reading book was introduced in all primary schools throughout Japan. Momo and his classmates liked their crisp new text-books, and felt that they were vastly superior to the old books with their silly bits about beans and umbrellas. The new books began: 'Blossom, blossom, cherry blossom. Here, here, dog, come here. Advance, advance, army advance. The sun is bright. The sunrise is bright. Flag of the rising sun, banzai, banzai.'

The children attended school six days a week, from Monday to Saturday, but the school terms were interspersed with many special days, such as 11 February (which commemorated the founding of the Japanese nation), 29 April (the emperor's birthday) and 5 May (Boys' Day), when they would receive half-holidays. On these days there were no lessons. Instead, in the morning, the whole school gathered in the gymnasium. There, at the back of the stage, was a little recess covered by a purple silk curtain. When they were all assembled, the deputy headmaster appeared wearing a pair of white gloves. He advanced to the recess and pulled the fine white cord which drew back the curtain to reveal a portrait of the emperor. As soon as he did so the children were expected to bow their heads and keep them bowed until they heard the whisper of the curtain closing again.

Then the headmaster came in, carrying a purple silk cloth in which was wrapped the school's copy of the Imperial Rescript on Education. He carefully opened it, unrolled the scroll, and began to read – or rather to intone – the Rescript in a sing-song voice and with agonizing slowness. It was strictly forbidden to fidget, cough, sniff or blow your nose during the reading of the Rescript, and as soon as the ceremony was over the gymnasium echoed with a chorus of relieved snuffling. After that, the children were given red-and-white rice cakes, and everyone could go home.

One day during the winter of his first year at primary school, Momo was on his way down the street from his home to the nearest sweet-shop when the frosty air was suddenly shattered by the wailing of a siren. Once it sounded and then once again. All over Tokyo, all over the Japanese Empire, the double siren was sounding that day, bringing the news that the empress had born a son. Later on, at school, Momo and his classmates learnt a special song to commemorate the occasion:

The sirens sounded, toot – toot,
A Prince is born.

On Sundays and holidays, unless the weather was particularly bad, the children played out of doors. Tokyo was growing outwards, into the sea, and near Momo's house were great expanses of rough newly reclaimed land where nothing had yet been built. On cold, bright days in winter this land was filled with the local children, flying their multicoloured kites. In the streets they huddled round in little groups, playing with *menko*, sets of cards decorated with the faces of popular *kabuki* actors or the generals of victorious wars.

Summer was the hunting season. There were cicadas, to be trapped with blobs of glue on the end of long poles and kept in bamboo cages where (if they survived) you could listen to their endless dry trilling. Momo and his friends were convinced that you could hypnotize a dragonfly by slowly rotating your finger before its eyes as it sat on a leaf, and all their unsuccessful attempts to capture dragonflies this way could not shake their faith in the validity of the method. A more successful trick was the one which was used to catch bats. In the warm summer evenings, when the bats came swooping and twittering down the narrow streets, the children would be out among them, flinging their wooden sandals high in the air. The trick was not to hit the bats but to break their radar beams, making them suddenly plummet down towards your outstretched hands.

But the most serious business of all was fly-hunting. In a city which was almost entirely without main drainage the flies multiplied by their millions in the hot, damp summers, and a reward of one sen was offered for every hundred dead flies which were presented to the local police-box.

From morning to night, the children were out on patrol armed with fly-swatters and an old pair of chopsticks, which were used to pick up the victims and deposit them in little white cloth bags. Each fly was carefully counted, not because the policemen actually bothered to check whether the bags contained a hundred, but out of some sense of the responsibility of the work.

Our nearest police-box was at Onarimon, which would have been about five minutes away at adult's walking speed. The policemen there all wore sabres on their belts, but they were friendly and smiling to us children. We were always popping in and out to ask them questions or consult them on our problems. I hate to have to admit this now, but I actually thought the police were wonderful at that time. I was only a child after all.

We also brought them rats, but rat-catching was done mainly by the grown-ups. The workers in my father's business used to do it sometimes. I remember that at first we used to take our catches round to the police-box whole, but all those dead rats lying around must have become a nuisance, because after a while they told us just to bring the tails.

For Momo in Tokyo, the events of the attempted rebellion of 26 February 1936 were both more immediate and more mystifying than they were for those who, like Saitō Mutsuo and Tsutsumi Ayako, heard of them only at second hand, through the reports of radio and newspapers.

On the night of 25–26 February 1936 heavy snow had fallen, and the following morning the residents of the capital woke to find the city deadened, not only by the lowering wintry weather, but also by a tangible chill of fear. Office workers in central Tokyo found streets inexplicably sealed off. Army vehicles sped through the icy roads. Groups of soldiers stood consulting one another in anxious huddles. Overheard phrases were picked up and flew like fire through the frozen city: mutiny in the army; coup; revolution; the sound of firing heard in the night. A foreign journalist later recaptured that obscure sense of crisis:

Hurrying down town I found an atmosphere of complete confusion, with a natural accompaniment of the wildest rumours. The Foreign Office was open . . . but there was no one there to hold the customary press conference with foreign correspondents. Troops were posted at the main street crossings in the central part of the city, but it was impossible to learn which were on the side of the government and which were insurgents. Indeed, during the early hours of the day it seemed doubtful whether any government was still in existence.[1]

Early news bulletins on the Incident did little to clarify the confusion. It was not until 8.15 that evening that the first official explanation of events was broadcast by the War Office.

The February 26th Incident must have been just towards the end of my third year at Primary School.

Yes . . . I remember that one very clearly. It was a cold day. In the books they always say that it was snowing then, but according to my memory that's not quite true. As I remember it there was no snow falling, only melting snow turning to slush.

It must have been sometime during the morning, in the middle of lessons, that we were all told to gather in the assembly hall. We lined up there and the deputy head came and spoke to us.

'There has been an Incident', he said (though he didn't explain what kind of an incident).

He told us that classes were being suspended for the day. We had to obey our class teacher's instructions and go home as quickly as possible. People who lived in the same direction were to go home together, in groups. Yes, I have a feeling that it was a cold, gloomy day and the streets were slippery with slush.

Early in the morning of the following day (Thursday), full-scale martial law was declared in Tokyo. During the course of the day, other aspects of the affair became public knowledge. The rebels began to distribute pamphlets, which a number of people managed to read before these were confiscated by the authorities and destroyed. From the style of their manifesto, the mood and background of the mutinous soldiers was easily understood.

The essence of the nation of Japan, as a land of the Gods, [they wrote] exists in the fact that the Emperor reigns with undiminished power from time immemorial down to the remotest future in order that the natural beauty of the country may be propagated throughout the universe, so that all men under the sun may be able to enjoy their lives to the fullest extent.

In recent years, however, there have appeared many persons whose chief aim and purpose have been to amass personal material wealth, disregarding the general welfare and prosperity of the Japanese population, with the result that the sovereignty of the Emperor has been greatly diminished.

The *Genrō*, senior statesmen, military cliques, plutocrats, bureaucrats and political parties are all traitors who are destroying the *Kokutai* . . . The Imperial work will fail unless we take proper steps to safeguard the Fatherland by killing all those responsible for impeding the Shōwa Restoration and slurring Imperial prestige.

May the gods bless and help us in our endeavour to save the Fatherland from the worst that confronts it.[2]

Although these ideas found some echoes in right-wing circles outside the army, it soon became clear that the rebels were going to receive neither widespread public support nor any sign of encouragement from the emperor himself. In the eerie stillness of Friday and Saturday morning, a fleet of warships sailed into Tokyo bay, and troops from other parts of Japan were brought into the capital. Appeals to the rebels to surrender were dropped from aeroplanes and suspended from advertisement balloons which floated over the city centre. On Saturday, all traffic in central Tokyo was stopped, and residents of the area close to the Imperial Palace were ordered to evacuate, as troops loyal to the government moved in for the final, silent confrontation which was to end with the rebels' surrender.

Afterwards, later in the week, we saw the balloons. They sent up gas balloons carrying messages to the soldiers, telling them that it was not too late to surrender and return to their barracks. I think they put up the balloons just above the Nichigeki Theatre. At least, when we looked out of our windows they seemed to be right above the theatre roof, hanging quite still there in the metal-coloured air.

The Iidas' flat, perched like an eyrie over the company offices, provided a vantage point from which the children could watch the intricate unfurling life of the city all around. In those days, before tall buildings were common in Tokyo, the top of their father's office block could be seen rising out of the sea of corrugated grey roofs even from Shimbashi Station, a couple of miles away. The terminus of the tram line was right in front of the building, and when the Tokyo tram workers struck in the early 1930s the Iidas watched with fascination as grey-suited gentlemen from the company management arrived to drive the trams and began to struggle clumsily with the long poles which were used to connect the feelers to the overhead wires at the beginning of each journey.

Early every morning, the whine and hiss of the trams was the first sound which Momo heard from his fifth-storey bedroom. The trams started up around 5 a.m., so there was still time to close his eyes and doze a little more before the next intruding noise, which was the cry of the *natto* (fermented soy beans) seller, doing his rounds in the street below: 'Nattō! Fresh *nattō*! Come and buy my *nattō*!' On mornings when they wanted *nattō* to eat with their breakfast, Mrs Iida would fling open a window and shout down into the street below: 'Wait a minute! We're just coming!' and Momo would be sent rushing and slithering down the steep flights of stone steps to buy a few sen's worth of the sticky, pungent mixture.

On other days they ate their rice with raw egg and soy sauce, washed down with a steaming bowl of bean-paste soup. From the windows, as he ate, Momo could look down at the great *Tōkaidō*, the main highway linking Tokyo with western Japan, and watch it gradually fill up with a surging tide of human beings: day labourers walking down to the docks to look for work. Each morning the road was lined with rows of tiny stalls and handcarts, and around them would gather a huddle of matchstick figures waiting to buy a cheap, filling bowl of noodle soup. Momo, surveying the scene from the family breakfast table, puzzled over these people who ate their breakfasts standing up in the cold, dusty street.

Then it would be time to set off for school, clutching his lunch box packed with rice, seaweed and pickles. Momo's school had a steam central heating system, so in the winter the children would balance their lunch boxes in rows along the radiators to make them warm before eating. The school was proud of its central heating, which was a symbol of modernity and progress, and even more proud of the solarium which it installed when Momo was in the fifth form. The solarium was part of a campaign against the vitamin deficiencies which were common in pre-war city children. It consisted of a large glass dome, under which the children could lie ten at a time. Each child would undress and be issued with a thick pair of dark glasses before stretching out to lie like a fish in a tropical tank, swimming in the warm light which flooded through the dome above.

Another thing we got was cod-liver oil. I experienced three phases in the evolution of cod-liver oil. First we got it straight, gulped down with a glass of water, but that tasted so disgusting that it was difficult to persuade us to take it. So then they produced sweetened cod-liver oil, made into capsules like little candies, and later still they gave us wobbly brown cod-liver jelly, which was supposed to be more palatable.

The school day started and ended early. About an hour after they had eaten their lunches it was already time to go home, or, in Momo's case, out on to the streets to play with his friends. Like most of the older primary school boys he now played baseball: baseball at break time, baseball after school, baseball at weekends and holidays and in every available moment of free time. Baseball had been introduced to Japan in the late nineteenth century, and by the Shōwa period the popularity of the game was so great that when the American star Babe Ruth visited Tokyo in 1934 the American ambassador remarked, somewhat ruefully: 'he is a great deal more effective Ambassador than I could ever be'.[3] Momo and his friends were fortunate, because their school was near Shiba Park, which provided them with a ready-made pitch. Bats and balls were easily acquired or improvised, but what every boy longed for was a real baseball glove.

About that time a sports shop opened just by the corner of Shiba Park. A sports shop was a very new and fashionable thing to have in the neighbourhood in those days, and we used to spend hours gazing wistfully at the smart, expensive sports equipment in the windows. I can remember my huge excitement and delight the day I persuaded Mother to go in and buy me a baseball glove. That glove was my most treasured possession, and I oiled it lovingly each week to keep the leather supple. We used to play in the park every evening until it grew so dark that you couldn't see the ball any more.

I believe the sports shop is still there today although it's changed its name since my time.

At the weekends one of the boys' fathers would sometimes take them to the park beside the Meiji Shrine, where they could watch the most popular sporting event in 1930s Tokyo: the Six Universities League. The league consisted of baseball teams representing (as the name suggests) six famous local universities, and a match between two league teams was staged every weekend during the summer months. When they were a little older, Momo and his school-friends would sometimes go to matches unaccompanied, setting off at crack of dawn so as to take advantage of the special cheap tickets which could be bought on the early morning trams.

When we couldn't go to see matches live, we listened to them on the radio. At that time the baseball commentator was a man called Matsuuchi, who gave the most wonderful, high-flown poetic descriptions, not just of the game, but of the green grass and the blue sky and the birds flying over the baseball pitch and so on.

With his father, he would go once a year to see *sumō* wrestling at the Kuramae Stadium. Together they would sit on the matted floor at the ring-side, eating their packed lunches and watching the ceremonial blessing of the contestants by brocade-robed referees, and then the heaving and grunting of the vast, fleshy wrestlers with their shining black top-knots, as they tried to lift and shove and trip their opponent out of the beaten-earth ring. *Sumō* at that time was dominated by the massive and seemingly invincible figure of the great Champion Wrestler Futabayama, who, although he was half blind, fought off every challenger from 1935 until 15 January 1939 when, after sixty-nine successive victorious fights, the seventieth finally brought defeat.

Momo's friends represented a fair cross-section of the social life of the area. Their parents owned shops and small businesses, or ran restaurants and bars and geisha houses. The children were absorbed into the adult world early: helping out in their fathers' shops after school and at weekends, listening, through the thin partitions which divided homes from workplaces, to the gossip of customers, the demands of unpaid creditors, the plaintive excuses of debtors. There was no room in this thronging, thrusting, vibrant community for concealment or prudishness, or for protecting the innocence of childhood.

From his earliest infancy Momo had listened in, intrigued and mystified, to the chatter of his father's young employees as they endlessly discussed their sex lives and the latest scandals from the newspapers.

One event in particular which provided days of whispered excitement and horror and laughter was the burning down of the Shirokiya department store in central Tokyo. The shop was one of the largest and most fashionable in the city, and in the fire fourteen people had died, and many more were injured leaping from top-storey windows.

It happened when I was at primary school. I heard the story from the apprentices at the factory, and it made quite a profound impression on me.

The apprentices described how the women customers who had been trapped on the upper floors of the store went down the firemen's ladders, and how the wind blew their kimonos upwards, so that all the crowd below could see under their skirts. As a result, several women refused to climb down the ladders. They stayed in the store and were burnt to death. There was also a good deal of talk about the pronouncements which were made by some prominent people after the fire, suggesting that all women should adopt the Western custom of wearing underpants.

The apprentices were always talking about things like that, making obscene jokes and so on. Being in the same building, I naturally spent a lot of time with them and heard many of their stories. Because of them, I have always remembered the Shirokiya fire.

Later, all the talk was of the gruesome Abe Sada case, in which the owner of a fashionable restaurant had been murdered and his body castrated by his mistress. The murderess, Abe Sada, when arrested, calmly confessed the crime and stated that she had been driven to commit it by her tormenting and jealous love for the victim. The idea of the composed, attractive young woman, whose photograph appeared on every front page, performing this grotesque act somehow made a deep impression on the public imagination. (Many years later, the case was to provide the Japanese film director Ōshima Nagisa with the subject for his famous film *The Empire of the Senses*.)

One of the boys in my class had a father who was blind, and, like a lot of blind people, he worked as a masseur. His customers used to come to the house and be massaged in the front room. Well, in those days a visit to the masseur's was like a visit to the barber's or the public baths: a great occasion for exchanging gossip. My friend used to sit with his ear to the sliding screens, hearing everything that his father and customers talked about. I remember when the Abe Sada case was reported in the papers. The more sensational parts of the case were censored – they just wrote that she had 'cut a part of his body' or something like that, so we didn't know what it was all about, but of course my friend the masseur's son soon found out, and had great fun explaining the anatomical details of the case to the rest of us.

There was another boy who had a passion for rude rhymes. His father ran a tea house and whether he picked up the rhymes from the customers or whether he made them up himself I don't know. But anyway he used to go around obsessively teaching these rhymes to his friends. There was one I can still recite which started off all about the emperor and empress going to the lavatory, and went on like that through all the usual litany of favourite schoolboy rude words.

Between the boys and their teachers there was more than the usual gulf of years and experience. The teachers were mostly country people, peasants' sons fresh from training college or military service, and burning with high ideals and disciplinary zeal. Teaching, like the army, was a profession which attracted many of the brighter and more ambitious sons of poor rural families, for the state-run teacher training colleges charged no fees, and actually paid a small grant to students. But the attitudes of the newly-graduated teachers to their pupils was complicated and complex-ridden, reflecting the feeling of hostility between town and country which was strong in pre-war Japan, as it is in many less prosperous countries today. The city-dweller looked down on the unsophisticated, clod-hopping peasant with a disdain which was perhaps all the greater because he was in many cases just a generation or two removed from the peasantry himself. Within a decade, the Japanese farmers were to have a brief but sweet moment of revenge on the townspeople. But when Momo was at primary school the teachers, conscious of their own uncultured rural backgrounds and their unpolished provincial accents, felt an added need to assert their authority over the flock of unruly, mocking urban children whom they taught.

In Momo's school it was usual for form teachers to be in charge of the same class for several years running. For the last three years of primary school his class was taught by a pale-faced authoritarian young man who came to them, velvet-headed, straight from military service. This teacher's favourite instrument of punishment was a wooden pole from which maps were hung in the classroom, and there was rarely a day which passed without some unfortunate child receiving a bloody nose or a lump on his head from the teacher's chastisements. Momo was rarely beaten, not because he was particularly studious or well-behaved, but because he was an exceptionally clever boy, who managed to come top of his class most years without any conscious effort on his part. So, when the final year at Sakuragawa Primary School arrived, and many of his friends were already preparing to leave school for good and work behind the counter or in the workshops of the family business, it seemed natural that Momo should be sent to take the entrance examination for the most exclusive and prestigious of Japanese state Middle Schools – Tokyo City No. 1 Middle School, normally known simply by its abbreviation, Ichi-chū. He passed with ease.

It was only afterwards that Momo understood that he had moved from one world to another.

In 1937 his father, whose flourishing business needed room to grow, moved the family out of their top-floor flat and into a new house which he had built for them at the edge of the geisha district of Shinmeichō, a short distance away. The house represented a further step away from Iida Toshifumi's ragged, hungry origins and towards solid bourgeois respectability. It had two storeys, with five rooms on the ground floor and four rooms upstairs. There were two maids to help with the housework and there was a garden with a pool filled with golden carp. The following year Momo left the rough but cheerful environment of his typical big-city primary school and moved to the self-consciously exalted and rarefied atmosphere of Ichi-chū.

Gradually, he began to notice the differences. In the past he had always loved to listen to *naniwabushi*, the long, rambling adventure stories which have been chanted by travelling story-tellers in the town and villages of Japan ever since the days of Edo. But at Ichi-chū, he discovered, it was not the done thing to re-tell your favourite *naniwabushi* stories. Instead, he started to cultivate more sophisticated pleasures. He joined the school tennis club; went to the theatre to watch the popular comedians of the day; listened on the radio to the quivering, melodies of singers like Awaya Noriko, who wove echoes of Japanese folk music with the softness of Western Blues to create a texture which is still much loved in Japanese pop songs today.

Most days, Momo travelled to school on the underground. The very first underground service in Japan had been inaugurated just over ten years earlier, in 1927, and the single underground line had not yet lost its shiny modern appearance.

Our school was right by the Akasaka Mitsuke underground station, so quite a lot of boys used to go to school that way. We were all very proud of travelling to school by underground. We never tired of watching the train conductors in their smart uniforms and their spotless white gloves as they blew whistles and pressed mysterious buttons. In those days it was the most fashionable thing in the world to be an underground conductor, and it all seemed to us to be the pinnacle of cultural achievement.

Momo continued to do well in his school work and in examinations, but his relationship with the teachers at Ichi-chū was not always a happy one.

I wasn't a particularly badly-behaved boy, but . . . well, it seems to me that there are just some children who manage to give a bad impression and who seem to get into trouble whatever they do, and that was what I was like at that time.

I remember when we had our school sports day. It was in the summer, and the sports day was held in the grounds of the Meiji Shrine. It started off with all the boys doing mass exercises. The parents and teachers and their friends were watching. I was in the back row doing my exercises with everyone else, when suddenly I heard the sound of gym-shoes scrunching over the ground towards me. It was the judo teacher. He walked straight over to me and flung me out of the way. To this day I have no idea what I was doing wrong, but I obviously must have been doing something which annoyed him.

Momo made several friends at Ichi-chū, and yet in a way he felt himself to be an outsider, apart from the companionship of school-boy life. Sometimes he would listen to his classmates chatting together about the normal schoolboy obsessions of sport and filmstars, teachers and exams, and their voices would seem to merge into an endless and meaningless babel of sound.

Momo would escape to books, hungrily devouring words in all their forms. Particularly he loved to read and re-read the books of the great modern novelist Akutagawa Ryūnosuke, whose tales of Japanese city life were set against backgrounds which Momo could easily identify with his own urban surroundings. Momo, fretting impatiently with the slow years of adolescence and dreaming of adulthood, set himself a private goal: to complete Middle School in four years rather than the usual five, and to enter Ichi-kō (the preparatory High School for Tokyo University) by the age of sixteen, in April 1942.

The war in China smouldered on. The capture of Nanking had been celebrated during Momo's last year at primary school. Just a few weeks earlier another event occurred which, although less immediately significant, in its own way helped to fuel the momentum of war. Japanese aeroplanes, attacking remnants of the Chinese army near Nanking, hit and sank the USS *Panay*, which was escorting ships carrying American civilians away from the war zone. A number of Americans were killed, and there were reports that Japanese army launches had also fired machine-guns at the survivors as they tried to swim to safety. The Japanese government responded with an instant apology and promises of an enquiry into the incident. Japanese public opinion, too, reacted with a sense of shock in which could be discerned a lingering hope that peaceful relations with the Western powers might be maintained.

One class of children at a Tokyo primary school wrote a letter to the American Embassy (doubtless on the suggestion of their teacher). It read as follows:

My Dear Ambassador,

The Japanese air force has dropped bombs by mistake on a man-of-war of your country, the United States of America! I was taken aback at being told so by mamma. I am sure that the mistake was due to the dense mist that hung over the river. There can be no reason why the Japanese air force would have aimed at an American man-of-war in dropping bombs if the airmen had been aware that it was an American ship. My great concern is that the mishap may have caused some casualties among the officers and sailors on board the ship, and I hope that nobody was injured in the unhappy incident.

My dear Ambassador, I sincerely wish that you would not take the matter so seriously but be generous enough to forgive the Japanese navy airmen, who are not to be blamed at all. It is my sincere wish that I may be allowed to apologize to you for the grave mistake of the Japanese air force. I like your country so much. 'Banzai' for America! Sayonara!

Fifth-year class,
Moriyama Primary School,
Setagaya-ku, Tokyo.[4]

But although the more official apologies were accepted and the incident was considered closed, it greatly aggravated the anti-Japanese sentiments which had been growing in the United States since Japan's annexation of Manchuria, and which were soon to be further increased as news of Japanese atrocities in Nanking reached the West.

By the following year, the economic effects of Japan's China campaign were clearly making themselves felt in Tokyo. Although the press was full of news of advances in China, the anticipated final victory did not come. Japan, unwittingly, was being drawn into one of the classical traps of twentieth-century warfare: the large, modern, well-trained army pitted against more poorly equipped but mobile and invisible guerrilla forces. The more they succeeded in capturing the cities, the more the control of the vast Chinese countryside, with its thousand-mile lines of communication, slipped from their grasp.

In 1938 the Japanese government introduced the National General Mobilization Law, giving the state extensive power of control over the requisitioning of materials, the mobilization of labour and production and distribution of goods. Japanese society was on a full war footing.

For Momo these events were no more than newspaper headlines, which did not directly impinge upon his life. Gradually, however, he became aware of a harshness and greyness, a sense of oppression which was infecting life in the capital. The demands of the war on the economy were growing daily, basic necessities were in short supply, and government pronouncements urged restraint and frugality.

Japan [wrote the journalist Hugy Byas in 1938] has reached the point where the length of a matchstick and the skin of a rat represent important economic factors in continuing the war with

China. So do toothpaste, toy balloons, tinfoil and chocolate bars, freckle cream and caviar, bathing suits and chewing gum, book-bindings and teacup decorations, golf balls and patent medicine and a thousand and one other things which might seem far removed from the 'sinews of war'. Japan is not a nation of raw products. The materials that go into these things must be imported, paid for abroad . . . Not even Germany in the [First] World War could have been so tightly laced as Japan is today. Chemists in the Ministry of Agriculture are tanning rat skins to find a leather substitute . . . Iron is scarcer than gold. It is hard now to buy a frying pan; a month from now it will be impossible.[5]

With the tightening economic situation came a surging tide of almost hysterical nationalism, as mounting foreign criticism of Japan's military involvement in China provoked a withdrawal into a protective shell of defiant xenophobia. Military and economic dif-ficulties were reflected too in a repressive mood of puritanism. People, it was felt, should be directing their entire energies to promoting Japan's success in the China War. Frivolous distractions from the grave international situation were to be discouraged, particularly when they carried with them the taint of foreign decadence. Momo and his friends, although now in their mid-teens, were not allowed to go to the theatre or cinema unaccompanied, and the newspapers carried frequent reports of groups of policemen raiding places of entertainment to pull out youngsters who appeared to be 'under age'.

I remember how shocked I was when I read in the paper that Awaya Noriko, my favourite singer, had been summoned to the Tokyo police headquarters. They made her sign a 'confession' apologizing for having corrupted the morals of the young. They also called in singers and actresses who used Western-sounding stage-names and made them change to proper Japanese names. There was a story which I heard at the time. It was about a then-famous comedienne who called herself Miss Wakana. She was summoned to the police station and told to choose a Japanese stage-name.

'Well, what are you going to call yourself?' they asked her.

'How about Mesu Wakana?' she said ['Mesu' being the Japanese for 'female'].

The great symbol of Western corruption was the permanent wave. Perms had become popular in Japan in the early years of Shōwa, and by the late 1930s most of the 800 or more beauty parlours in Tokyo had installed large, many-armed machines, looking rather like medieval instruments of torture, to coax the straight, thick hair of their customers into the cascades of curls. After the start of the China War, however, perms began to be scornfully described by the authorities as 'sparrows' nests', and in the summer of 1939 it was officially recommended by a subcommittee of the Japanese Diet that 'permanent waves and other ostentatious forms of dress and make-up which are unsuitable in a wartime situation should be strictly prohibited'. When he passed through the entertainment district of Ginza on his way home from school, Momo sometimes saw earnest-looking women in *mompe* (the baggy trousers which were to become a sort of national uniform for women during the Pacific War) handing out little cards on the street corners. The women were members of the Patriotic Women's League, and their cards carried warnings which were issued to any woman seen wearing high heels, silk stockings and other unsuitable forms of attire.

In November 1940, the Asahi newspaper carried the following report:

> On the night of 31st [October], the dancehall finally disappeared from the streets of this 'war economy' city. The period of grace which the halls had been given by the authorities to prepare for closure had at last run out. On the night of this last act of their drama, every hall was packed to capacity with crowds of people wanting a last dance to preserve in their memories. Between three and five times the normal number of people squashed and jostled one another like pebbles on a beach while noisy hordes pushed and shoved to get in until, more than two hours before the final dance, 'Sold Out' notices had to be pasted up on the entrances, and sweat-soaked dance fans were turned away into the night.[6]

Momo's instinctively negative reaction to these intrusions of nationalist morality into the world around him suggest the first obscure stirring of political consciousness – a consciousness which may also perhaps have been fostered by his school environment. Ichi-chū prided itself on its liberal traditions. There was no beating or bullying of younger boys by older ones, as happened in many other schools at that time, and relatively little attention was paid to the nationalistic celebrations which became increasingly common as international tension rose. But not even Ichi-chū could remain entirely untouched by the atmosphere of war.

A symbol of the liberal ethos of Ichi-chū was the quality of its English teaching. The English master, who, like most Ichi-chū teachers, came from an impeccable academic background, had many eminent friends in Japanese literary circles. But he was not popular with the boys. It was not that he was personally an unpleasant man, but his habit of talking about his famous left-wing literary friends who were now political outcasts, some of whom were even in prison, made them feel uncomfortable. So too did his foreign airs and graces. They nicknamed him 'the Western beggar'.

We also had an English conversation teacher, an American lady called Miss Guppy. That was another Ichi-chū speciality – it was very unusual in those days to have a foreign teacher in school. You know, I always liked to imagine that at Ichi-chū we weren't influenced by all the militarism and nationalism which was growing around us, but actually, when I remember what happened to Miss Guppy, I have to admit that we must have been subconsciously influenced in some way after all.

It happened quite suddenly one day. It was totally spontaneous. No one had planned it beforehand. Miss Guppy came into the class and, as always, she began to ask us questions in English. She used to start off with some quite simple question to get us going, something like 'What's the date today?' Well, on this occasion, she asked one boy, and he didn't answer. He just sat there and stared at her. She asked the next boy, and he wouldn't answer either. She went on round the class, and as she did, it turned into a sort of general rebellion, and of course Miss Guppy realized what was happening, and started to get desperate. No one would speak to her. At last she turned to the class prefect. He was a very good pupil, a real teacher's pet (he's a professor at Tokyo University now). Miss Guppy knew that he was her last chance.

The prefect stood up, with his book in his hands. I think he wanted to answer really, but every eye in the class was turned on him. We watched him, Miss Guppy watched him. He stood there, and his face grew redder and redder, and his hands began to shake, but he didn't say anything. Then Miss Guppy knew that she had lost, and she began to cry. She turned and went out of the classroom in tears.

After Miss Guppy there were no more English conversation teachers at Ichi-chū, and the next opportunity that Momo would have to practise his English was with the soldiers of the American army of occupation in 1945.

Even as late as 1939, there had still been a few who hoped that Japan's expansion in Asia could be carried out without conflict with the United States. After all, it was argued, the economic interests of Japan and America in East Asia were not fundamentally opposed, while both countries surely shared an interest in the defeat of the communist forces which were playing a growing role in the struggle in China. As a Harvard-educated Japanese businessman explained in a newspaper interview:

> Personally, I firmly believe that Japan and the United States must collaborate closely for the development of markets in the East since there is nothing to bring the two nations into conflict. Instead, interests of Japan and America in the Orient are rather coordinative . . . The trend of public opinion in the United States towards the Red movement has been changing considerably of late, and if we explain to them why the national spirit of Japan and Communism are incompatible, I believe the Americans will come to a clear understanding of Japan's position in the East as well as the meaning of the crusade being continued in China.[7]

As time passed, however, such hopes became increasingly forlorn. Later in the same year the American Secretary of State, Cordell Hull, refused to negotiate a new commercial treaty with Japan unless Japanese policy in China was reversed, and the following year this warning was followed up by the imposition of the embargoes on aviation fuel and scrap iron exports to Japan. Japan was now at an impasse. It was clear that no final victory in China could be achieved unless a new opening was found through which Japan could obtain the raw materials vital to her war effort. More and more the strategists of Japan's armed forces turned their attention southwards, towards Malaya and the Dutch East Indies from which (respectively) Japan imported 45 per cent of its iron ore and 20 per cent of its petroleum. The idea of a 'southward advance' had originally been espoused by elements in the navy, but by 1940 it was receiving considerable support also from the army, and Foreign Minister Matsuōka for the first time proclaimed Japan's policy of creating a 'Greater East Asia Co-Prosperity Sphere', whose aim would be:

> to bring all the people in Greater East Asia to revert to their innate and proper aspect promoting conciliation and co-operation among them, and thereby setting the example of universal concord . . . The Netherlands East Indies and French Indo-China, if only for geographical reasons, should be in intimate and inseparable relationship with our country . . . and relations of good neighbourliness secured for the promotion of mutual prosperity.[8]

With the coming of war in Europe, the Japanese government found the opportunity to take the first southward step towards the creation of that mutual prosperity sphere. The invasion of France left French colonies in Asia vulnerable, and in the summer of 1940 the French governor of Indo-China surrendered to Japan's demands and allowed thousands of Japanese troops to be sent into the north of the country. Then, after a border dispute between Indo-China and Thailand, the Japanese government seized control of the situation and, in return for arranging a settlement which was signed by Thailand and Indo-China in May 1941, Japan obtained the right to move her troops into the south also. On 28 July 1941 Japanese soldiers poured into Saigon, and the *de facto* occupation of Indo-China was complete.

The reaction from the West was immediate. America, Great Britain and Holland placed an economic embargo on Japan, and began a rapid strengthening of their military preparations in the Pacific. The much-feared economic and military noose of the 'ABCD line' (in which the 'ABCD' stood for the Americans, British, Chinese and Dutch) was tightening around Japan.

The economic embargo was imposed in July 1941. Already, for some months, regular meetings had been taking place between the Japanese ambassador to Washington and US Secretary of State Hull (who negotiated on behalf of Britain as well as the USA) to try to avert the impending disaster. Yet the views of the Japanese and American governments seemed as far apart as ever. Japan demanded that the United States and Britain should withdraw all support for the Chiang Kai-Shek regime in China. America was insistent that no settlement could be reached without a Japanese withdrawal from China and Indo-China. In September it was rumoured that an important meeting might soon take place between President Roosevelt and Japanese Prime Minister Konoe. But the month passed and no meeting took place. No settlement was yet in sight, and the impatience of the Japanese military was rising. Even at this late stage, however, there were many in Japan who were reluctant to risk war with the United States. In the media the insistent message was of a peace-loving Japan surrounded on all sides by intransigent enemies:

> What seems most important at this juncture [stated the English-language *Japan Times* on 18 November] is that the American Government should realise the all-importance of imparting to Japan a sense of security. The formidable cordon of naval and air bases which America has developed round Japan in concert with Britain, the Netherlands East Indies, Australia and Chungking constitutes a direct threat against the Japanese Empire. As long as this strategic situation persists, Japan can have little assurance of security or safety. If America desires no war in this part of the world, it should realise that it holds in its own hands the key to the solution of the whole situation.[9]

On 28 November the Japanese government received a set of conditions for the restoration of economic relations from the American secretary of state. The American terms were that Japan should withdraw all military, air and police forces from China and Indo-China; that Japan should deny support to any Chinese regime other than Chiang Kai-Shek's; that Japan should withdraw from the Axis pact with Germany and Italy; and that Japan should sign a non-aggression pact with the USA, Great Britain, China, the Netherlands, the Soviet Union and Thailand. After months of negotiation, it seemed that the Americans had not compromised on one iota of their original demands. The Japanese government reacted angrily. Prime Minister Konoe gave a speech condemning the United States and Britain for setting the peoples of East Asia against one another in order to advance their own power in the region. 'For the honour and pride of mankind', he said, 'we must purge this sort of practice from East Asia with a vengeance.'

PART II

Coming of Age – 1941 – 45

For an individual, one country's rise and fall is truly a great and important matter, but if I think of the movement of the universe, I know that such events are in fact infinitesimal.

(Uehara Ryōji, May 1945)

5

Saitō Mutsuo

The development of the radio during the 1920s and 1930s radically altered the way in which ordinary people experienced the major political events of their age. No longer did news come to them gradually, by rumours only later confirmed by the printed page of the newspaper. The outbreak and ending of wars, the deaths of political leaders, the overthrow of governments – all were now experienced with a new immediacy; and memories of such events came to be framed by the carefully-chosen words and dispassionate voices of the impersonal but authoritative radio newsreader.

So, for most Japanese people, the outbreak of the Pacific War on 8 December 1945[1] is remembered above all as the deep but slightly uneven voice of one Captain Hiraide crackling over the radio into the sudden silence of a winter's morning:

Here is an announcement by the Naval Section of the Imperial Headquarters:
1. Today, December 8th, before dawn, the Imperial Navy conducted a death-defying air-raid upon the American fleet and air force stationed at Hawaii.
2. Today, December 8th, before dawn, the Imperial Navy attacked and sunk the British Warship *Petrel* off Shanghai . . .

Of course in a sense we all knew that war with America was coming. Our teacher at the crammer had discussed it with us. Every day there had been reports of the diplomatic conflict with America. We knew that it was only a matter of time. But, all the same, it was a quite different thing to listen to that broadcast on the morning of December 8th and know that it had really begun.

Our first thought after we heard the news was that the Americans might start to bomb us right away. So what I did was –

97

I didn't go in to the crammer that day – I went down to the nearest cornerstore and bought some strong rice-straw paper and a pot of glue. It probably sounds rather silly now, but I spent the whole morning of the day that war broke out going round the house and covering the windows with sheets of paper to protect us from flying glass.

On that day the American reaction to the attack on Pearl Harbor was unknown, and anything seemed possible, but in spite of uncertainties and fears the atmosphere was one of euphoria. The months of tension, of frustrated peace talks and anticipated crisis had suddenly resolved themselves into a splendid Japanese initiative, a single dazzling spear-thrust at the heart of the enemy. In the Saitō household there was only one person who remained uninfected by the general fever of exhilaration and rejoicing: Mutsuo's father Kōsuke.

Later in the day we all sat around in the living room and discussed the war situation. Even then, when everyone was talking of victory, my father was pessimistic. You see, he knew about the outside world. He knew what sort of a country America was. He said: 'What do they think they are doing, going to war with America? Don't they know how rich and powerful it is and how strong American industry is? Japan can't hope to defeat a country like that.' Naturally, I argued with him. 'Didn't you hear what they said on the radio? We've wiped out the American fleet', I said, 'The whole Pacific is open to us now. Of course we're going to win.'

But it was a matter of education, really. Father had been educated in the Taishō Age. He'd been brought up with liberal ideas. We'd been taught to believe that Japan was invincible, the Land of the Gods and so on. But father, I think, believed that something terrible had started.

It was the first of many arguments between father and son during the early phases of the Pacific War. But Kōsuke's pessimism could not prevent his family from following the fashion of those heady months of Japanese military advance: pinning up on the wall a large coloured map of the Pacific on which they recorded each conquest with a tiny rising-sun flag, and each enemy vessel sunk with a little crossed-out picture of a warship. For all his certainty of victory, not even Mutsuo was quite prepared for the speed with which those paper flags would spread across the contours of Asia. When the map went up it was already necessary to stick a flag on eastern Malaya, and within the next couple of days Guam and Luzon were similarly adorned. Then came Borneo, Wake Island and Hong Kong in the last weeks of 1941; in January Manila, the Celebes, Rabaul; in the first weeks of February Java and Southern Sumatra. Caught up in the emotional tide of victory, Mutsuo was for a short while almost afraid that things would move too quickly, that the war would be over in a few months. History, he felt, might pass him by, leaving him a mere onlooker at Japan's moment of glory.

It wasn't that military life was ever really attractive. We heard rumours from time to time about the ferocious discipline meted out to army recruits. But in any case, once I was a High-School student, I would be eligible to become an officer cadet in the army, so I thought that wouldn't affect me. And somehow at that time we were all intoxicated with war. Reports of victories came from all around us, like bamboos exploding in a forest fire. We really thought that defeat was impossible then.

In February, Japanese troops advanced down the Malay peninsula to besiege Singapore. Although the 100,000 British, Indian and Australian troops stationed in and around the city easily outnumbered their Japanese attackers, they were ill-prepared to withstand an onslaught which was unexpected both in its speed and scale. The Japanese forces quickly gained control of the city's water supply and, when it became apparent that any attempt to defend Singapore would be tremendously costly and almost certainly doomed to failure, the garrison's commander-in-chief, Leiutenant-General Percival, surrendered. The Japanese army occupied Singapore on 15 February 1942, and immediately renamed the city 'Shōnan' – 'Shō' (as in Shōwa) meaning 'radiant', and 'Nan' meaning 'south'.

In Japan the southward advance was celebrated not only as a demonstration of invincible martial spirit but also as a crusade of liberation, in which Japan was breaking the shackles of Western domination in Asia.

The reconstruction of the southern region [ran a typical report in 1942] is making significant headway mainly due to the fact that our local military administrations are endeavouring their best to shape the growth of common prosperity life by permitting the southern peoples to contribute their legitimate shares. It may be noted that, following the outbreak of the current Pacific war, Japan immediately adopted an epochal policy of collaboration with the southern neighbours for mutual advantage and security. As soon as the southern military campaign was concluded in its favour it gave effect to this policy. In consequence, the southern peoples there and then recognised our good intention and naturally offered their cooperation.[2]

This propaganda cannot be dismissed as pure invention. It was true that in several areas of South-East Asia Japanese troops were welcomed by cheering crowds who saw them as liberators from colonial rule. It was equally true, but of course unreported, that most of those who welcomed them were soon to be disillusioned.

We only ever heard about the good side of life in the occupied areas of South-East Asia or in places like Manchuria. They kept a tight lid on all the rotten aspects of the occupation, so the smell of decay could never reach Japan. I believed that Japan was liberating Asia. We were brought up with the idea of 'Hakkō Ichiu' ['all the corners of the world under one roof'] and it seemed natural that if any country was to be the 'roof' of Asia it should be Japan. But actually, although I knew that liberating Asia was the ideal we were supposed to believe in, I always felt that it was of secondary importance. The most important thing was, quite simply, winning the war, because there is no point in fighting a war unless you win.

At the time of the capture of Singapore, Mutsuo was busy re-sitting his entrance exams for High School. Because the war had placed a new premium on scientific knowledge, physics had been introduced as a compulsory subject even for students planning to specialize in arts or social sciences. For Mutsuo, who had never liked science, this added to the burden of revision. He had decided to try for places in three colleges: the senior section of his old school, Waseda; Keio; and the state-run Hirosaki High School. Each college had its own examination, consisting of written papers in mathematics, Japanese language, classical (i.e. Chinese) literature, English and physics, followed by a rigorous interview. Mutsuo failed the interview for Hirosaki High School, but was offered places by both Waseda and Keio. He unhesitatingly chose to go to Keio.

My father had studied at Keio, you see, and I'd been brought up with stories of his student life there, and had known the Keio college anthem ever since I was at primary school. So it just seemed like a natural choice.

At that time there were two possible courses which you could take at Keio. Either you could go to the Preparatory University, which meant that you would automatically go on to do a university degree, or you could go to the Senior College, which did a diploma course, although it gave you the option of transferring to a degree course later. The courses at Keio Senior College normally lasted for four years, but because of the war they had been cut to three. I chose to do the three-year college course, because at that time the future seemed so uncertain that I didn't want to commit myself to doing a university degree. And as things turned out, I only did a year and a half at the college anyway.

When Mutsuo entered Keio it was already a large institution, providing education from kindergarten to university level. In Mutsuo's year at the Senior College there were some 150 students, mainly specializing in social science subjects. But Keio still retained traces of its origins as the little group of students who had gathered around one of the most famous figures of nineteenth-century Japanese Westernization, Fukuzawa Yukichi. Fukuzawa's aim in setting up Keio College in 1864 had been, he later wrote:

> . . . to create in Japan a civilised nation, as well equipped in both the arts of war and peace as those of the Western World . . .
>
> In my interpretation of education, I try to be guided by the laws of nature in man and the universe, and I try to coordinate all the physical actions of human beings by the very simple laws of 'number and reason'. In spiritual or moral training, I regard the human being as the most sacred and responsible of all orders, unable therefore, in reason, to do anything base. So in self-respect, a man cannot change his sense of humanity, his justice, his loyalty, or anything belonging to his manhood even when driven by circumstances to do so. In short, my creed is that a man should find his faith in independence and self-respect.[3]

Much had changed in the half-century since Fukuzawa wrote those words. But Keio still embodied some of the rationalist leanings of its founder. It also retained many of the trappings of Western

101

education which had been so enthusiastically adopted by the pioneers of Meiji education: the school song, the college baseball team, the carefully nurtured traditions. In the early 1940s the head of Keio was the eminent economist Koizumi Shinzō. Most of the students at college and university level were sons of business or professional people, while a fair sprinkling of Keio's intake came from the immensely wealthy *zaibatsu* families of pre-war and wartime Japan. The Senior College, which Mutsuo attended, was housed in a cluster of buildings around a grassy knoll in the Mita area of Tokyo. On top of the knoll was a large hall, in which all the main events of the academic year, such as entrance and graduation ceremonies, took place.

At our entrance ceremony, Professor Koizumi gave a speech which impressed me very much. His theme was the saying of Confucius that 'a people which is fed and clothed will behave with propriety'. But he turned the sentence round, and said: 'even without food and without clothes you must still behave with propriety'. What he meant was that we could not make excuses for ourselves even though life was harsh and there were shortages of almost everything you can think of.

For the tales of victory on every front could not fill empty stomachs, or conceal the fact that the Japanese economy was stretched to breaking-point. In May a law was passed requisitioning the gongs, bells and metal altarpieces of every shrine and temple in the country, to be melted down and re-cast as guns. By the end of the year shortages of manpower and resources were so severe that railway companies in some areas were introducing passenger trains without seats. (These had the dual advantage of fitting in more people and saving scarce raw materials). At the same time the government imposed a strict limit on household consumption of gas. All families who exceeded the limit had their gas supply cut off. In the early part of the war, however, the prospect of speedy victory softened the impact of material deprivation. In the towns people grew what vegetables they could in their window-boxes or miniature gardens, and filled out their rations of rice with wheat or bran. There were still opportunities for recreation – baseball matches; *sumō* contests; even the cinema, although the films now had titles like *The Naval Battles for Hawaii and Malaya* or *Spirit Warriors of the Skies*.

102

About a fortnight after I started college, Keio played Hōsei
University in the Six Universities Baseball League and I thought
I'd go along to support my new college's team. The match was
near the Meiji Shrine, which was only five or six minutes' walk
from our house in Sendagaya. It's funny, but I just can't
remember now which side won. Anyway, after the match I was
about to set off for home when I saw several planes flying very low
over the trees. A moment after I heard a sound of thuds coming
from somewhere in the direction of my old school, Waseda. I
hadn't realized that the planes were American, and it was only a
few minutes later, when the wail of air-raid sirens started, that I
understood what had happened.

The attack, by sixteen American B-25 bombers from the aircraft
carrier *Hornet*, was the first raid on Tokyo. The buildings of Waseda
school had in fact been raked by machine-gun fire, but the bombing
inflicted relatively little damage: so little, in fact, that it later became
the subject of a joke which derisively suggested that the *Hornet*'s
commanding officer had a name which summed up his capabilities –
Captain Doolittle.

Later in that month, April 1942, the people of Japan went to the
polls in a general election. Under the Constitution of 1889, which
remained in force until the end of the war, elections had never had
more than a limited impact on the activities of government. The
Japanese Diet, which, like the British Parliament, consisted of an
elected lower house and a hereditary House of Peers, was essentially
an advisory body. Although it had the power to pass laws, the
cabinet was ultimately responsible not to it but to the emperor.
From the Meiji Age onwards elections were dominated by two
conservative parties with closely similar policies, the *Seiyūkai* and
the *Minseitō*, but by the 1930s the established political parties were
becoming increasingly impotent in the face of the growing power of
the military and in 1940 the Prime Minister, Prince Konoe, ordered
existing political parties to dissolve themselves, and created in their
place the *Taisei Yokusankai*, which is translated into rather clumsy
English as the 'Imperial Rule Assistance Association'.

Konoe's aim in creating the *Taisei Yokusankai* had not been
merely to replace the existing parties, but also to create a political
counterweight to the power of the army. But as the military
tightened its hold on the government, and particularly after Konoe

was replaced as Prime Minister by General Tōjō in 1941, the *Taisei Yokusankai* became in effect a further instrument for the extension of military control over society. Its official role was 'to stand in relation to the government as one side of a coin does to the other; to channel the government's wishes to the people and the people's wishes to the government'. The 1942 election was the first to be held since the dissolution of the political parties, and in it the *Taisei Yokusankai* was given the right to nominate candidates in all constituencies. This did not mean that there was no opposition. A number of right-wing splinter groups also put up candidates in the election, while other individuals stood as independents, but any whose speeches departed too far from the government line were subject to many forms of official obstruction, and in most areas nomination by the *Taisei Yokusankai* was enough to ensure a candidate's election. To Saitō Kōsuke the election was the final degradation of the ideal of democracy.

My father had retired by this time, but he still kept in touch with many of his old contacts in the business world and friends from college. He would go out to meet them or ask them round to our house. They were mostly people of his generation, who had a similar outlook on things. One or two of them became quite well-known later, after the war, people like Professor Yoshioka from Waseda University and Obama Ritoku [later a well-known political commentator].

Well, just before the election, Father had a phone call from one of these friends, asking him to meet them somewhere. It was only afterwards that I heard what they did. On the evening of the 29th, which was the day before the election, they went to the Tokyo Assembly Hall [an exclusive club close to the Imperial Palace]. That was where the *Taisei Yokusankai* had its headquarters in those days, so Father and his friends went in there, into the lobby, and they all stood in a circle the way people do when they are drinking a toast, and urinated on the carpet. They were all elderly, respectable-looking gentlemen and I suppose that even if anyone saw them they didn't know how to stop them. It was a sort of last, hopeless gesture of their disgust at everything that was happening.

At Keio Mutsuo, untroubled by political events, settled into student life. His major subject was economics, which involved reading the works both of Japanese economic theorists, like Keio's own Professor Koizumi, and of Western economists such as Keynes. Mutsuo also studied English and German, while four or five hours of each week were devoted to military training. This was supervised by an army colonel who, for some reason, took an instant dislike to Mutsuo, and constantly gave him poor grades – a serious matter, since bad marks for military drill could jeopardize your chances of being accepted for officer training in the army.

As the tide of Japanese advance in the Pacific slackened, and news of victories became less frequent and less impressive, so the novelty and thrill of total war began to evaporate. The students at Keio looked at the future with divided minds. Sometimes their conversations reflected a knowledge that, sooner or later, they too would be called up to kill, and probably to die, for their country. At other times they sealed themselves off from this unsettling reality and talked, like ordinary, peacetime students, about exams, degrees, careers. They followed the course of the war mainly from radio broadcasts, listening frequently to the broadcasts of Prime Minister Tōjō, which invariably began with the same phrase: 'It is with great joy that we salute the succession of victories as the imperial forces advance on every front . . .'.

In June the Japanese people heard that the imperial navy had driven back the American fleet in a major encounter at Midway in the Central Pacific.

There was something odd about that report though: it was the first time that the loss of a Japanese warship had been officially announced. That made me wonder whether it had really been quite such a great victory as they suggested. Then, some time later, I heard a rumour from one of my friends at Keio (who I think had heard it from friends of friends of his parents, or something like that) to the effect that the survivors of Midway had been sent to a special place where they could be kept away from contact with the public. That made us speculate even more, and we began to think that perhaps it hadn't really been a victory at all. Perhaps even Japan had lost the battle. But we never guessed the scale of the defeat.

Midway was in fact the first disaster for the Japanese navy. All four Japanese aircraft carriers involved in the battle had been destroyed, for the loss of just one American carrier. The military authorities, aware perhaps that their reports of victory lacked conviction, tried to divert attention from the events of Midway by emphasizing other Japanese gains: advances in the Kurile Archipelago and the occupation of the tiny and remote island of Attu. But after Midway the radio reports, which until then had contained a fair measure of truth, were to become more and more remote from reality.

Some of the teachers at Keio understood what was happening, but because the possible presence of police informers could never be overlooked, their fears were carefully phrased.

Our English teacher, Professor Ikeda, often used to take time after classes to talk to us. I remember him saying to us: 'If you ever get to your graduation ceremony on top of Mita hill, you'll be lucky men. Not only you, we will all be lucky. Japan will be lucky if there are colleges like Keio still in existence in three years' time'. He also used to get very annoyed that so many schools had stopped teaching English, and that the government even discouraged the use of common English words in books and newspapers.

'Because we're at war', he used to say, 'that doesn't mean we should stop learning English. On the contrary, there's more need than ever to learn it now. Look at America. In America, when war seemed likely, lots of people started to learn Japanese. In order to beat your enemy you must first understand his mind, and in order to understand his mind you must first understand his language.'

And in fact as the war went on he did actually become stricter and stricter, and made us work harder and harder at our English lessons.

In August began the struggle for the control of Guadalcanal in the Solomon Islands, and soon after, a new word entered the vocabulary of military news bulletins: *'tenshin'* – a 'change of direction'. The meaning of this was explained to Mutsuo and his fellow-students during the week of military training which they spent at Narashino, to the east of Tokyo, during the autumn term of 1942. The week-long training camps were a regular feature of student life at this time, one being held every term. During that week the classrooms would be emptied and the students sent off to army camps for a brief period of total immersion in military life. At Narashino they slept in bunks in the shack-like wooden barracks around the perimeter of the camp. In the morning they were roused early, and tumbled out of bed to muster, shivering, in the half-dark of the autumn dawns for roll call.

From that moment on the day was a ceaseless, mindless cycle of drill, weapons training, food, more drill, until evening, when they gathered in the huts to listen to lectures on strategy.

At Narashino, one of the officers explained to us that the strategy at Guadalcanal was a great success. Its aim, he said, was to pin down an enormous number of American ships and men for as long as possible, leaving the Japanese forces free to advance on other fronts. We didn't really find that very convincing. The following term at Keio we had another seminar on military strategy. This was given by Captain Hiraide, the navy's chief press officer and the man who had made the broadcast about the attack on Pearl Harbor. He explained events at Guadalcanal differently. He admitted that the Japanese forces had been pushed back but he said: 'We can reckon that if the Americans continue to advance with the speed that they did at Guadalcanal, it would take them at least several decades before they reached Japan proper.'

The unsuccessful struggle to defend Guadalcanal lasted until February 1943. In that struggle 1600 American servicemen died and 24,000 Japanese troops were killed, or, in places where their supply lines were severed, died of starvation. One of those 24,000 was Koizumi Shinkichi, the only son of Keio's head, Professor Koizumi. A month after the retreat from Guadalcanal, the professor conducted a remembrance service in the hall on top of the little hill at Mita, for all former students of Keio killed in the war. Their number already came to several hundred.

Later Professor Koizumi, who was himself severely burnt in a bombing raid in the closing phases of the war, wrote a book about his son. In it, he included the letter which he had given Shinkichi, a naval lieutenant, when he left home for the last time:

We, your parents, are completely satisfied with you. We are proud that you are our son. If I were reborn to another life, and had to choose a wife again I would chose as I did in this life, and if I had to choose a son again, I would choose you. If a parent can say that to his son or daughter, that must surely be the best relationship there can be. For the past twenty-four years we have had every happiness that parents can expect from their child, so do not imagine that there is anything more that you should have done for us or for your sister. That is what I wanted to say to you today.[4]

As the dank haze of the rainy season closed in over Tokyo that year, the military High Command announced the heroic martyrdom of the defenders of Attu Island, who had fought to the last man in a vain attempt to prevent the island from falling into the hands of the enemy. The exaggeration was only slight; there had in fact been twenty-seven survivors out of a garrison of 2638. But all the honours heaped on the defenders of the strategically insignificant piece of land could not conceal the fact that it was the first official admission of a Japanese defeat.

The military authorities had to emphasize the heroism of the defenders of Attu, because you see, the Japanese army had no concept of surrender. Even if there was no hope of beating the enemy you were still supposed to fight to the end. That, we were told, was *Yamato-Damashii* – the Spirit of Japan. We were made to believe that there was something shameful in the way that American and British troops gave up the fight so easily, as they had done at Singapore and other places. The army had rules about what you should do when attacked by superior enemy forces, but General Tōjō produced his own little book of new rules. It began: 'No soldier should ever be captured alive. If you die in battle you will bring honour to your family.' We were made to think that it was the worst thing in the world to become a prisoner of war. I never actually encountered any American or British prisoners of war myself, but I was very clearly given the impression that they were inferior because they surrendered so easily.

In March 1943 Saitō Mutsuo had celebrated his twentieth birthday, and so was now old enough to be eligible for conscription. Compulsory military service had been one of the first measures of Westernization adopted by the Meiji reformers (three-year military service was introduced in 1873). High-School and university students, however, were exempt from conscription, their several hours a week of training and drill being seen as a substitute for full-time military service. But after the loss of Guadalcanal and Attu, Mutsuo and his fellow-students realized that it was only a matter of time before the exemption for students would be abolished. There was a feeling that this was going to be their last summer.

It seemed an occasion to do something, to seize some enjoyment from their youth and freedom before it was taken away from them. Mutsuo and two of his closest student friends, Komatsu and Koike, chose to spend the summer holiday travelling around Japan. Soon after the spring term ended they set off on the ten-hour journey by express train from Tokyo to Kyoto. They stayed in cheap inns, visited the famous sights of the city, and at night sat up late discussing their hopes and fears for the future.

We talked mostly about conscription – comparing different services, whether it was better to be in the army or the navy, and so on. One of us would maybe say:
'I hope I get sent to the navy, because they treat you better there. I've heard some nasty stories about what happens to army recruits'; or perhaps:
'I think naval uniforms are so smart. I fancy myself as a naval officer.' But another would say: 'I can't swim so I am not going on a warship if I can possibly avoid it.'
But the strange thing was, as often as not we'd wake up the next day, and the sun would be shining, and the war would just melt away out of our minds, and we would talk over breakfast about what subjects we were going to take at university, or whether your career prospects were better in banking or in industry.

The days when Mutsuo and his friends had played 'heroes' in the nearby temple grounds seemed infinitely remote. From Kyoto they went to Nara, the eighth-century capital where Buddhism first took root in Japan, and in whose ancient wooden temples the *sutras* brought to Japan by the Chinese monks of that age are still chanted:

Come, ye gentlemen, the human body is transient, weak, impotent, frail, and mortal; never trustworthy, because it suffers when attacked by disease;
Ye gentlemen, an intelligent man never places his trust in such a thing; it is like a bubble that soon bursts . . .
It has no power as the earth has none. It has no individuality as the fire has none. It has no durability as the wind has none. It has no personality as the water has none. It is not real and the four elements are its house. It is empty when freed from the false idea of me and mine. It has no consciousness as there is none in grasses, trees, bricks or stones . . . It is false and will be reduced to nothingness, in spite of bathing, clothing or nourishment. It is a calamity and subject to a hundred and one diseases. It is like a dry well threatened by decay. It is transient and sure to die . . .[5]

After Nara they travelled to Osaka, and crossed by boat to Shikoku, where their aim was to visit the famous shrine of the demon-god Kompira. The purpose of this part of their journey was principally to see for themselves a popular tourist attraction, renowned for its outstanding views over the sea and mountains of Shikoku. But there was also an element of half-joking superstition in their visit, for Kompira-Sama is the legendary guardian of those setting out on dangerous journeys. The shrine is on top of a steep mountain, and up the sheer slope rises an ancient flight of steps, worn hollow by the feet of countless pilgrims, some of whom might toil up and down the mountain-side a hundred times to obtain a wish or fulfil a vow, rather as a Western pilgrim might walk barefoot to Fatima or Lourdes.

It was a hot, sticky summer day, and walking up those steps your legs soon really began to ache. So about halfway up Koike suddenly sat down by the path and said he wasn't going on.

Of course Komatsu and I teased him about it. We said: 'Come on, lazybones. You'd better get to the top, otherwise who knows what may happen when you go off to war.'

But Koike just laughed and shook his head, and said he'd meet us later. So the two of us went on to the top, and paid our respects at the shrine, and looked at the view, which was every bit as breathtaking as it was said to be.

It was only a joke, of course. But it stuck in my memory. You see, because I'd failed my High-School exams first time round, I was a year older than most of the students in my class. Most of them weren't recruited into the forces until towards the end of 1944, so they almost all survived the war. But Koike was sent to Manchuria, and after the surrender he was taken to a prisoner-of-war camp in Siberia. He never came out again. Even his family doesn't know when or how he died.

Komatsu survived the war. He's in business now, the head of a *sake* brewing company.

The end of the spring term turned out in fact to have been the end of normal student life at Keio. By the time Mutsuo and his friends returned from their holiday, the government had announced that all students were to undertake compulsory labour service in factories or on farms, to strengthen a workforce severely depleted by war.

From then on, the books of economic theory and social history

110

remained on their shelves, unread. Each day Mutsuo was up at dawn, snatched a quick breakfast, and hurried out to catch a train to the industrial area of Adachi. By 7.30, a hundred bleary-eyed Keio students had gathered on the station for roll call. When all were accounted for, they lined up in four columns and set out at a brisk marching pace through the narrow streets to the cramped and grimy workshop where they would spend the rest of the day. What they were making there was something of a mystery, but there was talk that it was parts for some new kind of amphibious tank. Or perhaps it was a sort of boat which could also travel on land?

Whatever the purpose, the work was hard and numbingly monotonous. From morning to night Mutsuo bent over sheet after sheet of steel, filing and polishing each until it was mirror-smooth. His shoulders ached and his arms ached, and always there were the watchful critical eyes of the supervisors – the handful of teenagers and old men left from the factory's original workforce, whose job was now to train the soft, intellectuals' hands of the students into useful instruments of labour. Each day there was a quota to be fulfilled before you could leave the factory, and by the time he caught the train home to Sendagaya Mutsuo's face was grey and glittery with metallic dust, and an endless river of steel plates seemed to flow before his eyes.

The city was already in black-out for fear of bombing raids, and there were other signs that the government was preparing for an American onslaught on the 'Mainland'. Shortly after Mutsuo and his friends started work at the factory, a curious little ceremony took place in Tokyo: a memorial service for the spirits of the animals of Ueno Zoo. For the authorities, fearing that bomb damage to this, the largest zoo in Japan, might release hundreds of hungry and injured creatures on to the streets of the city, had ordered that all the carnivors in the zoo should be injected with a lethal drug, and stuffed. Buddhism, however, forbids the killing of animals, so the scientists at the zoo, following the centuries-old tradition of hunters and whalers in Japan, did not forget to atone for the killing by asking forgiveness from the spirits of their victims.

On 22 September came the expected news. The government had announced that all students over twenty years of age, except those specializing in medicine or science subjects, would be liable for immediate conscription.

For Mutsuo, the news jolted the war into a new perspective. It was no longer about heroic victories in places with unpronounceable names. It was close and inescapable, and he was very likely to die in it. A month later he, together with many hundreds of other students, went to a great recruitment ceremony held in their honour in the Meiji Shrine precincts, and attended by Prime Minister Tōjō and other dignitaries.

It was raining that day, and we marched in ranks through the drizzle. Because I was older than the rest, I was the only one from my class to go. The other Keio students there were all a year ahead of me. We marched in groups with our own college. The students from Tokyo University were at the front, and we came next.

Every now and then they show the old newsreel film of that gathering on television, and when I see it, I can always pick myself out from among all those rows and rows of students, because I was one of the tallest in my college, and I was marching near the front, next to the student who carried the school flag.

I was standing right in front of Tōjō when he gave his speech. He said something about 'you are fortunate and privileged to have been born into this imperial country, and to have the opportunity to sacrifice yourselves for His Majesty the Emperor'. Well, I had accepted by then that I was going to have to join the army, and that I would probably not come back alive, but I can't say that I felt there was anything particularly fortunate about it.

Mutsuo's instructions were to report to an army camp in Morioka, about two hundred miles north of Tokyo, on 1 December. As he packed his belongings and got ready to leave he was taken aside by his father, who informed him, gently and quietly, that it would be necessary to make preparations for Haruko's husband to adopt the name Saitō. Such 'adoptions' of sons-in-law are common in families which have no sons of their own to inherit the family name. The adoption would be put into effect only when Kōsuke lost his only remaining son. The stepmother who had treated Mutsuo as her own son, and whom he regarded as his own mother, could find nothing to say but inadequate phrases: 'Keep healthy; take care of yourself'.

Because we knew that all letters from army camps were censored, and that I shouldn't be able to write what I felt, Mother and I arranged a sort of code. We had five or six little words or phrases which would mean particular things. For example, 'Give my love

112

to Kaneko' would mean 'I am short of money' and 'sincerely' instead of 'with love from' would mean 'we are leaving here soon. Please come and visit me quickly'.

Later on I heard that Mother kept the paper with our code written on it by her all the time, and every time I wrote home she opened it up to check whether there were any secret messages in my letter. But actually in the end I hardly used the code after all.

On 29 November, Mutsuo set off for Morioka. All over Japan the 100,000 or more new student recruits were on their way to war that day, and the big station where Mutsuo was to catch his train was packed solid with nervous young conscripts; unweeping parents, filling awkward silences with platitudes; hearty groups of students in their peaked caps and uniforms, bidding a noisy farewell to class-mates, friends or brothers. The Keio send-off party had brought with them an old boy who was now a well-known singer to lead them in a rousing rendering of the school song.

Then it was time to board the train. Mutsuo's parents travelled with him as far as Morioka. That way they could spend one more evening together, as the night express rattled relentlessly through the huge, snow-covered darkness of northern Japan. They arrived at Morioka towards midday the following day, and stepped out on to the icy platform. And suddenly there was no time to say goodbye, for the army officers were ready waiting to order and direct the flood of new recruits into their proper places, and to issue each with a barrage of instructions and commands. Mutsuo found himself amongst a group of strangers being hurried off to the nearby inn where they were to spend that night.

We were divided into groups and sent to cheap lodging-houses for, as it were, our last night 'outside'. It was a strange sensation, sleeping in a room filled with other students from all over Japan, each with the same thoughts and fears in his mind. But none of us could speak our thoughts. We fell back on hollow expressions of bravery and artificial cheerfulness. And in between you could feel the tension and the aloneness of us all.

The next day, Saitō Mutsuo became a second-rank private in the Morioka Regiment of the Northern Command of the Imperial Japanese Army.

113

First thing in the morning, the new recruits to the regiment lined up outside their camp, each waiting for the commanding officer to shout out his name, and the name of the company and corps to which he was assigned. When his name was called he would run to stand with the other recruits to that corps, and then they all marched into the camp. They were shown to their quarters in the training section of the regiment. In each corps there were some twenty new student conscripts, who would share a room filled with two-tier wooden bunks. On every bunk lay a neat pile of folded military uniform. They were ordered to put on their uniforms, each with one star, signifying a second-rank private, and to tie their other clothes and belongings in a *furoshiki* (a large square of material, which is tied up by the corners to make a parcel) so that these could be returned to their families. They performed the act with a sense of its symbolism – they were stripping off the last trace of their student identities.

There was an unwritten rule in the army that, for the first three days, recruits would be treated as 'guests'. In Mutsuo's corps, one older soldier was attached to each student conscript for three days, to teach him every detail of the precise and intricate routine of army life: how to fold the blankets on his bunk, where to wash his clothes, how to collect his food from the canteen and where to return the dishes after eating. It was only when those three days were over that the recruit began his month's sojourn in which was, without great exaggeration, called 'the training section hell'.

For those first three days the older soldiers spoke to us pleasantly and politely, but the moment the third day ended, their whole manner changed, and they began to talk like gangsters. After that, we quickly discovered that we were not 'guests' any more.

Reveille was at 6 a.m. You had to get up, make your bed and put on your uniform fast enough to be lined up in the parade ground by 6.05 sharp for morning exercises. After exercises you washed, went to the kitchen, collected breakfast and ate at top speed. Next it was wash up, clean your table, return plates and utensils to the place where they belonged, but while you were still doing that the next bugle call would sound for the beginning of the morning training session, so you would rush back to the parade ground for training. And so it went on, non-stop, all day, until evening, when you collapsed in your bunk just in time for 'lights out'.

Then there would be silence and peace, for perhaps five or ten minutes, until the older soldiers came. They would walk in, turning on all the lights again and shouting: 'Come on, up, and out of bed all of you', and we would line up between the bunks. If anyone had made a mistake or failed to keep up during the day's training, everyone in the corps would be beaten, because we were all considered responsible for each other's mistakes. It wasn't so bad when they beat us with their hands, but often they would use belts or leather slippers. They struck your back or buttocks, or your face. All the time we were at Morioka, the insides of our mouths were full of cuts and swellings from their blows. But they knew how to beat people without causing serious injury if they wanted to. They were professionals, you see.

Some days we had made no mistakes in training, so they had to think of other excuses to beat us. They might check the recruits' shoes and clothes for tiny specks of dirt. Or, on other nights, they would order us to recite the Emperor's Directive to the Military. We were all reasonably intelligent and well-educated people, so we rarely had any difficulty reciting it by heart, but if we did not make mistakes they could always beat us for saying it too softly or too loud. I don't remember a single night that passed without someone being beaten for something.

For the first few days, of course, we felt angry about it, but there was never any real resistance. The reason why was this: from the moment we got up to the moment we slept we did not have as much as five minutes for our own thoughts. If human beings are deprived of time to think, do you know what happens to them? They become machines. That was the whole purpose of the system. We lost all sense of pride in ourselves and our achievements. We were left only with the two most basic instincts – to eat and to sleep.

The assault on the human personality was conducted not only through physical beatings but through many forms of psychological humiliation and intimidation which, over the years, had become institutionalized in the army training tradition. There was the 'nightingale dive', so called because it mimicked the way in which a nightingale swoops up and down the sides of valleys. In this the delinquent recruit was made to go from one end of his hut to the other, crawling under each bunk that he came to and whistling like a nightingale. Then there was the 'bicycle race', where the trainee would be forced to raise himself on his arms between two bunks and pedal his legs in the air like a cyclist. From time to time the older soldiers might shout 'up hill now!' – as a signal for him to pedal harder – or 'an officer is approaching!', which meant that the victim was obliged to salute, but, since he was supporting himself on his arms, it was of course impossible to do so without falling to the floor. A recruit who was found with traces of dirt on his boots was sometimes sent on what was called a 'tour of the company', carrying his boots by the laces in his teeth, and announcing to the senior soldiers of each of the company's ten corps: 'Second-Rank Private So-and-So, come to report failure to polish boots', after which, at each corps, he would be struck in turn by each of the older soldiers.

In the Japanese army, as in armies all over the world, the soldiers memorized the bugle calls with the help of little mnemonic jingles. The words which they fitted to reveille were: 'New recruits and older ones and everyone get up. If you don't the *hanchō-san* [corps commander] will surely punish you.' To the notes of 'lights out', they sang: 'Conscripts all, you are a sorry lot. Now you can lie down in bed and weep.'

The senior officers in the regiment had a curiously ambiguous, hypocritical approach to the system. Once a week our company commander, a lieutenant, would give us a speech at morning exercise time. Every week he said the same thing: that the army command was responsible for discipline, and that there should be no private beating of recruits by older soldiers. But each week he would go on, in almost the same breath, to say that everything must be done to increase the fighting spirit of the conscripts. And this was what gave the older soldiers their excuse. They could always argue that the reason why they beat us was not for personal revenge or pleasure, but to raise our fighting spirit.

The older soldiers in our corps, you see, were all first-rank privates. At that time they were one rank ahead of us, but they knew that, because we were college or university students, we would be eligible for rapid promotion, and in a year or so we would be cadet officers, while they would still be privates. So it was, in a way, their one golden opportunity to get at us. At Morioka, the higher-ranking officers all lived in quarters outside the main barracks, and at night the most senior person in charge

116

of the training section would usually be a young cadet officer. But it was the older privates who were the real lords of the night.

In the corps we were allowed to keep a small amount of personal spending money, but we always had to make a careful record of what we had spent and how much we had left. One day, I must have forgotten to write some small item down in my account book. When the older soldiers checked it, one of them found that the amount I had written didn't tally with the money in my pockets.

'What's happened to your money?' he roared at me, 'What have you done with it? Show me what you spent it on!'

After that they got a bench and turned it over. They made me balance on the upturned bench in front of the other recruits, with my feet on two of the legs and my hands on the other two, and they beat me again and again across the back with a wooden pole.

There were no deserters from our training section, because everyone knew that there was virtually no chance of getting away. You were almost certain to be captured and shot. There was one lad, though – he was from Shizuoka High School – and he was physically delicate and just couldn't keep up with the training. He became, as it were, their favourite victim. Day after day he got beaten for one fault or another. And then he made a very foolish mistake. He wrote a letter home, describing the awful life in the camp, and what made it even worse was that he criticized the whole system and wrote that this was not the way to turn people into good soldiers. Well, of course, we all knew that our letters were censored. The following day we were called to the parade ground. The company commander came and gave a speech. He said: 'We have one soldier in this company who is not loyal to his country', and he read us the offending parts of the letter.

That was all he did. He didn't order any punishment: it wasn't necessary to do that. We went back to our training, and the day continued normally until the evening and lights out. Then the older soldiers came and ordered the conscript from Shizuoka to go outside with them. Some time later they brought him back in again. He looked half-dead. The next day they sent him to a hospital outside the camp, and soon after I left Morioka I heard that he had died there.

It is probable that conditions in the Morioka training section were unusually harsh. The camp had previously housed the

117

Yamazaki Regiment, which had been slaughtered in the hopeless defence of Attu Island, and the ghosts of that regiment still haunted the
atmosphere of Morioka. Later, Mutsuo was to discover that other
camps operated a considerably less brutal regime. But Morioka was
certainly not unique. Many young recruits were treated in a way
which engendered lifelong hatreds. One such conscript, now a professor at Tokyo Economics University, has written of an incident
which occurred at Tsuchiura Naval Air Base, where he was trained.
On 14th February 1945, he and his fellow-recruits were punished for a
relatively trivial offence by being forced to sit for hours on a cold concrete floor and then being beaten with such force that one of his closest
friends suffered a fractured skull from which he never recovered:

> The person responsible for this was the squad commander,
> Lieutenant Tsutsui. We are still looking for that man. This is a
> quotation from my diary for that day. I wrote:
>   'I can hear horrible sounds, sounds of beating, of shouting,
> screams, the sound of breaking glass. I can hear the sound of
> floorboards cracking, of someone falling, of someone being
> kicked, and the dull, ominous sound of stick or knuckles upon a
> soft object. Between the shouted questions and the soldier's
> replies, I can hear another voice of an officer giving us some kind
> of lecture. We have had no supper. It is freezing cold. Now it is
> half-past ten, and I have been sitting in darkness on a concrete
> floor since four in the afternoon. I have meditated, and my mind is
> like that of a real criminal. I feel as though I am in prison. My
> mind is full of darkness like the mind of Dostoevsky's Murderer.'
>   If this incident had occurred not on 14 February 1945, but six
> months later, we would never have allowed that lieutenant to leave
> the army alive.[6]

Saitō Mutsuo, however, looks back upon his training in a
somewhat different way.

> I can still remember the names of some of the particularly brutal
> soldiers at Morioka – Private Iwasaki, he was the worst of all. I've
> never seen or heard of him since the war, and I have no wish to. I
> don't have any desire for revenge. It's all so long ago now. I can
> still remember every detail quite clearly, but it's like a snapshot
> pasted on some page of an album in my brain. All the feeling has
> faded out of it now.

Even at Morioka, however, life was not unrelieved misery. Recruits were given a holiday from training on Sundays and important festivals. On those days they washed and mended their uniforms, and were able to indulge in the supreme luxury of lying on their bunks undisturbed during the daytime.

One consolation of life in the training section was that we were all students. We came from backgrounds which were at least similar in some respects, so we could communicate with each other, and, on our days off, we could console one another.

There was only one other good thing about Morioka: the food. Food seemed to be reasonably plentiful there. I remember that, at our first meal in the camp, we were given red rice [rice mixed with red beans, normally served only for special celebrations] and I assumed that it was done specially to welcome us. But later I realized that they served red rice all the time, because it was a way of diluting the rice, which was then beginning to be very scarce. Generally we got good meals. The only problem was that the older soldiers took all the best bits, and we had to eat the left-overs. When they served *tempura* [fish and vegetables cooked in batter] all we could get was crumbs of batter. The best thing of all was curry and rice. That was because the curry was mixed together, so that it was almost impossible for the older soldiers to take out the good parts. I lived for the days when we got curry and rice. All the time at Morioka, I had the most ravenous appetite. I ate and ate, and if any one in our corps couldn't finish his portion, I would eat that as well.

During the month at Morioka, the recruits were invited to apply for a special pilot training scheme. Japan at that time had no separate air force. Both the army and navy operated their own air squadrons, which were stationed at different bases and flew different types of aircraft. (Inter-service divisions and rivalries, it will be noted, plagued the Japanese administration of the war. One army commander in South-East Asia was reported as remarking, perhaps only half in jest: 'This is not a war against the United States, It's a war against the Navy'.[7]) The attraction of the pilot recruitment scheme introduced by the army in 1943 was that it enabled student conscripts to become cadet officers immediately, rather than having to undergo a year's training to reach that rank. To the conscripts at Morioka, it seemed like a possible escape from the horizonless misery of a normal soldier's life, and almost all applied for entry to the scheme. The first stage of the selection process involved a rigorous medical examination. Only four of the two hundred recruits in Mutsuo's company were passed as being fit to go on to the second stage of selection – a series of aptitude tests to be held at the Aeronautical Research Station at Tachikawa, on the outskirts of Tokyo. Mutsuo was not among the successful candidates.

Even though I'd failed the medical exam, I still didn't give up. I went to the company commander, and told him that it was my greatest wish in life to fly aeroplanes for my country. The commander checked the records, and replied that my medical had shown that I wasn't physically suited to become a pilot. But still I insisted. I said: 'Please allow me at least a chance to devote my life to the nation in the air squadron.'

So at last he said: 'Well, since you are so determined, I'll have a word with the military doctor and ask his opinion about it.'

The doctor was called in, and he told me that there was hardly any chance of my passing the aptitude tests, but if I was particularly eager to become a pilot there was no reason why I shouldn't at least attempt them.

I didn't really want to be a pilot, though. I had a different reason, which was this: the railway line passed just behind our camp at Morioka, and every night, after the older soldiers had gone out and left us in peace I would lie in the dark in my bunk. And almost every night, before I fell asleep, I could hear the sound of the express train hooting as it went past our camp on the way to Tokyo. Every time I heard that sound, I was overwhelmed by a terrible sense of homesickness for Tokyo. I felt that the thing I most wanted in all the world was to be able to go to Tokyo just one more time in my life.

In mid-January 1944, Mutsuo achieved his ambition. He walked out of the gates of Morioka Army Base for the first time since the beginning of December, and boarded the Tokyo express on his way to Tachikawa Research Station. By then, however, his efforts had lost most of their purpose, for it had just been announced that the recruits, who had now completed their month of basic training, were to be transferred to Kashiwa, which was in any case within easy reach of Tokyo.

At Tachikawa, Mutsuo found that he was one of almost a thousand young student conscripts who had gathered from all over Japan to take the examination for entrance to the pilot training scheme. For several days they were put through tests of arithmetic calculation; tests to assess the speed of their reactions; and tests of balance which involved such things as standing on one leg with eyes closed for several minutes, or being spun round at high speed and then made to stand without showing signs of dizziness. The results of the examination would not be made known for two weeks, and in the meantime Mutsuo was sent to join his fellow-recruits at Kashiwa.

Even though I had only a glimpse of the city, it was marvellous to be back in Tokyo again. While I was at Tachikawa for the examination, my parents came to visit me and brought me presents of food.

But then, when I joined the others at Kashiwa, I began to feel that I had made a big mistake. The regiment which we were attached to there – the 4th Aviation Training Regiment, which taught recruits to service and maintain aircraft machine-guns – was nicknamed *Hotoke no 4-kyo* [Buddha's 4th Regiment] and after Morioka it really did seem like a paradise. I could hardly believe it when I saw it. Every corps' sleeping quarters were equipped with a radio, and we were actually allowed to lisen to entertainment programmes in the evening. There were fewer senior soldiers at Kashiwa than there had been at Morioka, and the atmosphere was generally more relaxed. Also it seemed so warm. It can't really have been very warm – after all it was early February – but it seemed like that after Morioka, where we had felt cold all the time. So then I longed to be allowed to stay at Kashiwa, and I began to hope very much that I had failed the pilots' exam.

The results were published on 10 February. After our training had finished that day, we were called to the parade ground and the company commander read us the results. In our company, only one person had passed: Private Akino, who slept in the bunk next to mine. That evening, I helped Akino to get ready. There were a lot of things to prepare. His uniform had to be sorted out, and new badges sewn on and so forth. While I helped him, I tried to cheer him up:

121

'It's bad luck, Akino,' I said, 'but never mind. Even if you become a pilot, it doesn't necessarily mean that you're going to die.'

We had just gone to bed that evening, when the duty officer came round. 'Private Saitō,' he called, 'come here. I have something to say to you.'

So I got up and went outside with him, and he told me that there had been some mistake about the results. I had passed as well.

After that, there was frantic activity. All the others in my corps got up and started to rush around helping me to prepare my kit for the next day. Now it was my turn to be told: 'Even if you become a pilot, it doesn't necessarily mean that you're going to die.' Somehow, it didn't sound all that comforting.

First thing the next morning, Akino and I left for Kumagaya Army Aviation Training Camp, to begin training as pilots.

The first stage of training took place on the most primitive of aircraft: simple gliders which were projected into the air by means of huge rubber catapults. Since there was only one glider to every fifty trainees, far more time was spent tugging on the heavy rubber strap of the catapult in preparation for other people's flights than was actually spent in the air. But gradually, during their two months at the base, they inched their way into the sensation of flying: first travelling the length of the runway with wheels on the ground, then being lifted into the air for fifty centimetres, then for a metre, until at last they flew alone for the full length of the glider's range – ten metres.

The great difference of life at Kumagaya Air Base was that we had all, overnight, become cadet officers. In most ways it was a pleasant feeling, but I discovered in my first few days there that there was one big problem about being an 'instant officer'. After all, as a second-rank private, which was the very lowest rank in the army, life had at least been simple in some respects. In that position you knew that any stranger you met was almost sure to be above you in rank, so as soon as you saw him coming you had to salute, and you mustn't stop saluting until the other fellow had lowered his hand. By now that had become a kind of automatic reflex, so that at Kumagaya I kept getting into embarrassing situations where I saluted someone whom I assumed to be of higher rank, and then we both stood there like statues, each waiting for the other to lower his hand first, until I realized that his uniform only had two stars on while mine now had three.

Mutsuo and his fellow-trainees were only the second group of recruits to enter the army's special pilot training scheme. There were six hundred of them at Kumagaya, divided into squads of approximately one hundred, each of which came under the immediate supervision of two senior cadet officers from the previous intake of trainees. In pilots, the army required something more than unreflecting obedience to commands, and their training therefore allowed time for thought and conversation, and omitted much of the dehumanizing violence which characterized other aspects of army life. But the cadet pilots remained to some extent at the mercy of their young, inexperienced and sometimes utterly unsuitable supervisors.

Although the actual training at Kumagaya was physically harder than anything I'd had to do before, there were far fewer beatings and humiliating punishments. But sometimes stupid incidents did take place.

One night one of the senior cadet officers, whose name was Hongō, made us all turn out on the runway at about 11 p.m. It was a punishment for something or other, but I've completely forgotten what we were supposed to have done wrong, so I imagine that it can't have been anything very terrible. Anyway, he made us line up on the runway in the dark, and he said: 'Take off your shirts', so we did. Then he said: 'Take off your trousers', so we all did that too. Next to the runway there was a very big open tank which was kept filled with water in case of fires, so he ordered us all to get into this tank of water. Well, this must have been February or March and the water was quite literally freezing. Afterwards, one of the people in our squad caught pneumonia and had to be sent to hospital. We felt very angry about that kind of idiotic treatment.

There was another incident which I was particularly involved in. It happened like this. Each time anyone went up in the glider, several of us had to stand on each side to pull on the rubber catapult, while others had to be ready to take away the blocks from under the glider's wheels, and a couple more would stand behind the glider to hold it steady until it took off. Stretching the

123

rubber catapult was actually extremely hard work. One day we were doing this while it was snowing, and there were piles of snow lying on the runway. Suddenly, I started to cough very hard, and when I looked down at the snow I saw that there was a splash of blood on it. Our supervisor had seen it as well, and he ordered me to go the medical room at once. The doctor X-rayed my chest, and told me to rest for three days. So while all the others struggled with their glider training in the snow, I had nothing to do but lie peacefully on my bunk for three days smoking cigarettes.

Now, one thing that they were absolutely fanatical about in the army was ashtrays. They were always afraid of fires, you see. So, even though we were cadet officers, we still had to count the ashtrays every evening to make sure that none was missing. On my third day in bed, one of the ashtrays couldn't be found. There was a great hue and cry about it, and eventually someone spotted it underneath my bunk.

I was called in to see the senior cadet officer – not the one who made us go in the water tank, but the other one, whose name was Kosaka. He was furious with me. He said: 'Anyone who smokes in bed is obviously totally lacking in martial spirit and completely unfit to be an officer. I am going to demote you to second-rank private immediately. Go and put on your dress uniform and present yourself to the commanding officer and inform him that you have been returned to the ranks.'

Now I knew that he wasn't really expecting me to do it. What I was supposed to do was to grovel and apologize, and plead with him not to demote me. But, in the first place I felt annoyed with him for making such a big fuss about what I thought was a rather small mistake, and in the second place I'd never really wanted to be a pilot anyway, and I quite liked the idea of being sent back to Kashiwa. So I just saluted and went back to the sleeping quarters and started to change into my dress uniform. Halfway through, Kosaka walked in. He took one look at me, and went completely crazy. He pulled out his sword and rushed at me, yelling something like: 'People like you aren't fit to live'. He really looked as though he would kill me, and all I could think was: 'One way I am absolutely not going to die is by being chopped to pieces by this lunatic', so I just turned and fled down the corridor in my carpet slippers. Meanwhile the other trainees had grabbed hold of Kosaka and tried to restrain him. They started saying that he should treat the whole squad as being responsible for the error, and that if he was going to demote me he would have to demote all of them too.

By this time the squad commander had heard the uproar, and came to find out what was going on. He heard the story, and then he said to Kosaka: 'Just wait a minute. I can see that you're partly right, but I can see that there's another side to the argument as well. Please go back to your office and allow me to settle this.'

Then the squad commander called me in to see him in private. He said: 'I believe that Cadet Officer Kosaka acted unreasonably, but at the same time it is clear to me that you have behaved badly. You are to write a statement of your mistakes in your diary and show it to Cadet Officer Kosaka, and you are to offer your apologies.'

I did exactly what he said. I wrote out a description of what I had done wrong. Then I took my diary along to Kosaka's office and held it out to him open at that page.

Kosaka didn't even bother to look. He said: 'I'm not interested in what you write in your diary', and he pulled out his sword again and slashed straight through the page, knocking the book right out of my hands.

Since the war we've had regular reunions of the trainees from Kumagaya, and every time we have one of our get-togethers, someone always brings up the story of Kosaka and the ashtray, and we all have a good laugh over it. It wasn't so very funny at the time though.

For those of Saitō Mutsuo's generation who survived the war, service in the armed forces created a specially powerful and close network of friendships, which in many cases remained with them for the rest of their lives. In Japanese society it is rather more common than in Europe or America for the most important and enduring of personal friendships to be formed at high school or university: in the words of the sociologist Nakane Chie, 'the sharing of experiences during the critical period of the teens and twenties has life-long effects'.[8] Amongst the generation of students who were conscripted in the war, the shared experiences of college life were to some extent displaced by the shared experiences of military service, a bond which was made all the stronger because it involved a sharing of the most profound of human feelings: the fear of death.

One of my friends at Kumagaya was a trainee called Uehara Ryōji. Uehara was from Keio University. We'd both been recruited at Kumagaya, so we often used to chat together, reminiscing about college and that sort of thing. Uehara had very liberal views for that time. I remember him once remarking that he didn't believe that a totalitarian state could ever defeat countries which had democratic governments – that was a rather risky comment to make in the circumstances.

Uehara didn't have a father. He'd been brought up by his mother, and she was a really devoted parent and used to come and visit him at the camp as often as she possibly could. She and my mother used to meet quite often when they came to visit us at Kumagaya, and for a while they kept in touch with each other and became quite good friends.

Another person I came to know very well was Konno Shigeru – that's the Konno who is now the head of the Japanese Rugby Union. Konno and I were together right the way through military service, so we became close friends. Konno had been brought up in England, and he often used to talk about his time there. Something I noticed, not just about Konno but pilots in general, was that they didn't have any feeling of personal hatred towards the enemy. Of course people at that time were encouraged to believe that they were 'American and British Devils', but none of the pilots that I knew seemed to have that sort of attitude at all. People in the air force, you see, never saw the enemy. If they dropped a bomb, they never saw the bodies of their victims, and if they were shot down they would never see the face of the person who had killed them. So their attitude was not one of hatred at all, but just – well, that this was war and it couldn't be helped. They regarded it as – I know this is a bad analogy to use for something as terrible as war – but they regarded it in a way as something like sports. It wasn't a matter of good and evil, just a matter of winning or losing.

At the beginning of April 1944 Mutsuo and his fellow-cadet officers completed their initial training on gliders, and were divided up amongst several flying schools where they would learn to pilot real planes. Mutsuo was sent to a branch of Kumagaya Flying School, which was situated just outside the nearby town of Honjō. They trained on small 480-horsepower biplanes, which were nicknamed *Akatonbo* (Red Dragonflies). The first weeks were spent in intensive practice of the techniques of taking off and landing, and after this they graduated to solo flying. In normal circumstances training would have taken one year, but these were not normal circumstances: the long and costly Battle of Imphal on the Burmese-Indian border was gradually turning into a disaster from the Japanese point of view, and three months after Mutsuo arrived at Honjō, on 7 July 1944, the Americans took Saipan. In view of the worsening war situation, the cadet pilots were required to complete their training on the *Akatonbo* by August.

There was one thing that happened while we were at Honjō which made a great impression on me. I remember that it was three days after the fall of Saipan – that would have been 10 July. We were doing our normal training on the *Akatonbo* when suddenly, out of the blue, a big transport plane came circling round and landed on the air-strip, and out got several officers wearing more stars and stripes and braid on their uniforms than any of us had ever seen before. Their arrival was totally unexpected and everyone, including our commanding officer, Flight Lieutenant Asai, was thrown into a complete state of panic. Eventually we were all ordered to assemble in one of the hangars, where a kind of makeshift platform was erected, and one of the officers stepped up on to it. Then we realized who it was: it was General Tōjō. Well, you can imagine that, as this was just after Saipan, Tōjō must have been feeling quite hysterical. Anyway, he got up on to the platform, and without any kind of introduction he said, in his staccato, military way: 'Situation: you are flying an *Akatonbo* during training at so-many metres. Enemy bomber appears above you, aiming for the airfield. What do you do? Flight Lieutenant Asai, answer.' [The significance of the question lay in the fact that the *Akatonbo* was purely a training aeroplane, and carried no weapons.] Well, we all knew exactly what answer he was expecting, and Asai must have known as well. But he didn't give it. Instead, he said: 'I would order an emergency landing of all planes and command the students to evacuate the airfield, Sir.'

It was obvious from Tōjō's face that he wasn't pleased with that. He said, in a louder voice: 'Students, what would you do?' and he pointed to one of us to answer. The trainee who was pointed out hesitated for a moment, and then gave the expected answer.

127

'Even though it might not be possible to bring down the enemy bomber, Sir,' he replied, 'I would fly up and try to crash my plane into it.'

'Right,' barked Tōjō, 'Flight Lieutenant, your student answered more correctly than you. Your reply shows lack of military spirit.' But even then Asai had the courage to answer back.

'Sir,' he said. 'the army air training regulations, article so-and-so, stipulate that in the situation you described the commanding officer should order every student to make an emergency landing.'

Tōjō looked very annoyed now. 'That may be so,' he shouted, 'but you have still shown yourself lacking fighting spirit. As a punishment you are to run to the wind-sleeve at the far end of the airfield and back again.'

After Tōjō had left, all the recruits discussed what had happened. We all felt a great respect for the way that Flight Lieutenant Asai had acted, and in a way we felt ashamed that we had given in to Tōjō's pressure. Normally, commanding officers weren't particularly popular with cadets, but after that Asai came to be greatly liked and admired.

There was another thing about him that impressed us. Every now and then at the camp we had entertainment evenings. Usually some local people would come and sing folk songs or put on a play, but as we were all college students, we didn't particularly enjoy that kind of thing. However, one of the trainees at Honjō was the younger brother of a very famous soprano singer called Hosokawa, so one day we went to Flight Lieutenant Asai and asked permission to invite her to give a concert at the camp. He agreed, so we organized this concert with Miss Hosokawa and a well-known cellist, and also a very good pianist. The three musicians turned up on the appointed evening, and gave us a concert in the dirty, dingy hall where we normally ate our meals. First, I remember, they played a cello sonata, then there were some songs, and after that they played our requests – Chopin and Liszt and so on. We felt like people who had found water in the middle of the desert. We clapped and clapped, and shouted 'encore'. The concert was supposed to end at 8.30, but it just went on and on until about 10 p.m., when Flight Lieutenant Asai stood up and thanked the musicians, and told us that it was time to end now. And he said to us: 'These musicians have put their whole hearts into playing their music for you. From tomorrow I expect you to fly your aeroplanes with as much dedication as a musician playing an instrument.'

We enjoyed that concert so much that afterwards we had another idea. As cadet pilots, we had a salary of 60 yen a month. It wasn't a great fortune – I would suppose it was about the same salary as a college-leaver would get in his first job – but at the camp we had nothing at all to spend the money on. So we decided that we would use some of our money to set up our own entertainment room. We went to Flight Lieutenant Asai to ask his permission, and he told us that there was a store shed among the trees on the airfield perimeter which we could use. We each contributed 10 yen, and we elected a committee to run the entertainment room. I was one of the people on the committee. The first thing we did was to take the money (two hundred and fifty people had joined in, so there was plenty of it) and go to town and buy a good electric gramophone and big collection of records. After that, most evenings when we had finished training we would go off to our shed in the woods to relax and listen to records. Very often, when you came in through the gates of Honjō camp, you could hear strains of Beethoven or Mozart wafting mysteriously from among the trees. I'm sure there can't have been another military camp like that in the whole of Japan.

When they completed their four-months' training on the *Akatonbo*, the pilots were invited to state which which type of plane they would prefer to fly. There were four possible options: fighters; reconnaissance planes; heavy bombers (which flew horizontally and carried 1000 kg bombs); and light bombers (which carried 500 kg to 800 kg bombs and were adapted for dive-bombing raids). In Mutsuo's squadron, the majority applied to fly reconnaissance planes. This was chiefly because the Type-100 reconnaissance plane was considered the most advanced of Japanese army aircraft, and could normally outfly any enemy planes which it encountered. But this choice did not suit the army authorities. At that time the greatest need was for fighter pilots, and the cadet pilots of Honjō were therefore informed that their preferences would be disregarded and they would be allocated for further training in accordance with military needs. About two-thirds were sent to train as fighter pilots, and the remainder divided equally between the three other categories.

They were not told in advance when or where they would be going, but for several days in early August transport planes would arrive at the base, and the names of those who were to board the planes would be read out. Some went to Java or the Philippines, to China or Manchuria. Mutsuo, who had stated a preference for flying reconnaissance planes, found himself on his way to Yōkaichi, in the western Shiga Prefecture of Japan, to train as a pilot of light bombers.

On 25 October 1944, the first officially planned suicide mission was carried out by a Special Attack Squadron (*Tokubetsu Kōgeki-tai*, usually abbreviated to *tokkōtai*) set up by the naval air force at Clark Field in the Philippines. (The word 'kamikaze' was not used in wartime Japan. The suicide squadrons were referred to by the term *Shimpū* – an alternative reading of the characters 'Divine Wind' – or more commonly by the term *tokkōtai*.) The army, who had also been preparing plans for suicide attacks, created similar squadrons soon after, and between October 1944 and 15 August 1945 it is believed that 2530 pilots from both forces died on suicide missions. In a sense the creation of the squadrons may be seen as a logical extension of the military philosophy, particularly evident in the closing phases of the war, that men were less valuable than equipment. But even in terms of the use of scarce equipment, the attacks were often of limited strategic value. For example, on 4 April 1945 seventy-nine pilots were sent on suicide missions off Okinawa. The total result of their action amounted to one aircraft carrier damaged, one destroyer damaged, and no vessels sunk.

To a great extent, it is necessary to understand the creation of the *tokkōtai* in the context of the military's great emphasis on the psychology of warfare. One of the pilots who served under Vice-Admiral Ōnishi, the man who was responsible for the creation of the first *tokkōtai* squadron (and who was himself to commit suicide on the day of Japan's surrender), recalls the vice-admiral as explaining the motives like this:

> First, in order to obtain a ceasefire quickly, it was necessary to show that Japan had the will to fight to the last man. If Japan were to be occupied, it would be absorbed as a state of the United States, and the Japanese would be treated like American Indians, and would cease to exist as a nation. It was in order to show their determination to avoid this that Japan had to appear willing to

fight to the last man and in that way it might be possible to obtain a ceasefire quickly and on reasonable terms. Next, by means of the suicide missions, it would be possible to impress upon the Emperor and his advisors the gravity of the military situation, and thus persuade them to make a ceasefire. And then again, whatever conditions Japan might have to accept to obtain peace, the fact that these young people had been willing to sacrifice their lives in the *Tokkōtai* for the sake of Japan, and the fact that the Emperor had accepted a ceasefire for this reason, would mean that some day, even if it was fifty or a hundred years from now, the Japanese people would have the strength to recover from the consequences of the war.[9]

Soon after I was sent to Yōkaichi I became a fully-fledged flying officer, and so I was eligible to eat in the Officers' Mess. One subject of discussion which was often raised at mealtimes was the *tokkōtai* mission from Clark Field. Several times, our commanding officer remarked that it was necessary for us to work out in our minds whether we would be willing to do the same thing, but at that time I had no idea that the army was seriously planning to set up its own suicide squadrons.

It was not until November that we first heard about it. We were summoned to listen to a special speech from the commanding officer. He explained to us that the army was to set up its own *tokkōtai*, and that it was starting to train pilots for the purpose at Hokota Air Base, on the Pacific coast. Pilots from our base, he said, were being invited to volunteer for the *tokkō* squadrons. Then he went into one of the hangars, and we were called in one by one to see him. He gave us each two pieces of paper, and we were asked to write our name on one of them to indicate our feelings about joining the *tokkōtai*. One piece of paper said 'eager'. The other one said 'very eager'.

'In that case,' I said to the commander, 'I hope that you will not mind if I only write myself down as being "eager".'

As far as I know, everyone else in the squad did the same thing. No one really wanted to join the *tokkōtai*. Of course we knew that, as pilots, we had a 99 per cent chance of being killed anyway, but that 1 per cent hope of surviving made all the difference in the world. If you have a 1 per cent hope of survival you look at life completely differently from the way that you look at it when you know for certain that you are going to set out on a journey and never come back.

A few days later, our squadron was divided in two. The better pilots were sent to Hokota to train for the *tokkōtai*, and the rest remained at Yōkaichi. Luckily for me, I was not one of the better pilots. So for the time being I stayed at Yōkaichi and went on practising my dive-bombing.

By now Japan's military collapse was visible, not only in the desperate shortages of materials and equipment, but also in the growing inability of strategic planners to put the available men and materials into effective use. Pilots were trained at top speed only to discover that there were no planes for them to fly, or, in other areas, that there were planes but no fuel to fly them with. At Yōkaichi, Mutsuo began by learning to fly two-propeller light bombers, known as Type-99. After a few months at the base, he was ordered to begin bouncing-bomb training. The object of this was to drop bombs in such a way that they struck the relatively vulnerable sides of enemy ships, rather than the more heavily armoured superstructure. For several weeks Mutsuo and his fellow-pilots practised the difficult and dangerous techniques of the bouncing-bomb attack over the calm waters of Lake Biwa, near Kyoto – diving down to within ten metres of its surface to 'bomb' a target fishing vessel moored in the lake. But in November, one by one, the Type-99 light bombers began to be taken away for use by the *tokkōtai*. For a brief period Mutsuo was sent away to another base to train on heavy bombers, but these too were in short supply, and he soon returned to Yōkaichi. Next he was told to prepare for fighter training, but he had made no more than a few flights on the *Toryu* ('Dragon Slayer') fighter plane when these also began to disappear into *tokkōtai* service.

By December the American forces were steadily advancing on Manila, and the army threw its best resources into the final defence of the Philippines. The fourth (and last) generation of fighter plane to be developed by the Japanese army had just come into service, and the new planes were hastily dispatched to the battle front. The planes themselves were believed to be highly effective, but they were so new that few pilots had the experience to fly them, and there were shortages of spare parts and trained engineers to maintain them. In early December, therefore, a sudden request came for all the senior pilots and maintenance staff from the Yōkaichi Air Base to be sent to

132

the Philippines. They left in the airfield's own planes and for a month Mutsuo and the other less experienced pilots remained in a training camp without instructors, without ground staff and without aeroplanes, filling in time as best they could while, little by little, Japan lost the war.

At New Year of 1945 it was learned that the emperor had not celebrated the festival in the normal manner. Instead, he had been offered, with his traditional New Year meal, the food which was commonly presented to the *tokkōkai* pilots before they took off for their last flight: red rice, snapper and a cup of *sake*. When he heard the news of the first suicide attack in October, the emperor was reported to have said: 'To think that it has come to this! And yet, they have done nobly . . .'.

We were all told about the emperor's comments on the *tokkōtai*, and of course in a sense I found them moving. But at the same time, I felt that I was the one who was going to have to die that way, sooner or later, and nothing that the emperor said made me feel any less troubled by the thought. I often talked about it with the other pilots, and I think that most of us agreed that it was not really a proper way to fight a war.

Besides, I never believed, during the war, that I was fighting for the emperor, and I don't think that any of my friends believed it either. Of course people talked about 'dying for the emperor', but we didn't feel that way. If it was necessary, I was prepared to die for Japan and for Japanese people. That was something that I could understand and identify myself with. But I did not want to connect the thought of my death with some abstract cause like saving the emperor.

By this time, frequent air-raids were taking place throughout Japan. Since Yōkaichi had no fighter planes to ward off enemy attacks, each time an air-raid siren sounded it was necessary for the pilots to race to their light bombers and fly them to the safety of an air-strip in the surrounding mountains. Frequent accidents occurred as the relatively inexperienced pilots threaded their way between the mountain peaks in the snow and mists of the Japanese winter. In spring came the invasion of Okinawa, and Mutsuo was sent back to his old base at Honjō, to rehearse another desperate tactic of the closing phases of the war: landing at night on an unlit runway This training was part of a scheme, thought up by the military command, to send plane-loads of soldiers into the bases which the American air force had established on Okinawa. The soldiers were to land under cover of darkness and sabotage as many American aeroplanes as possible while they stood on the runway. Surprisingly, at least one such attack was successfully carried out, although, as was expected, none of the Japanese soldiers involved returned alive.

We practised with heavy bombers. First we had to land with the runway lit up, but then they would turn off the landing lights – just a few at first, then more and more every night until we were landing in total darkness. Our planes had small lights on their wings, but we had to keep these turned off until the altimeter read zero. Then we had to flick the lights quickly on and off, to give ourselves a moment's glimpse of the ground in front of us as we landed. We landed without undercarriage, as this prevented the plane from overshooting the runway.

As you can imagine, with such a ridiculous method of training there were many accidents. One night about ten people at the base died when a propeller fell off their plane as they were preparing to land. Another time a plane missed the runway altogether, and seven more people were killed.

We were still doing that training when the order came for pilots from our squadron to go to the *tokkōtai*. Three pilots went first, but I knew that it would be my turn next.

In July, Mutsuo was called in to see the commanding officer. He was told that he was being sent to Kumagaya Air Base, close to the training camp where he had begun his career as a pilot, to lead a suicide squad. At the same time he was promoted to the rank of flight lieutenant.

Becoming a suicide pilot also required its own special training. By the closing months of the war almost every available aircraft, including the little *Akatonbo* training planes, were used by the *tokkōtai*. In Mutsuo's squad they used ancient, two-propeller train-ers, which were specially adapted to carry the one large bomb to be used on the mission. Because it was too dangerous to carry a real bomb during training, they practised by loading each plane with a straw rice-barrel filled with earth. The unaccustomed weight made the planes cumbersome to fly, but at the same time it was particu-larly important to achieve great control and accuracy in flying, in order to be sure of striking the enemy target at its most vulnerable spot.

When the command came to leave on their mission, they would have only one hour to prepare. Everything had to be ready. At all times their uniforms were kept clean and smart, and with their belongings in the sleeping quarters they placed their wills, letters to their parents, and the traditional Japanese mementos of the departed: a lock of hair and clippings from their nails. At first they expected that the order would be to fly initially to Chiran, in Kyushu, in order to attack the American fleet off Okinawa, but later they understood that their function was to repel the attack upon the Mainland itself.

There aren't any words to describe my feeling about joining the *tokkōtai*. I knew it was the end. It was only a matter of when the command would come. While we were training we were too busy to think about it, but afterwards, in the evenings, there was plenty of time to think about death. I suppose that all our minds were similarly empty and bleak and, perhaps for that reason, we often used to get irritable, and to quarrel over silly, petty things. But all the same, human beings are funny, aren't they? Although we knew we had to die, still somewhere there was a tiny corner of hope left, a hope that in some way or another something would happen . . . Without that tiny bit of hope it isn't possible to live at all.

My family's house in Sendagaya had been destroyed in the bombing raid of 24 May 1945 and my parents had been evacuated to Kiryu, a small town not far from the base, so quite often in those weeks I went to visit them. They understood the situation, but none of us ever mentioned it when we met or wrote letters. I didn't want to talk about it, and I suppose that they didn't either.

A glimpse of Mutsuo's family's feelings during his eighteen months' service in the army air force is provided by the comments of his sister Yasuko:

In 1944 I was newly married and living in Iidabashi [in central Tokyo]. My parents were still in Sendagaya at that time, and one day I had a telephone call from Mother. She said: 'Mutsuo has joined the army air squadron'. Her voice sounded strange on the phone, so I hurried over to their house as soon as I could. It was

135

evening, and when I arrived there were no lights on in the house, and it looked empty. I opened the door and went into the living room. Mother was there, sitting in the darkness by the window, with tears running down her cheeks. She kept muttering; 'We've only got one son left. Why has it got to happen to him?'

I asked where Father was, and she told me that he had put on his *haori hakama* [traditional men's formal dress] and gone to see the elder brother of Haruko's husband Hachirō. Hachirō and my sister were away in Taiwan then, and Hachirō's brother was the head of that family. Afterwards I heard that on that visit Father said: 'Our son has become an army pilot so we must consider him as being dead. When he dies we shall have no one to inherit the family name, so if you will give your permission, I should like your younger brother Hachirō to be adopted as a member of our family and inherit our name.'

It was such a worrying time, that. For days I could not eat at all. I kept thinking: 'What's to become of us? Father is getting old, and Haruko and I are both married. How are we going to manage?'

Then later that year my eldest son Kazuo was born. My brother was so pleased about that, because now he had become an uncle for the first time. Every time he wrote to us from his camp his letters were full of questions about Kazuo. He wanted to know all about him.

One day I went to visit my brother at the air force base. It was very difficult in those days. Getting a ticket and travelling on the train was terribly difficult, particularly with a baby. But first, before I went, I bought some red beans and sugar on the black market, and Mother and I made some sweet rice cakes for Mutsuo, because we knew he always had such a sweet tooth. Then I went down to the base by train, carrying Kazuo on my back. You weren't really allowed to bring presents for the pilots, so I had to slip the rice cakes to Mutsuo furtively, when no one was looking, and he ate them, there and then. But it was so hard to have to say goodbye. My brother came to the gate of the camp and waved. The airfield was all flat, you see, in the middle of rice fields, and you could see it from miles away. I kept turning back and waving. I could see Mutsuo, because he's so tall, but I was still looking back and waving until he looked tiny, no higher than a little bean.

At Kumagaya the *tokkōtai* pilots found themselves suddenly strangely free of the normal regulations of military life, and accorded all the special liberties allowed to those condemned to death. In the evenings, after training, they were permitted to leave the base, and if they chose not to return until morning no one would ask questions. If they stopped to bid the time of day at one of the neighbouring farms they would be invited in, welcomed as honoured guests and begged to accept the best food and drink that the house had to offer.

In those weeks, everyone had his own way of finding comfort. People who liked to drink might go to a local *sake* brewer's house and virtually take up residence there. People who wanted to could spend all night in the brothel. There was one thing, though, that we had very strict morals about: we believed that we should not form serious relationships with local girls. In the circumstances, that was felt to be wrong and unfair. There was one pilot in our squad who fell in love with a farmer's daughter from nearby, and when the others in the squad found out they beat him up as a punishment.

I did a funny thing at that time. I used to go and visit an old man who lived near the camp. This old man kept several horses and carts, and ran a little business carrying goods to and from the farms all around. There were only two people in his house: the old man himself and his grandson, who was a boy of about thirteen or fourteen. In the house they happened to have an old hand-turned record player, and many hot evenings I used to walk over there to chat to the old man and the boy and listen to music on their scratchy gramophone.

In those days it was impossible to find out what was happening to anyone outside the close circle of the base and its immediate surroundings, so Mutsuo had no news of the fates of his friends who had entered the *tokkōtai* before him. In most cases it was only after the war that he heard what had become of them:

For example my friend Uehara from Keio, who'd been on the first training course with me: I only discovered what had happened to him several years after the war, when I bought a book called *Listen to the Voice of the Sea*. It's a collection of writings by student conscripts who died in the war, and there, on the very first page, I found the name Uehara Ryōji, economics student from Keio University.

Uehara died on 11 May 1945, in a suicide attack on an American aircraft carrier. He was twenty-two. The book also prints Uehara's last letter to his mother, in which he wrote this:

I have supported freedom because, for Japan to survive for ever it is necessary to have freedom. Perhaps you think I am a fool to say this. At present, Japan is enveloped in the atmosphere of totalitarianism. But if you open your eyes wide, and think of the essence of human beings, then the belief in freedom can be the only reasonable ideology.

If you wish to judge the winners and the losers of a war, I think that this can be best done by looking at the ideologies of nations. It is clearer before my eyes than fire, that the country whose ideology satisfies the natural essence of human beings must win.

My belief has been made empty and defeated. For an individual, one country's rise and fall is truly a great and important matter but if I think of the movement of the universe, I know that such events are in fact infinitesimal.[10]

There was another friend whom I only heard about afterwards. His name was Watanabe and he was in my squad at Yōkaichi. Watanabe was one of the first group to be posted to Hokota Air Base for training in the *tokkōtai*. After his training there, he was sent off to another base further up the Pacific coast.

One day in 1945 the pilots who had stayed at Hokota saw a strange plane circling over the airfield. It was a navy Zero fighter. It landed on the runway, and out got a rather pompous young navy pilot, who started demanding fuel for his plane. The people at Hokota were annoyed at this, because fuel was so scarce in those days, and the navy had no right to demand fuel from army bases. But, at any rate, they refuelled the plane. Then the pilot asked for food, so they grudgingly let him share their evening meal, and were relieved to see the back of him. Later that evening, after it had got dark, they heard a plane circling over the runway again, as if asking permission to land. Someone said: 'It must be that navy pilot back with engine trouble. Let's ignore him.' So they did, and later the plane flew away. First thing the next morning, there came news that a plane had crashed into a mountain near the base during the night. But the plane that had crashed was not a Zero, but a Type-99, an army plane. A group of pilots from the base were sent to the wreckage, and in it they found their friend Watanabe.

Later, they pieced together his story. He had been dispatched on a suicide mission earlier the previous day, and had presumably failed to find the target. *Tokkōtai* planes did not usually have enough fuel for a two-way journey, so Watanabe presumably made for Hokota because it was nearer than his home base, and because he knew that he had friends there.

But there was another thing. The friends who recovered his body found that it was all covered in perfume. His face was painted with thick white powder and his lips were bright red with lipstick. On his feet was a pair of unmatching shoes, and round his neck he wore the white scarf of the *tokkōtai*.

Although my mind was blank inside, all those weeks that I waited for the order to fly my *tokkō* mission I managed to keep quite calm. But you could never tell, and to this day I can't tell, what would have happened when the order actually came. To this day I can't be sure that, when that happened, something might not have snapped inside me, as it must have done in Watanabe.

At Kumagaya Air Base, mysterious rumours flourished about the progress of the war: rumours of unexpected and miraculous events, even that America and Russia had started to fight each other, so now America would cease to attack Japan. Everyone understood that a Japanese victory was no longer conceivable and yet – here they were, trained pilots, waiting for the command to fly to their deaths, and out there on the runway stood the lines of aircraft, oiled, fuelled and ready. How could Japan possibly be defeated?

The news came of the 'new, special-type bomb' which had fallen on Hiroshima. The military authorities, however, announced that wearing white cloth could protect you from the weapon's as yet unspecified effects, and Mutsuo and his fellow-pilots therefore assumed that it was only some minor adaptation of the normal American bombs. The night after the attack on Hiroshima, when the air-raid siren sounded at Kumagaya, the pilots ran to the shelter covering their heads with white sheets, and were lucky not to have suffered severe casualties, for they must have made a perfect target for night bombing.

Then came the news of Russia's declaration of war, and Mutsuo understood that Japan had been defeated.

I knew that we had lost when I heard that. I expected then that the American and Russian forces would invade Japan, and that there would be a long guerrilla war. I didn't want Japan to surrender, even though I knew that it would save my life. I suppose that was just the way I had been educated – I believed that we had to fight and never admit defeat, but I thought also that this would be the end of Japan as a nation. The government made a lot of propaganda in those last few months about what would happen if the Americans came – how they would make us into slaves, and all the women would be raped. Later I thought about that, but not at this time. At this time all I felt was: 'Anyway, I shall not be there to see it.'

6

Tsutsumi Ayako

In the attack on Pearl Harbor, Japan had admitted only nine casualties – the crew of one midget submarine sunk during the action. The military High Command did not at first make these deaths public knowledge, perhaps because they wished to present the attack as an unqualified success. But in March 1942, they announced the creation of 'Nine Military Gods'.

The Japanese view of the universe has not traditionally drawn any sharp line between the natural and the supernatural, or between the human and the divine, and in past centuries it was quite common for dead or even living persons of fame and virtue to be treated as *kami* – 'gods'. It was therefore in keeping with this tradition that the nine unknown and unremarkable young men who died at Pearl Harbor should be posthumously awarded the distinction of divinity.

It was just after the beginning of my second year at Kōshū Girls' School [in the spring of 1942] that we heard about them. Our school had an auditorium where they used to show films, and one day we were all taken in there to watch something. The lights were turned out, and there was solemn music playing. Then, one by one, these nine photographs of faces flickered on to the screen, and there was a commentary explaining how they had died. We hadn't heard that anyone had been killed at Pearl Harbor until then.

They were all so very young and handsome-looking that most of us in my class instantly fell in love with them. We each had our own favourite god, and used to argue fiercely about who was the most beautiful and heroic-looking of all.

At Girls' Schools throughout the empire, as at the boys' Middle Schools, there was compulsory military drill, although in the girls' case their training was based, not on that of a soldier, but on that of a

141

battlefield nurse: making first-aid kits, rolling bandages, carrying stretchers.

The man who came to take us for drill was a young lieutenant who had been invalided out of the army. Lieutenant Oshimi was his name. There was a girl in our class called Shimomura, who had a desperate crush on Lt Oshimi. Every time he went anywhere near her, her temperature would rise. She would come rushing up after drill and say: 'He spoke to me! He actually spoke to me!'

It was all imaginary romance, though. Real relationships with boys were strictly prohibited. Sometimes, when there were special festivals or ceremonies or that sort of thing, we would visit the local Japanese boys' school, but every time that happened we would get a special little lecture first, telling us that we mustn't have private conversations with any of the boys, and we mustn't let our eyes wander unnecessarily.

In a small, close community like ours anyone who walked out with a boy was likely to meet someone who knew them, and then there would be a terrible scandal, and gossip at the *tonarigumi* meetings, and the story would probably get back to the headmaster. If that happened, he would call the girl into his study and give her a good talking to, and she would have to make a public apology or, if it happened more than once, she might be suspended from school. I suppose that there were one or two girls in my class who had boyfriends, but they weren't in my group of friends, so I never really knew anything about them.

Japanese teenagers tend to define themselves as being '*nampa*' or '*koha*', 'soft group' or 'hard group'. The 'soft group' consist of those who pursue the sexual dreams of adolescence, and the 'hard group' of those whose fantasies are directed towards the military or (in the post-war period) to motorbikes and martial arts.

I was very definitely '*koha*' – 'hard group'. I was so patriotic, in fact, that the other girls in my class used to look a bit askance at me. They would look at me, as they say, with the whites of their eyes.

It was a school regulation then that we all had to wear our hair in a pigtail. Most girls used to decorate their plait with some sort of hair-slide, but I never wore anything like that. One day, our class teacher noticed this, and I think he must have said something to the Head about it. In any case, the next day at assembly the Head gave us a speech on the subject. He singled me out by name and said how my not wearing a hair-slide showed that I had the right attitude in this time of national emergency. At the end of assembly all the other girls in the school had to bring their hair-slides to the Head, to be donated to the war effort. But they were a bit annoyed with me about it afterwards, and said it was all my fault for being so silly.

It is hard to imagine that a few hundred girls' hair-slides can have had any material effect on the Japanese war effort, but such gestures were encouraged, as much as anything, for their psychological value in creating a sense of civilian participation in a great national struggle. Neighbourhood associations vied with one another in the collection of old newspapers, empty bottles and cast-off clothes for donation to the war effort. School-children were told that every scrap of used tin-foil must be preserved and surrendered to the authorities for use in the aircraft industry. (One child of that generation was later to recall that, as a result, he lived through the years of the war with the unshakable conviction that all Japanese aeroplanes were made of silver paper.[1])

In a similar spirit, Ayako's years at Girls' School saw a gradual modification of school uniforms. When she entered the school, her parents had bought for her the traditional navy-blue skirt and sailor-suit top which are still the uniform of Japanese High-School girls today. The following year, however, new pupils arrived at school in uniforms shorn of their large square collars, since these were regarded as a waste of valuable material. At the same time, and for the same reason, the wide flared skirts became narrower, and later in the war the girls were encouraged to divide their skirts into loose breeches, which were considered more economical and more in keeping with the mood of the time.

By Ayako's last year at school, therefore, her class was arrayed in a curious motley of costumes, in which only traces of the original trim blue uniforms remained.

The officially instigated spirit of self-sacrifice, which pervaded even the smallest and most personal corners of life, was consciously contrasted with the hedonistic attitude of civilians in the enemy nations. In the build-up to Pearl Harbor the Asahi newspaper had reported, in an article sarcastically entitled 'American Patriotism', that:

. . . for American women, difficult diplomatic issues like the crisis

143

in the Pacific are much less important than the current lack of silk stockings in the shops, and the attendant panic-buying. Big stores like Gimpels, Maceys and Alexanders have now rationed stockings to between three and six pairs per person, but every day tens of thousands of Yankee girls rush to the stocking counters, and some have been injured in the crush. Such is the exalted status which women enjoy in the United States, that this silk stocking crisis has resulted in the government agreeing to a partial lifting of its embargo on silk, and to the release for consumer use of some of the stockpiles of silk which it had been retaining for parachutes and other military uses . . .

To sum up, while America's material preparations for war are daily becoming more intense, spiritually the nation is unfit to fight. At present, a campaign is underway in the United States to persuade people to contribute their aluminium pans to the war effort, but even this is conducted in typical Yankee fashion, for although people willingly contribute their old pans, as soon as they have done so they immediately hurry out to buy new ones![2]

But the effect of war upon education was not merely a matter of uniforms and hair-slides. In August 1942 the government announced that the period of time which children spent at Middle Schools, High Schools and Girls' Schools was to be reduced by one year.

This meant that Ayako would graduate from Kōshū Girls' School in the spring of 1945 rather than in 1946, as she had expected. Just one month earlier, other changes had been introduced in the Ministry of Education, who had decided that:

. . . in the present war circumstances, secondary education for girls should focus upon the subjects of housework (particularly hygiene and the rearing of children), science, and home economics. School discipline should also be strengthened. In order to provide time for these developments, the teaching of foreign languages in Girls' Schools will be phased out. Where foreign language education is specially required, this should be on a voluntary rather than a compulsory basis.[3]

In the circumstances of 1942 it would have been a foolhardy parent or teacher who requested special facilities for English teaching, and the announcement meant in effect that in Ayako's school, as in almost all Japanese Girls' Schools, English Language disappeared from the curriculum, and was replaced by increased sessions of cookery, needlework and drill.

So in the end I only had one year of English classes, and even in those they didn't really teach us anything about what sort of countries America and Britain were. But what we did learn, because we heard it repeated so often, was to think of them as *Kichiku Bei-Ei* – American and English Devils. And when you hear something said so many times you really do start to imagine, as I did, that they are somehow inhuman and awful.

From the point of view of Ayako's family, the war brought certain short-term blessings. Her father's business thrived, and often he was away from home for weeks at a time, supervising newly obtained military contracts for work on roads and fortifications in distant parts of the peninsula.

My elder brother was sixteen when the Pacific War started, and Father was very keen that he should join the navy. Right from the day the war broke out, he kept going on at my brother to take the exam for the naval cadets' school. Father, you see, had been turned down for military service in peacetime because he was too short, and I think that had perhaps given him some sort of a complex about it. But in fact my brother didn't really seem enthusiastic about going to war. In the end, it was decided that his whole class at Middle School should apply to become naval cadets. At that time it was still voluntary in theory, but as all his friends were going to apply, my brother more or less had to try as well. In any case, he failed because his eyesight wasn't up to standard, and later he went off to a pharmacy college in the Mainland, so he never did get conscripted.

But still my father used to go on complaining: 'Isn't anybody in this house going to go and serve their country?' At that time, towards the end of my second year at Girls' School, I'd become friendly with a girl called Okada. She was always the top of our class. She was one of those people, you know, who is good at everything: she was pretty and she always came top in maths and she was good at music and had a lovely clear speaking voice. I can't really think how I came to be friends with someone like that. Anyway, in the winter of Second Year Okada and I made a vow that we would go every morning to the Kōshū Shrine to pray for

145

victory. It was very, very cold at that time of year, but I would get up early and eat breakfast, and then I would walk up to the shrine through the frost and mist, and meet Okada-san there, and after we'd prayed we would go to school together.

From those early morning meetings we developed another idea. We decided that, by the time we finished school, it might already be too late to offer ourselves for service to our country, so instead we would leave school right away and volunteer for the nursing corps. We told our teacher about the plan, and he must have been quite impressed by our determination, because I remember that he got in touch with a man from the local newspaper, who came and took our photographs and wrote a little article about us, how patriotic we were and so on. For me, I wanted to do it, partly out of patriotism, but partly because, since girls couldn't be conscripted, it seemed like the only way for us to take a main role in the great drama which was taking place.

The nurses' training school was in Seoul, so Father took us there, and we had an interview with one of the teachers. She was quite kind, but she told us very firmly that the best way to serve our country was to go back to school and study hard. In those days, you see, there were two ways of joining the nursing corps. There was a lower-level training course which you could take after finishing primary school, and a higher level course which you entered after Girls' School. The teacher told us that, as we had almost finished two years of Girls' School, it would be best to continue there until graduation and then come back to take the higher-level exam. Of course we felt frightfully disappointed, but we knew she was right really.

It's funny, although I knew that being a front-line nurse was very dangerous, I never thought about the danger or the possibility of dying when I went to volunteer. When you are fighting for your country I suppose you don't think about death.

It was hard to return from the heroic heights of the nurses' college in Seoul to the mundane reality of Kōshū Girls' School. But at least Ayako and her friend Okada could comfort themselves with the knowledge that their school curriculum was becoming more and more relevant to their unrelinquished goal of nursing. Not only were there the weekly hours of drill; even the annual school Sports Days had been altered to reflect the horrors of war. Sack races and hurdling were replaced by stretcher races or team games which involved carrying buckets of water to quench imaginary fires.

In Third Year I was in my class liaison team for Sports Day. What we had to do was this. First of all, one person had to pedal as fast as they could on a bicycle to one end of the field. Then they had to pick up a message and pass it in semaphore to the next person in the team. Then she had to write it down and hand it on to someone else, who would carry it by bicycle to the finishing line. It was a preparation for the sort of communications which we might be needed to do in an emergency, you see. We practised and practised.

On Sports Day, I was the person who had to take down the semaphore message. The message was: 'Let us wield the pen with the spirit of wielding a weapon'. But the silly thing was I just couldn't understand the word 'pen'. I managed to get all the other, more difficult bits down, but I just couldn't figure out 'pen'. It wasn't simply that it made me look stupid, but, worse still, it slowed the whole team down, so our class did badly in that race, and I felt terribly responsible about it.

Oh yes, and there was another embarrassing thing which happened around that time. We were supposed to bring a first-aid kit to school every day, but one day I forgot mine. When the teacher found out she said, in front of everybody: 'Really, Tsutsumi! You were the person who wanted to become a front-line nurse, and you forget your first-aid kit. You, of all people, ought to be the one to bring two kits, rather than forgetting to bring one altogether!'

She didn't really mean that I ought to bring two, of course. That was just a manner of speaking. But after that I never did forget my first-aid kit again.

Meanwhile, Ayako and Okada kept their spirits high by rehearsing the anthem of the nursing corps, which they sang on winter excursions to the forests, to gather pine-cones for the school stoves; in spring, when their class was sent to the country to help weed the rice fields; and at harvest time, when they went to winnow wheat on the farms, sending clouds of chaff swirling to the brisk but plaintive rhythm:

In the silence after the bursting shells,
The silence when even no insects cry,

The bodies of wounded strew the field
And the military nurses come running.
To the heroic Japanese soldier,
And to the enemy who speaks a foreign tongue,
We will bring life and healing
With the red cross on our hearts.

Girls, like boys, were required to perform labour service in the last two years of the war. So from the Third Form onwards Ayako spent almost half her time in silk-reeling factories or on farms, where her task was to catch grasshoppers – not only to protect the crops from their ravages, but also because grasshoppers, boiled with soy-sauce and sugar, make a strongly flavoured and protein-filled sweetmeat. In the Fourth Form many days were also spent in the mountain forests around the city, digging pine-roots. The roots were dug out with heavy shovels, chopped into pieces, and delivered to an army supervisor who would take them away to be boiled down for their resinous oil. By now, pine-root oil was a vital supplement to the desperately short supplies of fuel oil for the Japanese forces in their struggle to control South-East Asia and the Western Pacific. Civilians were taught that 'wherever there are pine trees, there are the oil fields to supply fuel for Japan's warships'. Within the school itself most lessons were also acquiring a new practical dimension.

Until the end of Second Year we were still doing ordinary needlework lessons – learning to make and tie *obi* [kimono sashes]. But from the beginning of Third Year we had to spend our lessons sewing buttons on military uniforms. We turned it into a sort of competition, which made the job more fun: we used to try to see who could get the most jackets done in an hour.

In cookery lessons at that time we were making our own school meals. We each had to bring a box of ready-cooked rice with us from home, and then in class we would cook something to go with it, usually a dish of boiled vegetables or something like that. I remember there was quite a long prayer which we had to say before we started eating, and it always made me want to laugh, because it started off in a very grand way: 'Again this day we can receive sustenance, thanks to the grace of heaven and earth and of our ancestors . . .' But it ended up on a suddenly practical note, with 'We will not complain whatever our food is like'.

We were also given a lot of advice about how to avoid wasting

148

things, how to preserve and reuse everything from paper to potato peelings. The funny thing about that was that it never really mattered much during the war, because in Korea we Japanese people never had any serious shortages, but after the war I found that all those tips I had learnt at school were essential for survival.

At the beginning of Ayako's third year at Girls' School, the military High Command announced the death of Admiral Yamamoto Isoroku, the architect of the attack on Pearl Harbor and of Japan's early naval successes in the war. He had been killed on 18 April 1943 when, during the struggle for Guadalcanal, his plane was shot down over the Solomon Islands.

We were all told to go into the assembly hall, and the headmaster gave us a speech explaining about the death of Admiral Yamamoto. I remember that a lot of the girls were crying, and I felt a sad ominous sort of feeling when I heard that news, but all the same, I still believed very strongly that Japan was the Country of the Gods, and couldn't possibly be defeated. Even afterwards, although we knew that the American forces were approaching Japan day by day, we still felt sure that at the last moment there would be some kind of dramatic reversal, and everything would be all right in the end.

The headmaster who gave us that speech was a new one, who had just come to our school. I really liked and admired the new Head. One thing which he did was to introduce meditation sessions. We all had to make our own little cushions, and once a week we would take them to the hall and sit on our heels on the cushions for an hour without moving. I'm not really quite sure what the purpose of the meditation was supposed to be, but it was a very good discipline.

Another thing that the new Head did was to choose a school song. We already had one school song, but he made another special one which we used to sing at assembly each day. The words he chose were a *tanka* [thirty-one syllable poem], which I think was written by the wife of the Emperor Meiji, and he got the school music teacher to write a tune to go with them. The words went:
'Although in summer
The weeds flourish tall and strong
Still you will find them
Wild white lilies, standing proud,
Noble in the wilderness.'

What it meant, you see, was that even in Korea Japanese girls could grow up to be noble like the white lilies. I thought that was lovely.

My favourite teacher at Girls' School, though, was a man called Mr Niimi. He was our form teacher in my last year at school, and I respected him a lot and felt that he really influenced me. There are two things in particular that I remember about Mr Niimi. One thing, I think, happened the very first time I had a lesson from him. In any case, it made a great impression on me. He walked in through the door and wrote in big letters on the blackboard: 'Minobe Tatsukichi: The Emperor is an Organ of State', and then he drew a firm cross through it. He went on to explain to us about Professor Minobe's theory,[4] and how wrong and evil it was to try to reduce the emperor to a mere branch of the constitution, like any old ministry or local government office. I felt at once that Mr Niimi was absolutely right, and that I could never think of the emperor just as an 'organ of state'.

The other thing I remember concerned a notable Japanese lady, who was the wife of a prominent figure in the colonial administration of Korea. This lady had seen some foreign prisoners of war being used as labourers, to carry heavy loads on and off the Shimonoseki–Pusan ferry, and she had said that she thought it was a shame for them to be made to do such hard and dirty work. This remark was very widely reported in all the papers at the time, and one day Mr Niimi discussed it with us in class. He criticized the lady very sternly, and said that in the middle of a war you couldn't afford to have such soft and sentimental thoughts. Actually, although I respected Mr Niimi such a lot, I couldn't help disagreeing with him and agreeing with the lady about that. It *did* seem to me to be a shame.

The widening net of conscription caught not only male students but also more and more middle-aged men, among them several of Ayako's teachers. In November 1943 the upper age limit for conscription was raised from forty to forty-five, and the Japanese press commented:

The state has proclaimed those up to forty-five years of age to be 'in their prime'. We have an expression that forty is 'the beginning of old age', but now we should erase that expression from our minds. Moreover, those who find themselves newly classified as being 'in the prime' must see to it that they truly are as fit in mind and body as the young. The way to win this war is to regard the forties as 'the prime of life' and the fifties as 'middle age'.[5]

From Kōshū Girls' School, the Japanese language teacher was the first to go. As was customary, the girls inscribed their names and messages of good luck on two large rising-sun flags, which the teacher would tie like sashes across his chest when he set off for war. His pupils accompanied him as far as the station, waving flags and singing songs, and raising a last cry of 'banzai' as the train drew out of the station. Later, four other teachers were called up, including the deputy headmaster, who only went for reserve training, and returned a few months later. There were other, less cheerful, ceremonies which became more common as the war continued:

Several of my school-friends had older brothers who were killed in the war. When someone from a family we knew died, we would all go with the parents to the station to receive the ashes when they were brought back to Kwangju. In the first part of the war there were always crowds of people accompanying the family on occasions like that, often hundreds of people or even thousands if it was someone important. But as the war went on, and deaths became more common, the number dwindled until there would usually be no more than, maybe, five or six close friends.

Families whose sons were killed in the war were given little plaques saying 'Military Patriotic House' to hang on their gate-posts. Every time we passed a house which had one of those plaques, we would stop and bow our heads in respect. But that was also something that people got more lax about as the war went on, because in the end it reached a point where you could hardly walk down the street without having to stop and bow half-a-dozen times.

The loss of five teachers out of a staff of only fifteen put increasing strains on those left behind. More and more women continued working after marriage, or even while pregnant. This would be unusual in Japan today, and until the 1940s would have been unheard-of for anyone in a middle-class occupation such as teaching.

I remember that in Fourth Year our needlework teacher went on working while she was expecting a baby, right up until the very day before she gave birth. Afterwards our headmaster made a little

151

speech about it, praising her and saying how good she had been to do something like that for the sake of her school and her country.

The needlework teacher's condition, however, prompted some quiet speculation amongst the girls, who received no formal sex education apart from advice on dealing with periods. Ayako's knowledge of the subject, like that of many other girls, came from the whispers of her school-friends, and from the explanatory supplements which women's magazines included from time to time, either for educational purposes or to boost their circulation.

A friend at school showed me a little booklet explaining how sex works, and, well, I was just terribly shocked. Somehow I had been living in this kind of idealistic, romantic world, full of thoughts about 'the Land of the Gods' and so on, and that kind of thing didn't seem to fit in with my ideas at all. For a while after I looked at that book I felt as if the whole world had turned grey and sombre around me. But in the end the feeling passed off, and I got used to accepting the way things are.

As the last term of school approached, Ayako began once more to look forward to becoming a nurse. In the early spring of 1945 she and Okada, together with one of the Korean girls in their class, whose Japanese surname was Aomatsu-san, went to Seoul to sit the entrance examination for the higher-level nurses' training course. The examination consisted of written papers and a medical check, and after these had been completed they returned to Kwangju to wait for their destiny to be decided. The results arrived just before their school graduation ceremony. Okada and Aomatsu were accepted; Ayako had failed. It was a bitter disappointment, and one over which she shed many tears. But in the end there was nothing to do but dry her eyes, and consider alternative ways of contributing to Japan's victory.

Out of our class, there was only one girl who went on to higher education. She applied for medical school, but that was very much frowned upon by the rest of us. There was a sort of unspoken feeling that it was a crime to go on to higher education at a time like this. The rest of the girls either stayed at home to help their families or applied to work for the military in some way, mostly in the army or navy supply divisions. On the whole the navy was more popular, because naval officers were considered smarter and more attractive than army officers. But in the end I applied to go to the Army Supply Section in Inchon, where there was a big munitions factory. My father had really wanted me to be a front-line nurse, and he had been disappointed, too, when I failed, but he said: 'Since you haven't managed to get into the nursing corps, you may as well go and work in Inchon.'

For some reason, I don't remember much about my graduation ceremony from Girls' School. It didn't leave any great impression on me. We just all exchanged addresses and promised to keep in touch with our friends, and then we went our various ways.

Inchon is a town on the Yellow Sea some twenty miles west of Seoul, and a place whose name was to become well-known abroad five years later, during the Korean War. But in 1945 it was a bustling, rather grimy port, full of the comings and goings of Japanese ships and troops. The Imperial Army supply Section itself occupied a sizeable area of the town with its barracks, munitions factory, offices and dormitories for civilian workers. The dormitory where Ayako was to live for the next four months was occupied entirely by young Japanese Girls' School graduates of about the same age as herself.

We slept about ten to a room. In the morning, we would get up around 6 a.m., dress in our work uniforms and have breakfast in the dormitory dining room. Then we'd all walk together down to the munitions factory, which was maybe five or six minutes away on foot. We had to be there by 8 a.m. for the works assembly, which was held in the garden of the factory. We used to line up in front of the flagpole in the garden, and the colonel who was in charge of the supply division would arrive at eight o'clock sharp and raise the flag. Then he'd give us a little speech about our tasks for the day, and he might tell us something about how the war was going. Sometimes he mentioned things like the air-raids on Tokyo, but he never went into any details, and mostly he talked in an optimistic way, saying that although the situation was serious, there was all the more reason to work hard and ensure Japan's victory. So I never realized how bad the bombing was until afterwards. When the colonel had finished his speech we would sing some songs, and then we'd go in to start our work.

My job was in the office. One of the things I had to do was to make up the pay packets for the other girls. I remember that when

I started I was a bit puzzled, because there was one Korean woman who worked in the office, and although she was in a senior position her pay was less than mine. I thought there must have been some mistake, so I went to the supervisor. But he explained that there was no mistake: her pay, he said, was the normal basic wage, but Japanese workers got a bonus of between 40 and 60 per cent for working overseas. I'd never heard of that before, and thought it was a bit odd.

Anyway, at midday we would go back to the dormitory for about an hour for lunch, and then we returned to the office and worked until five or six in the evening. We worked every day, including Saturdays and Sundays. Most people did that, of course, in those days – what they used to call working 'Monday, Monday, Tuesday, Wednesday, Thursday, Friday, Friday'. I can't remember how much I got paid – I'm always hopeless at remembering that sort of thing – but at any rate it was just enough to live on.

In the last two years of the war, the recruitment of women into the Japanese empire's labour force was greatly expanded. Although young women had for some time formed a large part of the workforce in certain industries, such as textile spinning and weaving, they were now, through force of necessity, being employed in what had traditionally been men's occupations. In 1944 a Women's Volunteer Work Brigade had been set up to recruit groups of female workers directly from Girls' Schools or neighbourhood associations, and more and more women were being drafted into shift-work in the aircraft factories, which now operated twenty-four hours a day. The trend was encouraged by frequent news items praising the sacrifice of women who volunteered for heavy manual jobs. One such article, headlined 'Flowers of the Rear Guard Forces', noted:

In the field of transportation an army of women is now beginning to supplement the ranks of men depleted by the needs of war.

Since 24th May [1944] women have been training at the Tokyo Railway Drivers Training Centre, and on 22 August thirty-four girls qualified to drive heavy goods vehicles for the road haulage section of the National Railways in Tokyo.

At Tokura Station, the management of the Shin–Etsu railway line has begun training fifteen women employees to control the points on the railway. Four girls aged between fifteen and twenty-two have already successfully completed training: Negishi Keiko (22), Shimizu Tamai (18), Ogawa Mitsue (16) and Yoshiike Nakako (15) have been selected to begin work on the line.[5]

Her job in the Army Supply Section at Inchon, however, did not live up to Ayako's expectations. She had envisaged herself as being actively engaged in producing and handling the guns and bullets which the imperial army so urgently needed in its mortal struggle with the enemy. Instead, she found herself sitting in an office, filling in attendance registers and checking pay packets, or, as often as not, tidying her desk or making cups of tea, because there was nothing else to do with the long, empty hours of the day. At first she tried to argue with the system. She went to her supervisor and asked to be transferred to the factory production line, but was told that her clerical work was every bit as vital to the nation as the work performed by the factory girls. For a week or two she managed to convince herself that this was true, but gradually frustration and boredom began to creep back, and she tried again.

There was an army captain who used to come in to check our work in the office, and one day I went and explained to him that I wanted to be transferred to the factory. But he was quite adamant about it. He said:
'The people who work in the factory are all young Koreans. Japanese girls work in the office.' So that was that.

The only break from the monotonous routine of office life were the occasional national holidays: Meiji commemoration day, Taishō commemoration day, and the emperor's birthday. It was on one of these holidays – perhaps the latter, which occurred during Ayako's second month at Inchon – that she decided to visit her friends at the nurses' college in Seoul.

I managed to get the train to Seoul and find my way to the college where I had been for the nursing exam. But when I got there I had such a shock!
    Okada-san had been a very pretty girl, but when I saw her that day she looked awful, just like a skeleton, with great dark lines under her eyes. She told me that life in the nursing corps was a nightmare. They had to work terribly long hours, and the trainees were constantly bullied and beaten by the older nurses. The

Korean girl, Aomatsu-san, wasn't there. She had run away because she couldn't stand it any more.

Okada said to me: 'You don't know how lucky you were to fail that exam.'

There was, however, one distraction within the routine itself, which began to absorb Ayako's attention more and more as the months passed by. She had been assigned the duty of delivering the daily attendance register each morning to the headquarters of the Army Supply Division, which was some ten minutes' walk from her office.

Each day I had to hand the register over to the same young soldier in the headquarters. He must have been about eighteen, and I heard that he had just graduated from Middle School. We never said anything to each other apart from the usual greetings, but after a while I began to feel that he was looking at me in a sort of special way. Sometimes our eyes met, and I could feel something like a tension in the air between us. I was sure that he could feel it too. One day, after I'd been going there every day for three months or so – it must have been towards the end of July 1945 – I took the report in one morning and as I gave it to him our hands accidentally touched. And then suddenly, he put the report down and caught hold of both my hands and held them in his. I can't really remember what he said, or whether I said anything, but I know I went out with my head whirling, feeling in my heart that I had found my destiny, and that this was the man I would spend the rest of my life with.

Who knows, it might really have turned out that way! Only of course I didn't have any opportunity to see him except on official duty, and after the war ended a couple of weeks later, work in the munitions factory and the office ended too. I couldn't think of any excuse to go off to the army headquarters on my own after that, and so I never saw him again.

7

Iida Momo

On the day the Pacific War started, I remember the atmosphere of excitement at school. We all discussed what had happened. One boy in my class was particularly impressed because, on the train on his way to school, an old army veteran had suddenly stood up in the carriage and started to make a speech to all the passengers in a shaking, emotional voice. He had said that this was not just an expansion of the war, but something entirely new, a total conflict the like of which we had never experienced before. He said that now the conflict had started, there would be no going back. Japan was facing the greatest challenge in its national history, and whatever the cost we had to overcome it.

The force of these words was not immediately apparent. Naturally, there was a new mood of excitement in the air; there were the daily reports of victory in the press and on the radio; there was the growing shortage of material necessities and the increasing regimentation of everyday life. But for those of Momo's generation, there was no overnight change in their routine of lessons and homework, their talk of text-books and exams, their hopes and their ambitions. It was only little by little that their lives would be sucked into the totality of war.

The events of December 1941, therefore, made less impact upon Momo than the event which took place in April 1942: for in that month he achieved his personal goal, graduating from Ichi-chū and entering Tokyo No. 1 High School, the preparatory college for Tokyo University, at the unusually early age of sixteen. It is hard to exaggerate the prestige enjoyed by Tokyo Imperial University and its associated High School in a society where so much was determined by academic success. The university (which since the war has dropped the word 'Imperial' from its title) has provided and continues to provide recruits to all the best positions in the Japanese bureaucracy and in the largest and most famous industrial and financial concerns. It has also produced many of the leading figures of Japanese literary and cultural life over the past hundred years. The students of Ichi-kō and Tokyo Teidei (to use the common prewar abbreviations for the High School and University) were a breed apart.

Each time I changed schools – first when I moved from primary school to Ichi-chū and then when I moved from Ichi-chū to Ichi-kō – it somehow made a complete change in my whole life and attitude. It was, I think, something to do with the fact that I came from a basically culture-less background. We didn't have a single book in our house, and my father's idea of culture was to take us to whatever happened to be on at the local cinema. So I was always tremendously impressed and influenced when I encountered, as it were, higher levels of culture.

If I think back, I can remember very clearly how my consciousness of things changed after I went to Ichi-kō. I suddenly became much more socially aware. And I can also remember particular incidents from that time which came as a real shock to me, and which must have helped to cause that change in consciousness.

One of these things was our entrance ceremony to Ichi-kō. There was a programme posted up on the door of the school hall saying that the ceremony would last for however long (about an hour and a half, I think it was) and that there would be speeches by the vice-chancellor and various other people. Well, we went into the hall and stood through the speeches, and it all went according to plan, but then at the end of the ceremony the teachers walked out and we were told that we would have a speech from the head of the Students' Autonomous Committee of Ichi-kō. So this older student stepped up on to the rostrum, surrounded by other young men who were obviously his committee members, and he started to talk to us about the history of the Students' Autonomous Committee, and how at various times they had won the right to organize their own meetings and run their own dormitories and so on. He went on speaking for almost eight hours. Every time his voice flagged the committee members, who were all carrying bamboo *kendō* sticks [used for a form of martial art], would drum them on the floor to urge him on. It was then that I realized that it was the students who really controlled life at Ichi-kō, and I was amazed at their power.

There was another thing which happened a few days later. At our first class meeting we had a brief talk from one of the professors, and then he went out of the classroom and a second-year student came in. He stood at the front of the class and surveyed us for a moment.

'You're a funny lot', he said finally, 'You're really a different generation from us, aren't you? I was watching you all, while the vice-chancellor gave his speech at your entrance ceremony. Each time he mentioned the words 'His Imperial Majesty', every one of you stood to attention. I could see all your shoulders going straight and hear a sort of shuffling sound as you put your feet together. Here *nobody* stands to attention for anyone, emperor or no emperor!'

At Ichi-kō, Momo chose to specialize in law with English as a first language. His main interest in that first year at the college, however, was in philosophy, for he soon discovered that a basic knowledge of philosophy was essential if you wished to join in the intense, impassioned intellectual arguments of the other students. So, just as the focus of his interest had once moved from adventure stories and rat-catching to theatre and popular music, now it moved again to Descartes, Kant and Schopenhauer. The reputation of Ichi-kō students was so formidable that their opinion was courted and feared even by the most famous figures of Japanese cultural life.

There were several legends of Ichi-kō which were popular at that time, and which I heard soon after I started there. One concerned Yokomitsu Riichi, the novellist, who before the war was immensely respected, regarded almost as a 'cultural god' [*bunka no kamisama*]. I think it was about a year before I went to Ichi-kō that he'd been invited by the Students' Committee to give a talk there. Well, Yokomitsu at that time was obsessed by a kind of religious mysticism, and when he started to explain his ideas to the students, they just tore them to shreds. He couldn't answer the questions they put to him, and in the end he had to admit that his views were logically indefensible. As far as I know, his reputation never recovered from his encounter with the students.

Another Ichi-kō legend in my first year was about the Hitler Youth Movement. A contingent from the Hitler Youth Movement had paid a visit to Japan in 1938, and one of the places they went to was Ichi-kō. Although I didn't see it myself, from what people told me I can just envisage the scene: there were the beautiful young men of the Hitler Youth, in their smart uniforms, coming marching in perfect goose-step through the gates of Ichi-kō. And there were the Ichi-kō students, who were about the dirtiest, scruffiest-looking lot you could imagine (the way a lot of university students still are today). In my day the students all used to wear open-toed wooden sandals and grimy black capes. The purpose of the cape was that you could use it as a blanket, and lie down for a nap wherever and whenever you wanted. My memory of Ichi-kō is that there were always people lolling about on the classroom floor or in the corridors or on the grass outside. Well, that's what it must have been like when the Hitler Youth arrived – a whole lot of students lounging around in the grounds, either completely ignoring them or shouting insults in a kind of hybrid of Japanese and German. What they must have thought of it all I really can't imagine.

All the students of Ichi-kō lived in dormitories, but Momo, because his home was near by, made frequent visits to his family – visits which were occasioned partly by filial affection and partly by the poor quality of food in the college refectory. Eating arrangements, like all other aspects of college life, were run by the Students' Autonomous Committee. In the sparsely-furnished dining room stood two massive buckets, one containing rice and one containing bean-paste soup, from which the students would help themselves. As the war went on, the contents of the rice bucket changed from white polished rice to brown rice, which although richer in vitamins was usually so badly cooked as to be indigestible.

When the bucket was empty, one of the students would yell: 'Oy, boy! Rice!' and a cook would come grunting and running in with a full bucket. You see, in spite of the liberal attitude of the students, it was all quite medieval in some ways. Sometimes, when the food wasn't good enough, the students used to occupy the kitchens. But when that happened the cooks always managed to get their revenge on us. One of the things they used to do was to put dandruff in the rice – it was invisible, but you found out about it afterwards because it caused the most terrible diarrhoea.

Another time, a bit later in the war, we went into the dining

160

room and instead of rice we found pieces of paper on each table with great mountains of sugar piled on them. I suppose the sugar must have been requisitioned from the occupied areas of South-East Asia. But although it was all right in small quantities, we soon discovered that a main meal consisting of nothing but sugar is quite inedible.

Each time he went home to see his family, Momo had a chance to observe how the war was eating away at the vitality of city life. One week the *sake* shop down the road was shuttered and silent: supplies of alcohol had dried up. The next week the nearby geisha house had vanished, its occupants packed off to provide consolation to soldiers on the battle front. The Iida family business was changing too. No one now wanted to sunbathe in front of ultraviolent lamps, and besides, supplies of raw materials were virtually unobtainable unless you were engaged in some form of military production. Iida Toshifumi therefore converted his factory to make valves for X-ray equipment to be used by the armed forces.

One day in 1942, when Momo dropped into the company office to speak to his father, he was surprised to find, sitting behind the manager's big wooden desk at the far end of the room, a young and rather nervous-looking army officer: it had been decided by the authorities that a military supervisor should be appointed to all factories engaged in production for the armed forces. For weeks Momo's father went about with a bitter expression on his face, sighing and muttering behind the officer's back, while the young man himself, who understood nothing whatever about the running of the business, fussed fretfully round the office, getting in everybody's way. Eventually, the army itself must have recognized the ineffectiveness of the arrangement, for a little later the young officer vanished as suddenly as he had arrived. But not even the military supply contracts could keep the little factory going on its original scale. Workers were drafted into the army, and the bustle of the workshops diminished as the war went on. Iida Toshifumi, with unimpaired ingenuity, began to cast around for alternative ways to maintain the family's living standards, and soon hit upon the idea of selling off a portion of the raw materials allocated to him by the army to those businesses which were not fortunate enough to have contracts with the military. Within a few months, he had established an active and highly profitable side-business in the black market.

My father had absolutely no ideological feeling about the war whatsoever. His war was all about how to cheat war: how to get enough food for his family; how to keep his business going; how to prevent his son from being conscripted. Of course everyone was encouraged to believe that it was a glorious and noble thing to send your sons to the army. But my father, well, he'd spent much of his life as a virtual outlaw, and he had learnt not to pay any attention to what the authorities told him. His motto was live in a 'back street of the war'.

One thing he found particularly hard, though, was the lack of *sake*, because Father had been a heavy drinker for years. Soon after the war started it became very difficult to find *sake* in the shops. For a while you could still get it in restaurants, but there you were normally limited to one small flask per person, so as often as he could, Father used to take the whole family out to meals. That way we could get five flasks of *sake*, and he would drink them all himself. Later on, after we moved out of Tokyo, he started to experiment with methyl alcohol, which was one of the raw materials that the army supplied for his factory. Towards the end of the war I remember the whole of this room where we're sitting being filled with all kinds of peculiar contraptions which Father had dreamed up to turn the methyl alcohol into some kind of strong-smelling but drinkable spirit.

In this respect his father's views coincided with Momo's own, for Momo, like most students at Ichi-kō, had an attitude to the war which varied from the negative to the apathetic. There were, it was true, some exceptions. One boy, the son of a famous and passionate Japanese nationalist, followed Japan's military advance with enthusiasm. A handful of others, who formed a Nichiren Buddhist study group and held regular meetings in the college dormitory, would speak in high-flown terms of Japan's mission to liberate Asia, and frequently criticized their fellow-students for their cynical egotism. But for most, the war was only one thing: it was the fact that they, having reached the goal to which every schoolboy aspired and having become the bearers of Japan's richest intellectual tradition, were likely to be sent in their twenties to a battle-front where they would fight and suffer and die. And in that they could find no meaning.

Momo discussed these things most of all with a young man named Hidaka, who had quickly become his closest friend at college.

Hidaka had in fact entered Ichi-kō a year earlier than Momo, but, as often happened, had been kept down at the end of his first year. It was he who passed on to Momo the legends of the college, and became his guide and mentor in the traditions of student life. Although they read and talked avidly, Momo and Hidaka attended few classes. Most days they would wake around midday, and wander down to the refectory in time to snatch some glutinous remains of the communal lunch. After that they strolled around the city, or sometimes spent an afternoon in the cinema. At night they went to Dogenzaka, a small hill in the Shibuya district of Tokyo, whose streets, during that first year of the war, were lined with restaurants and little stalls selling black-market alcohol. They drank, less perhaps for pleasure than to satisfy an obscure feeling that this was a necessary part of their mental self-image, and they talked. They talked about life and death, about literature and art and reality and history and sex (although the latter, because of the restrictive circumstances of the time, remained until the final phase of the war no more than a topic of academic speculation).

Hidaka also taught me what to read. In particular, I remember, he introduced me to two books. One was called *Twelve Essays on Modern Ideology* – about Schopenhauer and Kierkegaard and so on – and when I had read that I felt that I knew all there was to know about philosophy. The other was called *Twelve Essays on Modern Drama*, and it covered the works of dramatists like Chekhov and Ibsen. Once I had read that book, I felt that I knew all there was to know about drama. In fact, I felt so full of knowledge and confidence that I immediately started to write a play of my own, which I gave to the editor of the Ichi-kō literary magazine. He was planning to publish it, but just at that time he was conscripted into the army, and my play went with him and was never seen again. That was a pity really. Afterwards, Hidaka used to say to me that it was the best play he had ever read.

As an Ichi-kō student Momo had access to all the great figures of the academic and intellectual world. It was not considered strange for him, a High-School student barely turned seventeen, to catch a train to the green and beautiful town of Kamakura, some miles south of Tokyo, to knock on the doors of men like Nishida Kitarō, the most famous twentieth-century Japanese philosopher, or the writer and critic Nakamura Mitsuo who, after the war, would become the

doyen of the Japanese literary establishment. Everywhere the reputation of Ichi-kō gave him access, and he could sit, sipping bitter
tea in the peaceful, leaf-shadowed salons of Kamakura, and listen
while masters and disciples discussed the burning questions of
contemporary life: politics and art and war. It was through these
encounters, rather than from formal lessons, that Momo received his
education and developed his ideas.

Classes at Ichi-kō in any case ceased abruptly halfway through
Momo's second year, and, like all students, he was drafted into the
labour force. Whenever possible, however, Momo would escape
labour service, pleading colds, fevers or imaginary aches and pains,
and slip away quietly to spend the day reading or talking with his
new-found eminent friends. But it was not possible to evade the
realities of war entirely. In summer Momo was packed off for several
weeks to a farm in Chiba, where he slept on the rough, dung-scented
floor and spent the days pulling sweet potatoes in the flat, black
fields. In winter there were long and tedious hours in a Tokyo
factory, cutting and sewing parachutes and army uniforms. It was at
that time that many of Momo's fellow-students were conscripted for
military service, and went to take their places in that great student
recruitment ceremony whose massed, dark-uniformed ranks also
included Saitō Mutsuo.

I was the youngest in my class – what they used to call an 'express
train' – you know, the sort of boy who shaves his face every
morning, not because there's anything there to shave but because
all his classmates do it. There were only a handful of others in my
class who were anywhere near me in age. You see, because of
Ichi-kō's reputation a lot of the students there had been trying to
get in for years, and people were happy to be accepted even if they
were way past the normal age for high school. In fact, I had quite a
shock when I first walked into the classroom and saw people
sitting there who looked almost old enough to be my father. I
remember that the oldest student in my class was thirty-five, and
the second oldest twenty-seven. So of course all those people were
caught by the draft of students in 1943.

It was a strange day, that day of the student recruitment
ceremony in October '43. It was raining – cold and grey with a
small rain falling. Hidaka and I were lying dozing in the Ichi-kō
literary club's common room, which was on the first floor of our

164

dormitory. We were all supposed to go to the ceremony – the students who were being conscripted were to march in the parade, and the rest of us to cheer them on – but most of us refused to go.

There was such a heavy, oppressive atmosphere over the dormitory that day. It was very quiet. Most people had shut themselves in their rooms. But every now and then you would hear raised voices, and the sound of doors opening and closing, and a moment later a student in uniform, carrying a rifle, would wander out into the drill yard, which was just below the window of the room where Hidaka and I were resting. Everyone was supposed to gather there before leaving for the Meiji Shrine grounds, where the ceremony was to take place. As the time for departure grew nearer, a little cluster of dark, uniformed figures began to form in the yard.

They were just about to leave when suddenly, from beneath us in the dormitory, came a great shout: 'Wait for me! I'm coming too!' Hidaka and I leaped to the window and looked out. Out from the door below us a student came running. It was a young man who was the most brilliant figure in our literary club and the person most vehemently opposed to war. But now he came rushing out from the dormitory calling: 'Wait for me! I'm coming too!' And somehow it made a shiver go down my spine.

I never heard what became of that student afterwards. But strangely enough, when I looked in a newspaper a year or two ago, I saw an article about someone of the same name who is now a prominent professor of medicine. Studying medicine, of course, was one of the ways you could avoid conscription, so I thought that perhaps, in spite of that last-minute cry, he had in the end been unable to face the thought of going to war after all.

At about this time a new element entered Momo's ideas: Marxism. Marxist thought had been introduced to Japan in the late nineteenth century, but until the First World War had made little impression on a political and intellectual world where the main radical impulses came from Christian socialism and anarchism. It was only after the Russian Revolution, and the disastrous Japanese military expedition to Siberia, that the ideas of Marx and Lenin began to have any significant impact in Japan.

Between 1919 and the mid-1920s a host of new Marxist study groups and journals were created, one of the most influential being the Shinjinkai (New People's Association), set up by students of Tokyo Imperial University in 1918. In 1922 the Japanese Communist Party was founded by a group of largely university-educated young men, some of whom (such as Tokuda Kyūichi and Arahata Kanson) were to have a long-lasting influence on Japanese political life. This period of the early 1920s saw, too, the expansion of trade unionism and the growth of social-democratic ideas as a force in Japanese politics.

All but the most moderate of socialists, however, were subject to the attentions of the police, who under the laws of the time possessed wide powers to suppress 'dangerous thoughts', particularly those which incited the people to bring about a 'revolutionary change of the National Polity (*Kokutai*) or abolish the system of private property'.

When the first election under the new system of manhood suffrage was held in 1928, four left-wing parties, one of them closely linked to the Japanese Communist Party, put up candidates. Between them, they won eight seats: a result which was sufficient to alarm the authorities into redoubling their efforts at suppression. Within a month of the election, over one thousand left-wing sympathizers had been arrested under the Peace Preservation Laws.

From then until the mid-1930s, when its active life was finally extinguished, the Japanese communist movement struggled to maintain a precarious existence, again and again re-creating its political structure as one leader after another was arrested. Membership of the Party, which had never exceeded 1000, dwindled to a mere handful. As a result its leading members tended to be young and often immature, and the faction-fighting which had plagued Japanese communism from its inception intensified. Morale was further weakened as several prominent Marxists recanted their views – some under police torture, others apparently out of sheer disillusionment with the cause.

By the time Momo entered Ichi-kō, political activity in Japan had congealed into the great unwieldy structure of the Imperial Rule Assistance Association. But Marxism, although it no longer existed as a political force, still exerted a certain covert influence on intellectual life. Marx's social and historical analysis had had a particularly powerful appeal to the Japanese intelligentsia of early Shōwa, in part no doubt because its theoretical structure provided a clear and coherent contrast to the romantic, emperor-centred nationalism propagated by the authorities. Perhaps, too, radical-minded Japanese recognized in their own society those very conditions of exploitation and poverty which had so impressed Karl Marx in the Britain of the mid-nineteenth century.

Momo first encountered Marxism not at Ichi-kō, but at the home of his former class teacher from Middle School. Mr Takada was in his twenties and had himself recently graduated from Tokyo Imperial University. He had been one of Momo's favourite teachers at Ichi-chū but, inhibited by a convention that pupils should not visit their form teachers at home lest this should be seen as a sign of favouritism, Momo had never been to Mr Takada's house until after he left Middle School. In 1942 and 1943, however, he paid regular visits to Mr Takada, to discuss his progress at college, to recount his experiences, his new friendships, his explorations of philosophy and literature, and to borrow books from the tier upon tier of bookshelves which lined the walls of Mr Takada's living room. Among these volumes Momo discovered, in neat, uniform paperback editions, the collected works of K. Marx, F. Engels and V.I. Lenin.

Looking back on it, it surprises and somehow impresses me that Mr Takada lent me those books so readily. After all, he must have known the consequences of what he was doing. I was young and rather foolish – I had the courage of ignorance, and used quite cheerfully to read the books on the train or the bus where everyone could see me, without even trying to hide the covers. But as Mr Takada must have known, if I had ever been caught by the police they would certainly have traced the books back to him, and in those days that was a very serious matter indeed. It was pure luck that nothing like that in fact happened.

It must have been late in 1943. I was on my way to the place where I was doing my labour service, travelling on the Sōbu Line train, and I was reading Lenin's *Imperialism*. I can still see in my mind the carriage where I was sitting, and the book open on my knee. As I read, quite suddenly, it seemed as though a great dark mist which had surrounded me vanished and in an instant everything became crystal clear. Until then I had known that it was my destiny to be sent to the war and killed but I hadn't understood why: I hadn't been able to fit it in to the universal pattern of things. But now suddenly I understood. This book explained to me that what was going on was an emperor-controlled imperialist war. And I was part of it. Not only that, but other things became clear as well. All the bits and pieces of history which I had learnt but never connected with one another fell into place, like the pieces of a jigsaw puzzle. I understand why they had executed Kōtoku Shūsui [a noted Japanese Anarcho-Socialist writer, executed in 1911 for alleged complicity in a plot to assassinate the emperor], why Korea had been made a colony, why the Manchurian Incident had taken place. Now, of course, those kinds of ideas are familiar to everybody but, because I had never encountered such an explanation before, it hit me like that, like a flash of light.

I became overnight, as it were, a single-cell Leninist. I saw the war then in very straightforward terms as a struggle between imperialist Japan and its opponents. But what mattered was that I knew now that Japan had to lose – both that it was a good thing that Japan should lose, and also that it was inevitable. Knowing that meant crossing an invisible but terribly powerful line. I had taken a step which was decisive for the rest of my life.

From then on avoiding labour service was not just a haphazard exercise to be pursued as the mood took him, but became a conscientious and purposeful plan. He began to feign the symptoms of tuberculosis and, being in any case pale-complexioned and slightly-built, was so successful in persuading the authorities of his frail health that they eventually allowed him to remain with a small group of other students in the dormitory, performing ballistic computations for the navy.

Soon after this, Momo officially graduated from Ichi-kō to become a fully-fledged student of the Law Faculty of Tokyo Imperial University, though the elevation of status in fact brought with it few practical changes, since academic life at both High School and University had already ceased to exist. In his free time Momo continued to mix with the same group of student friends, and, with that 'courage of ignorance' with which he had read Lenin, unconcealed, on the suburban commuter train, he could not now resist the urge to discuss with them his newly-discovered and dangerous vision of the truth. Amongst his friends there were, he soon found, five or six who, far from being hostile to his ideas, had arrived at a similar understanding of events themselves.

All of them were now transfixed by the steady approach of the moment when they would reach recruitment age. From morning to night they discussed what they would do when that time came, what were their chances of survival. They clearly perceived that they were engaged in a battle with time: if the war ended before they reached that fateful twentieth birthday, their lives would be spared; if not they would die. Hidaka was the optimist among them.

'Be rational,' he would say, 'consider what an immense disparity there is in strength between Japan and the countries she is fighting. Japan is in a hopeless situation, and there must be people in high places who realize the fact. Who knows, we may wake up tomorrow and find it's all over.'

But Momo was more cautious: 'You may be right about the disparities in strength, but you've got to remember that Japan has a huge military machine, and that machine is still in some sort of working order. This is not something the military will give up easily. For them, after all, everything is at stake. They're not going to spare one drop of our blood if it will help to stave off a defeat.'

For a while, as the months of 1944 passed by, it seemed that Hidaka's hopes might be justified. Observing events from the viewpoint of the Ichi-kō and Teidai students, the signs of the end were already apparent. Japan's ally Italy had surrendered; there were reports of advances in South-West China, but news from the Burmese front suggested that Japan was trapped in a hopeless conflict there. In Tokyo, ever-growing groups of silent figures came to bow their heads before the Yasukuni Shrine, to which the spirits of dead soldiers were said to return, in memory of husbands, brothers, sons or friends. Then in June came the news that American forces had overrun the Marianas and captured the island of Saipan. For the first time in the war, Tokyo lay within the range of land-based American bombers.

In the garden of the house in Shinmeichō, Momo's father began to construct an air-raid shelter – but reluctantly, and with little hope that it would be of any use. By now he was increasingly enmeshed in a small but vicious struggle with the petty bureaucracy of war, the host of little dictators of the *tonarigumi* and Civil Defence (*Keibō-dan*), into whose hands circumstances had thrust powers almost of life and death. It irked him to have to smile and cringe before the pompous and officious head of the local *tonarigumi*, yet he knew that if he did not, he would find the best part of his family's rations withheld on one pretext or another. He quietly but firmly ignored the Civil Defence regulation that an air-raid warden should be posted in his factory every night, but each time the nocturnal Civil Defence patrols found the building empty they would wreak revenge by smashing open the padlocked gates, not because it was in any way necessary, but in order to demonstrate that they would tolerate no awkwardness or insubordination. But Iida Toshifumi had two qualities which stood him in good stead in the final year of the war: a sublime disregard for the opinion of others, and a deep-seated instinct for self-preservation.

In the autumn of 1944, he decided that the time had come to evacuate his family from Tokyo. The fact that the neighbours regarded his flight as cowardly and ignominious mattered to him not one bit. Besides, he happened at that time to hear of a house in the seaside town of Fujisawa, thirty miles south-west of Tokyo, which was for sale at a bargain price. The house, it emerged, had belonged to a wealthy businessman and politician who, realizing the direction in which events were heading, and fearing that Fujisawa might be a site for a possible enemy landing in Japan, had fled to a yet remoter area in the mountains of Shikoku. The war had made Toshifumi reticent and secretive, even towards his son, whom he knew to be politically incautious, so it was quite without warning that Momo discovered one day that his family and possessions had been moved out of the home where they had spent the past seven years, and installed in a large, rambling wooden building among the pine-forested sand dunes of Fujisawa. A few weeks later the Americans launched their first fire-bombing raid on Tokyo, and in it the Iidas' Tokyo house, together with the entire surrounding area, was destroyed.

Between November 1944 and the following May, when the American military decided that Tokyo had ceased to be a significant target, there were seven major and many minor raids on the capital. In them 110,500 people were killed and more than half the buildings in the city were destroyed. In one raid, that of 10 March 1945, more people were killed in Tokyo than were to die in the atomic bombing of Nagasaki five months later. At the time of Pearl Harbor, the population of Tokyo had been almost seven million: by the last days of the war, bombing and evacuation had reduced it to two-and-a-half million.

I was always fascinated by the way that different people reacted to the bombing raids. Some people who were quite brave in other

ways would go pale and tense when they heard the sound of the
sirens, and would stumble off in a daze towards the nearest air-
raid shelter. I watched many raids, particularly over Mitaka,
where the Nakajima aircraft factory was situated. At night the
fire-bombing had a weird, fantastic beauty, like a curtain of light
falling through the air, accompanied always by this strange sound
– za-za-za – like the beating of a torrential downpour of rain. It
wasn't because I was brave that I watched the raids, but because I
was like my father – I didn't trust air-raid shelters.

One of my best friends at college was a student called Ishimoto.
He came from Kobe. His father was high up in a big trading
company (I forget which one), and they were very rich and had a
grand house up in the hills behind Kobe, where many of the
wealthy business people lived. In 1943 Ishimoto invited me there,
and I spent a few days with his family. At that time his father was
in detention in America, because he had been working for his
company there when war broke out. Later I heard that he'd been
sent back to Japan on the *Awamaru*,[1] you know, the ship which
got torpedoed, and of course he was drowned with all the rest.

Anyway their house in Kobe where I stayed had a huge garden,
and in it you could see this sort of lump, like a small hill. I asked
what it was, and was told that it was the air-raid shelter. They
were quite proud of this air-raid shelter, and Ishimoto's mother
showed me round it. You could reach it through a tunnel from
under the house. When I went in, I just couldn't believe my eyes.
The little space was lined with rows and rows of barrels and tins.
Mrs Ishimoto explained to me that they had enough food and
water in there to keep the whole household alive for a month.
Well, I was amazed, but also there was something I didn't quite
like about it. It's not logical I know, and in any case I was in no
position to criticize because I was busy trying to keep myself alive
while everyone else was going off to die in the war, but still I
found the thought of staying alive in your shelter while everything
around you was obliterated somehow a little repugnant.

But in the end, when Kobe was bombed in 1945, it didn't turn
out that way. My friend Ishimoto was in Tokyo at the time so he
survived, but all the rest of the family were in that shelter. Only
there was one thing which they hadn't been able to prepare for.
The shelter didn't collapse, and it didn't catch fire, but what no
one had realized was that the fire storms created by the bombing

would suck the oxygen out of the atmosphere. They all suffocated to death.

At the very beginning of the bombing of Tokyo, Momo's private race with the tide of war encountered a half-expected obstacle. On November 1 1944, the age-limit for military service was reduced from twenty to seventeen. Until that day Momo had not fully realized how much he had pinned his hopes on the small but real chance that the war might end before he reached recruitment age. Now there was no possibility that he would 'miss' the war, and he and his closest friends began to plan in detail the ways in which they would resist conscription. The first line of defence was the army medical check, which preceded formal recruitment. Starving yourself for several days before the medical could produce impressive effects of pallor and dizziness, and might result in your being awarded the desired classification of C or D – 'Unfit for military service'. But, as an additional precaution, it was recommended that you should drink large amounts of soy sauce in the period preceding the examination, as this was believed to induce heavy perspiration and an uneven pulse-rate.

For those who failed to fail the medical, there was a second course of resistance. It was reported that, before each new group of conscripts was formally admitted to military service, they would be lined up outside the barracks and those who believed themselves to be unfit for service would be given one last chance to step forwards. There was, of course, great moral pressure against such action. In addition, those who claimed to be unfit without good cause were liable to be court-martialled and shot. Momo and his friends, however, agreed that this was the point at which they must break ranks with the ethics of militarism. Whatever the cost, whatever the pressures, they would take that one step forward. To face execution, they argued, could be no worse than to face death in battle, and no one who joined the Imperial Japanese Forces in the autumn of 1944 could reasonably expect to survive. But they were so aware of the effort which might be required to take that one step under the gaze, perhaps, of thousands of disapproving eyes, that they prepared themselves by rehearsing, again and again, the scene which they envisaged at their recruitment, and each movement which they would have to make.

Beyond that, there lay one final act of defiance. In October 1944 the Naval Air Squadron had announced the creation of a Special Attack force – the *tokkōtai* – whose task was to perform suicide missions. The suicide pilots were officially reported to be volunteers, but widespread rumours suggested that recruitment to the force was far from voluntary. Momo and his friends assured one another that, if in the end they could not escape recruitment, they would allow no threats and no persuasions to force them into the *tokkōtai*.

One day, towards the end of the war, I saw an American B-29 fly over. They came by quite often then, even in broad daylight. Every time they passed, I had to watch. They were so big and beautiful, like great shining flying fish, and the sound they made was always recognizable – a deep, distinctive drone. This time, as I watched, suddenly, near the B-29 there appeared another plane, which looked just like a tiny mosquito. I heard the splutter of its engine as it flew up, up, and then struck the B-29 and exploded into a shower of fragments. But, incredibly, the American plane simply went on flying. From what I could see, it did not even seem to have been seriously damaged.

Later, I described what I had seen to one of my friends, and from that we went on to talking about the *tokkō* pilots. It was something that, well, I felt in two minds about, and I suppose I still do now. In a sense I wanted to say: 'It's your own fault. You have no one but yourselves to blame'. After all, even if it wasn't really voluntary, there must have been some way of escaping, and if you really understood the context of what you were doing, then you had a responsibility to escape, to resist. But then in another way, looked at from a long-term point of view, they were also caught up in a historical situation which they could not control. In a sense they were also victims.

The New Year of 1945 was a sombre occasion. New Year specialities like herring's roe and chestnut sweets were long since unavailable, and even the cakes of pounded rice, which formed the basis of the season's feast, were strictly rationed. In the Iida household, the only drink to be had was Toshifumi's potent but unpleasant-tasting illicit brew. No one dared to contemplate what the coming year might bring.

In January Momo received a letter informing him that he was to report, in ten days' time, to the local government office of Shiba district (where the family register was lodged) for his pre-recruitment medical examination. In those ten days there were two things to be prepared. First, he had to go and purchase a *fundoshi* – the traditional Japanese loin-cloth. This was not something that Momo possessed, since young men of his generation normally wore Western-style pants. It was, however, required dress for the army medical. The remaining days were spent in a concentrated assault upon his body. He ate practically nothing, and forced himself to drink cup after cup of soy sauce, although the thick dark liquid, drunk neat, brought tears to his eyes and made his throat gag with nausea.

At the Shiba local government office, there were about two hundred other students waiting for their medicals. We all stripped down to our *fundoshi* and stood in line to be called in for the examination. There were several soldiers there, keeping us in order and calling out our names, and there must have been something about the way I behaved that offended them, because one of them – a sergeant, I think he was – suddenly came over and called me out of the line.

'You!' he said, 'You stand over here!' So I stood and waited, while the others went in and were examined and left. It was January, and I stood in nothing but my new *fundoshi* on the stone-cold floor of the hall for hours. Other officers passed by and glanced at me, but they didn't say anything. I suppose that for that sergeant, it was just a little chance to show his power, and he couldn't resist it. Always you get people like that in our society, don't you: those sub-leaders, the ones who hold the bottom line of power. It's inevitable really that people should behave like that if you suddenly put into their hands the right to be tiny feudal lords. If you look at those sub-leaders, you can always see the ugly side of the system in all its nakedness. The other students, who watched me as I stood there and shivered, didn't say anything either, but their eyes seemed to be saying: 'We're sorry for you, but if he hadn't picked on you, it would have been one of us. So it's all for the best really.'

At last, right at the end, I was called in for my check-up. The examining doctor was a civilian, and quite pleasant. When he looked at my papers he said: 'You're a law ststudent at Tokyo Imperial University; hm'; in quite an impressed tone of voice, and for a moment I had a surge of hope that he might help me, he

174

might write down something which would make them have to reject me. But then, when all the checks were over, I was sent into the room where the chief military medical examiner sat behind his high desk. He had my file open in front of him, and he thumbed through it for a few moments, and then gave a cursory glance in my direction.

'Passed 2-B!', he shouted.

2-B was the lowest grade of those eligible for service in wartime. Momo returned home, numb with disappointment, to await the arrival of the dreaded Red Paper, the distinctively-coloured formal notice of conscription to the armed forces.

At the same time, one of Momo's fellow-first-year students at Tokyo University was also waiting for the post to bring him his Red Paper. His name was Hiraoka Kimitake, and at that time, since university classes were suspended, he and Momo had never met, although they were later to have a number of friends in common, and to travel paths into the worlds of literature and politics which, though divergent, were in some ways curiously intertwined. Precisely what happened at Hiraoka's conscription is unclear. One version of events is that he was mistakenly identified by an army doctor as suffering from tuberculosis, and was bitterly disappointed at being denied the opportunity to serve his country. But in the semi-autobiographical novel which he wrote under the pen-name Mishima Yukio – the name with which he was to earn international literary fame and political notoriety – Hiraoka himself presented a rather different picture. His reflections on his conscription are worth recording both because they present a view of the war which was rather different from Iida Momo's and because they have some bearing on later events in Japanese history:

Why had I looked so frank as I lied to the army doctor? Why had I said that I'd been having a slight fever for over a year, that my shoulder was painfully stiff, that I spit blood, that even last night I had been soaked by a night sweat? (This happened to be the truth, but small wonder considering the number of aspirin I had taken.) Why, when sentenced to return home the same day, had I felt the pleasure of a smile come pushing so persistently to my lips? Why had I run so when I was through the barrack gate?

I realized vividly that my future life would never attain the heights of glory sufficient to justify my having escaped death in the army, and hence I could not understand the source of the power which had made me run so rapidly away from the gate of the regiment. And that completely automatic reaction which always made me dash so breathlessly for an air-raid shelter – what was this but a desire to live?[2]

Momo received his Red Paper a month later than Hiraoka, in March 1945. It instructed him to present himself in one week's time to the Supply Division at Kashiwa (the military base where, the year before, Saitō Mutsuo had spent his brief sojourn in 'Buddha's 4th Regiment'). He had one week: it seemed like the last week of his life.

On the first day of that week, Momo went to the home of a literary friend in Kamakura. This friend had in his possession a copy of some unpublished writings by the famous nihilist and poet Nakahara Chūya, who had died a few years earlier, and these Momo borrowed, took back to the family home in Fujisawa, and began, painstakingly, to copy out by hand. At that time, not only his own future but the future of all things seemed to be uncertain. More and more destructive bombing raids were expected, and it was likely that irreplaceable fragments of culture, irrecoverable ideas and thoughts and dreams would disappear in the final conflagration. At least, if he did not do anything else with his nineteen-and-a-bit years of life, Momo felt that he might help to save one piece of Japan's literary tradition for future generations. As he deciphered the scrawl of faded, handwritten characters on sheet after sheet of yellowing paper, Momo had time to consider his situation. Kashiwa, where he was to be conscripted, was, he knew, close to a long, level stretch of coast. There were reports that the beaches in that area were being fortified and that trenches and gun emplacements were being dug. The Kashiwa Supply Division was, he guessed, intended to service the front line of the last battle: the battle for the mainland of Japan. Momo finished copying his manuscripts on the evening before he was due to be conscripted.

The neighbours had heard that I was leaving for the army, and first thing that morning a little group of women from the local *tonarigumi* turned up at the door, waving rising sun flags and shouting 'Banzai, banzai'. I looked at them and thought: 'Here am I going off, as it were, like a lamb to the slaughter and all you can do is shout "banzai" about it. Well, it may be "banzai" for you, but I certainly don't feel I've got anything to cheer about.'

My father came with me to Kashiwa. The headquarters of the Supply Division, when we found it, turned out to be located in an abandoned primary school. My father waited with a group of other parents who had gathered nearby as I went and joined the rest of the recruits. It happened exactly the way I'd expected. Just outside the gates, they made us all line up. There were, I should think, about two thousand of us, standing in straight ranks outside the headquarters. Then the commander of the Division came out through the gates and addressed us.

'Once you pass through these gates,' he said, 'you must understand that you will be members of the Imperial Armed Forces and subject to military law alone. Because you have all passed a medical examination, you will receive no further check here. If, however, you have special reason to believe that you are physically unfit for service, when I give the command you will step forward. I do not imagine', he went on, particularly slowly and emphatically, 'I do not imagine that any of you here present would wish to do such a thing, but if any of you should claim to be unfit for service without good cause, I must warn you that you will be sent to a military court for trial. Those who wish to have a second medical examination, step forward now.'

I looked straight in front of me, and took that one large step which I had rehearsed so many times. The students who had stepped forward were made to come and stand at the front, and the rest marched into the army headquarters. I found that there were five of us left – me and four others. We were taken in to a little building which was the Division's medical centre.

As I stood and waited for the doctor to come and examine me I could see, outside the window of the medical room, the other students who had been recruited. They were each issued with their military uniform and equipment, and sent off to change. A little later, you could see officers taking neatly tied bundles of civilian clothes and possessions to the gate, to return them to the waiting parents. Then I saw some of the new recruits walking past the window in their army outfits, and I really understood at that moment that the end of the war was near: they were carrying, not rifles, but the sort of wooden model guns that used to be used in Middle Schools for drill. Instead of water flasks and canteens they had been issued with the hollow pieces of bamboo. Even their boots were not the sort of leather boots that you always imagine soldiers wearing; they were made out of canvas.

I had staked everything on a guess: my guess was that the headquarters wouldn't have any X-ray equipment. You see, I knew a certain amount about that, because after all my father's business was to supply the things, and we had reckoned that a little place like the Kashiwa HQ probably wouldn't have one. And when the doctor came in and started to tap my chest, I knew the gamble had paid off. After that, it was just a kind of war of nerves between me and the doctor. I mustn't show any doubt or hesitation. As he tapped me, he asked questions, and I described to him every symptom of TB that I could think of: my temperature went up in the evenings; I had diarrhoea all the time; I coughed phlegm and sometimes it had flecks of blood in it; and so on.

My father told me afterwards that he knew that something was going on, because one by one the bundles of clothes were brought to the gate, and names called out, and the parents went off bearing their son's bundle, and little by little the crowd around him melted away until there were only himself and a few others left. In the end, three of us were released. As for the other two, they were just shouted at and sent to join the other conscripts. As we had guessed, the bit about the military court was only bluff. At that time they really couldn't afford to shoot reluctant recruits.

As I walked out through those gates my first thought was 'I've done it!' and I felt: 'Perhaps I am going to survive this war after all!' But I knew I couldn't smile, because all the people outside were watching, so I tried to look as miserable and downcast as I could. I could tell that my father was doing the same thing, but as we set off down the road towards the station, we just couldn't stop our faces relaxing into smiles. I remember that it was a very long straight road, between flat rice fields, and every now and then from far off we would see a military figure coming towards us, and each time that happened we would instantly look solemn again, just like a couple of children playing truant from school.

It was dark when we got home, and for several days I stayed in the house and didn't dare show my face outside. But in the end I went round to all the neighbours and told them that I was ill and had been sent home and now heartbroken I was not to be able to fight for my country, etc. The ironical thing about it was that of course not so long after I really did get TB, and my mother also later caught the disease and died from it. So all the neighbours round here still believe the story that that was why I never served in the army.

From then until the end of summer Momo found that he had all the free time he had ever wished for. There were no classes at university, and, since he was supposed to be ill, no labour service to perform. Long, idle days stretched ahead, and yet, now that his time was suddenly his own, he had little to do with it but contemplate the probability of approaching death. For, once the euphoria of escaping conscription had passed off, he found himself confronted with another nightmare: the end of the war. In Okinawa, a ferocious struggle was at that time taking place between the advancing American forces and the defending Japanese army, while the civilian population, trapped between the two, was steadily decimated. By the time the island was surrendered in June, 100,000 Okinawan civilians had died.

Towards the end of July the press carried reports on the Joint Declaration which had been issued by the American, British and Republican Chinese governments, meeting at Potsdam. The Declaration was brief and to the point. Its principal clauses stated that Japanese sovereignty was to be restricted to the four islands of Honshu, Hokkaido, Kyushu and Shikoku and others 'to be decided by the Allied powers'; that the imperial forces were to be totally disarmed and demobilized; and that the Japanese government was to surrender unconditionally. Otherwise, the Declaration concluded, the Japanese empire would face 'prompt and utter destruction'.

Momo, like many other people, expected the Okinawan pattern to be repeated throughout Japan itself. He foresaw his family's house being caught in a no-man's-land within two lines of fire, and himself dying a meaningless dog-death in a war which he did not wish his country to win.

It was rather stupid really, but in those months I had this sudden urge to dress up in a smart three-piece suit every time I went out. You see, at that time, everyone else was wearing uniforms. Even civilians all wore *kokuminfuku* ['Citizen's Dress' – a shapeless approximation of military uniform]. Wherever I went there seemed to be a great sea of khaki all around me, and, dressed up in my smart blue suit, I liked to be the only dot of a different colour in that sea. It was, well, a sort of way of asserting myself, of showing that I was still alive. I can't think why the Military Police never stopped me, because I stuck out like a sore thumb. But perhaps that was exactly why: perhaps, as I was the only one going round in a suit, they must have assumed I was someone important.

Momo now lived in a strange, distant proximity to the military: a company of soldiers had been billeted in his district of Fujisawa, and the company commander and two of his men had installed themselves in a wing of the Iidas' large old-fashioned house. From opposite sides of the big garden of pine and sand, officers and draft-resister observed each other with remote curiosity.

Little by little, news of the fates of Momo's college friends filtered through.

I heard that one of our group, a student called Ōta, had also taken that 'one step forward', but at the medical check he had failed to persuade the doctor that he was really ill, so he was recruited into a supply division in Tokyo. But Ōta didn't give up that easily. He went on insisting that he had all kinds of peculiar symptoms, until at last they sent him to an army hospital. He spent some time there, but the doctors couldn't decide what was wrong with him, and eventually even he started to get bored with lying in bed, so, as he could speak very good English, they put him to work interrogating American pilots who had been shot down during the bombing raids. I kept in touch with him then and after the war. He's done very well for himself now – he's on the board of one of the big banks.

Hidaka had been recruited before me. He didn't manage to avoid conscription either, and was sent to train on anti-aircraft guns by the Sumida River [in central Tokyo]. Almost at the end of the war his division was dispatched to China, but on the very day they left he collapsed with an attack of TB – a genuine attack, that was – and was left behind. He spent the end of the war in hospital, which was fortunate for him, because I heard that only half of the men in his division who were posted to China ever returned.

I visited Hidaka quite often after he was recruited. But always there was a slightly strange feeling of him being on the 'inside' and me 'outside'. I used to want to talk about the same old things that we had always talked about before – girls and so on. But Hidaka

was no longer interested in that kind of thing. He said that I could
not possibly imagine the misery of being a soldier.

To fill the dying days of the war Momo resumed the study of
Russian, which he had started to learn while at Ichi-kō. He found
himself a private tutor and spent many summer hours working
laboriously through Pushkin's *Queen of Spades* in the original, and
distantly dreaming of escape to an imaginary Russia, a mirage
country which arose in his mind from the pages of Dostoevsky and
Lenin. He also took up Latin, and with his friend, the writer
Nakamura Mitsuo, went to classes at the house of a Latin teacher in
a nearby small town. And he read – incessantly pursuing insights
into the historical predicament into which he and his friends had
been drawn.

There were two books which I discovered at that time. One was
Herodotus's *History*. Mind you, it seems extraordinary really that
in the middle of a war in which everything was scarce, including
paper, publishers should have been allowed to produce things like
two-volume translations of Herodotus, but for some reason or
another, they were. The other book that I read then was Caesar's
Gallic Wars.

From Lenin I had acquired a theory of modern war, but from
Caesar and Herodotus I learnt something new. Of course it was
possible to see that many things had changed since those books
were written and that history had in many ways outgrown the
concepts of those times. But there, in the middle of the most
technologically advanced war the world had ever known, I could
still learn from these books how human beings can find a
justification for any war and a political rationale for any act.
Reading Herodotus, in particular, somehow gave me a great
overall vision of history. It was almost like viewing the world from
another planet.

A long life [wrote Herodotus, putting his words into the mouth to
Solon] gives one to witness much, and experience much oneself,
that one would not choose. Seventy years I regard as the limit of
the life of man. In these seventy years are contained, without
reckoning intercalary months, twenty-five thousand and two
hundred days. Add an intercalary month to every other year, that
the seasons may come round at the right time, and there will be in

the seventy years, thirty-five such months, making an addition of one thousand and fifty days. The whole number of days contained in the seventy years will thus be twenty-six thousand two hundred and fifty, whereof not one but will produce events unlike the rest. Hence man is wholly accident.[3]

On the afternoon of 6 August, Momo heard over the radio that the American air force had that morning dropped 'a new type of highly destructive bomb' on the city of Hiroshima in western Japan. More attacks of this new type of bomb might occur in other areas, and citizens were advised to wear white clothes as a protective measure during attacks.

In our house we understood right away that it was an atomic bomb, partly because there had been occasional reports about nuclear research in Japan – I have a feeling that some politician had even asked a question in the Diet on the subject – and partly because my father was in any case interested in that sort of thing. I remember him explaining to us earnestly that with nuclear power, a bomb the size of a matchbox could burn up the whole of the world. Of course, we realized that the bit about the white clothes was ridiculous. It was just a typical example of the military taking a scientific fact – that white things repelled radiation – and making nonsense of it. But during those last few days after August 6th I overcame my fear of air-raid shelters, and every time that I heard a report of an American reconnaissance plane being seen in the area I would dash for the nearest shelter as quickly as anyone else.

Two days later the Soviet Union declared war on Japan, and Momo understood that Japan's imperialist adventure was almost over.

In the last few days of the war I went round to visit some of my friends who had been conscripted, because I knew that in the army it was difficult for them to discover what was really going on. I remember particularly that, when Russia declared war, I went to see my friend Ōta at his base in Tokyo. Visits to the military camps were strictly regulated, but I managed to invent some sort of emergency as an excuse to arrange a special visit. When no one else was listening, I told Ōta quietly what had happened, and I said to him: 'The war can't possibly go on for more than another week, so keep going, and take care of yourself. If they order you to do anything stupid, don't do it. Whatever happens don't go and die now.'

And I also said, to encourage him: 'If we survive this war, when it's over, it's going to be our generation's turn, and we're going to do things differently, aren't we?'

8

15 August 1945

At noon on 15 August 1945 a message from the Emperor Hirohito, which had been recorded the previous day, was broadcast to the nation. It was the first time that the voice of an emperor had ever been heard on the radio. What he said was this:

To our good and loyal subjects: After pondering deeply the general trends of the world and the actual conditions obtaining to Our Empire today, We have decided to effect a settlement of the present situation by resorting to an extraordinary measure.

We have ordered Our Government to communicate to the Governments of the United States, Great Britain, China and the Soviet Union that Our Empire accepts the provisions of their Joint Declaration.

To strive for the common prosperity and happiness of all nations as well as the security and well-being of Our Subjects is the solemn obligation which has been handed down by Our Imperial Ancestors, and which we lay close to heart. Indeed, we declared war on America and Britain out of Our sincere desire to ensure Japan's self-preservation and the stabilization of East Asia, it being far from Our thought either to infringe upon the sovereignty of other nations or to embark upon territorial aggrandisement. But now the war has lasted for nearly four years. Despite the best that has been done by everyone – the gallant fighting of the military and naval forces, the diligence and assiduity of Our servants of the State and the devoted service of Our one hundred million people, the war situation has developed not necessarily to Japan's advantage, while the general trends of the world have all turned against her interest. Moreover, the enemy has begun to employ a new and most cruel bomb, the power of which to damage is indeed incalculable, taking the toll of many innocent lives. Should We continue to fight, it would not only result in an ultimate collapse and obliteration of the Japanese nation, but also it would lead to the total extinction of human civilisation. Such being the case, how are We to save the millions of Our subjects; or to atone Ourselves before the hallowed spirits of Our Imperial Ancestors? This is the reason why We have ordered the acceptance of the provisions of the Joint Declaration of the Powers.

We cannot but express the deepest sense of regret to our Allied nations of East Asia, who have consistently co-operated with the Empire towards the emancipation of East Asia. The thought of those officers and men as well as others who have fallen in the fields of battle, those who died at their posts of duty, or those who met with untimely death and all their bereaved families, pains Our heart day and night. The welfare of the wounded and the war sufferers, and of those who have lost their homes and livelihood, are the objects of Our profound solicitude. The hardships and sufferings to which Our nation is to be subjected hereafter will certainly be great. We are keenly aware of the inmost feelings of all ye, Our subjects. However, it is according to the dictate of time and fate that We have resolved to pave the way for a grand peace for all the generations to come by enduring the unendurable and suffering what is insufferable.

Having been able to safeguard and maintain the structure of the Imperial State, We are always with ye, Our good and loyal subjects, relying upon your sincerity and integrity. Beware most strictly of any outbursts of emotion which may engender needless complications, or any fraternal contention and strife which may create confusion, lead ye astray and cause ye to lose the confidence of the world. Let the entire nation continue as one family from generation to generation, ever firm in its faith of the imperishable-ness of its divine land, and mindful of its heavy responsibilities, and the long road before it. Unite your total strength to be devoted to the construction for the future. Cultivate the ways of rectitude; foster nobility of spirit; and work with resolution so as ye may enhance the innate glory of the Imperial State and keep pace with the progress of the world.

14th day of the 8th month of the 20th year of Shōwa.[1]

Saitō Mutsuo

For some reason, on the morning of 15th August our training had taken us outside Kumagaya Air Base. But we had been warned that at midday there would be a very important broadcast which we all had to listen to, so we had gone prepared with our full dress uniforms.

At noon we assembled in the nearest convenient place, which happened to be the village hall of the little village, called Takekawa, where we had been training. We stood to attention in front of the radio, all in our formal uniforms, with swords in our belts. Unfortunately, the radio in the village hall was very bad, and it was hard to hear what the emperor was saying.

Afterwards, we began to argue about what it meant. One person said: 'It's because of the Russian declaration of war. His Majesty is just making a special appeal to us to fight harder.' Then someone said: 'But what was that bit about "peace for all the generations to come?" Doesn't it mean they're accepting the Potsdam Declaration?' 'In that case', said a third person, 'it's surrender.'

In the end, we decided to send someone back to the base to find out what it meant. The hall, like most village halls, had a big matted room on the first floor, which they used for parties and the like, so while we were waiting for him to come back we all went up there and sat on the *tatami* [straw matting]. Then he returned, and told us that the government had accepted the Potsdam Declaration, and that we were all to behave calmly and sensibly. At the base, you see, they had a proper radio, so they'd understood what the emperor said.

It was very hot. We all sat collapsed on the *tatami* in our formal uniforms. None of us said anything. I kept thinking: 'What have we been doing for the last year and a half? Every day we've been facing death. So many people have died. What was it all for?'

I felt full of regret and bitterness, but at the same time I also thought: 'Perhaps I am going to survive. Perhaps this thing they call peace is going to come . . .'

The next day, several things happened almost at once. First, an officer arrived by plane from Atsugi Naval Air Base nearby and gave us a speech. He said: 'The broadcast which you heard yesterday was a fake. It was made by evil, defeatist elements among the emperor's advisers. His Majesty's true wish is that we should fight on to the very last soldier.' When we heard that, most of us felt that it must be true. After all, it fitted in with everything that we had been taught for the last four years. Other aeroplanes also came over from Atsugi and Honjō, and dropped leaflets saying the same thing.

But then, soon after, a man from the Imperial Headquarters arrived and gave us another speech, saying that the broadcast was true. The emperor, he said, was concerned with the fate of future generations, and we were to remain calm and ignore agitators. We were still none the wiser when we went to bed that night, but the next morning when we woke up we realized that, at least as far as we were concerned, the war was over, because during the night someone had removed the propellers from every aeroplane in the base. Whatever the rights and wrongs of the matter, there was nothing in the world that we could do with planes which had no propellers. Later that day, one of the lads in the squad – he'd been a volunteer who'd gone straight from school to military cadets' college – he took a machine-gun and pointed the barrel into his mouth, and he put his foot against the trigger and fired.

That evening I was sent into the town of Kiryu to take a message to someone. When I arrived at Kiryu, I suddenly understood for the first time that peace had come. For the blackout had ended. Every window was lit up, and along every street stretched great lines of light. I just stood and stared, as if I was seeing it for the first time in my life. I had never realized that electric lights could be so beautiful.

Tsutsumi Ayako

That morning we were told that His Imperial Majesty would make a broadcast at noon. We all went back to our dormitory and sat on the *tatami* matting to listen to the broadcast. He spoke in very formal court language, and I couldn't understand what he was saying. Some of the girls started to cry, but I'm not sure whether they were crying because they understood the broadcast, or just because they knew it was something very serious and solemn.

After that, when we went back to work they explained what the broadcast meant and we were told to make arrangements to go home as soon as possible. First, though, there were lots of things to sort out in the office, so I stayed on there for about another week. One thing I noticed was that, right away that very afternoon, the workers in the factory stopped using their Japanese names and began to use Korean names instead.

I think it was the next day, or perhaps two days later, that I saw two girls from the factory when I was on my way to work. I had only ever seen them in their factory uniforms before, but now they were riding on a see-saw. It was a bright, windy day, and as they went up and down the multicoloured skirts of their national dress fluttered against the sky. They looked so happy. That was the first time that it had occurred to me that this terrible thing might actually be a cause of joy for some people.

On the night of 15th August I had a dream which kept recurring afterwards. Somewhere I had read that, when the Emperor Go-Daigo went into exile, one of his *samurai* retainers wrote to him saying: 'Whatever may happen, here I am, loyal to you'. In my dream I was kneeling on the ground in front of the *Nijūbashi* outside the Imperial Palace – I had never seen the Imperial Palace at that time, but I knew what it was like from photographs. I was kneeling there, bowing my forehead to the ground to apologize for failing in my service to His Imperial Majesty, and over and over again I was saying: 'Whatever may happen, here I am, loyal to you'.

Iida Momo

In my memory of August 15th 1945, I have two clear images of events which took place in different parts of the day, but, strangely enough, I have no memory at all of anything in between those two moments.

The first image is like this. At that time, in the last months of the war, three of us – myself and two friends whom I'd known since Middle School – used to visit a lady who was the mistress of the head of Nihon University [a large private university in Tokyo]. She was a good fifteen years older than us, and she used to teach classical Japanese music. We were round at her house that day, having one of our little amorous adventures. It was very hot, and afterwards we were all sitting together inside a big mosquito net, listening to the radio, when we heard the mutter mutter of the emperor giving his speech. We understood at once that this was the thing we'd been waiting for: the end of the war.

Several years later I met that lady again, and she reminded me of something which I'd completely forgotten. She said to me: 'Don't you remember, right after the broadcast we all started to say: "What's going to happen now?" And straight away you said: "There will be a massive inflation. All paper money is going to be worthless, so what you must do is cling on to any gold or jewels you have for dear life, and if you have any money, buy things with it quickly before it turns into trash." No one else had even thought of such a thing at that time, but there were you, scarcely dry behind the ears, and you'd got it all worked out.'

Apparently from that time onwards she'd been under the illusion that I was some kind of prophet. It was just a pity that my political beliefs prevented me from putting my own advice into practice!

Anyhow, later in the day I must have come back here, to Fujisawa, because in my memory I am here in the house, and the garden is full of soldiers. The company commander who was billeted in our house had summoned all his company together. It was a sign of the times, I suppose, that although this was said to have been the most modern technological war, the company at Fujisawa had only one means of communication with the rest of the army: a horse. The broadcast had been very crackly, and they probably didn't have a good receiver either. Evidently, none of the soldiers had understood what the emperor's broadcast meant, and when I got home one of them had been sent off on the horse to the Divisional Headquarters at Ōfuna, to find out what was happening.

A little later he returned, and the company commander made all the soldiers line up among the pine trees, and gave them a speech explaining that they had lost the war. I watched them from the house. I can remember that very distinctly. They stood in lines, listening, and their faces were quite blank and without emotion. It was so hot. They stood there sweating in the heat, and from all around came the cascading sound of the cicadas crying.

PART III

Choosing Directions – 1945 – 60

We have seen Hell, we have known Heaven, we have heard the Last Judgement, witnessed the fall of the gods and witnessed before our eyes the creation of heavens and earth.

(Ara Masato 1946 – Translated by J. Nathan[1])

9

Saitō Mutsuo

General Douglas MacArthur, Supreme Commander for the Allied Powers, landed at Atsugi Air Base on 30 August 1945. Three days later he supervised the formal acceptance of Japan's surrender on board the USS *Missouri* in the port of Yokohama, and from then until April 1951 his powerful, if eccentric, personality was to dominate the development of Japanese political life. Theoretically, the general directions of policy for Japan were formulated by a Far Eastern Commission, representing eleven Allied nations, and conveyed via MacArthur's Tokyo headquarters to a reconstituted Japanese government headed (in the first months of the occupation) by the emperor's cousin, Prince Higashi-kuni. In practice, Japanese people understood that their future would be determined by the stream of directives which issued from the Supreme Commander's office overlooking the Imperial Palace moat – an office which became universally and simply known as GHQ.

Within six months of the surrender, GHQ had ordered the Japanese government to produce plans for a new constitution based on popular sovereignty, universal suffrage and freedom of thought; a new landholding system which would remove the last traces of the old, feudal landowning class; the dissolution of the industrial combines (*zaibatsu*) and the promotion of free enterprise and competition; and a new labour law to allow the creation and development of independent trade unions. In short, the occupation had placed into the hands of GHQ's largely young and idealistic staff the power to perform a unique experiment: to construct a version of the American Dream in the unfamiliar and improbable setting of a bomb-blackened Japan.

Even before MacArthur had reached Japan, the colossal task of demolishing the ruins of Japan's imperial military structure had begun.

Disarmament and demilitarization [stated the American occupation authorities' first post-surrender directive, issued on 29 August] are the primary task of the military occupation and shall be carried out promptly and with determination. Every effort shall be made to bring home to the Japanese people the part played by the military and naval leaders, and those who collaborated with them, in bringing about the existing and future distress of the people.

Japan is not to have an army, navy, air force, secret police organization or any civil aviation.[1]

For Mutsuo and the other pilots at Honjō Army Air Base, this meant that day by day, one by one, they would be called in by the commanding officer and given their last military order: to return their army documents to the place where they had first registered for service, and then to go home. They were each provided with a military pension of two thousand yen, some packed food, chocolate and a large sack of flour. By sending them away separately and in different directions, it was thought that organized resistance to the surrender might be avoided. By sending them with money and food, it was hoped that a throng of impoverished ex-servicemen, adding a further element of instability to a hungry and uprooted society, would be avoided. But the process of demobilization took several days to complete, and meanwhile the pilots hung around the base without work or purpose or discipline.

One day, while I was waiting for my papers, I went by train to visit my parents at the house where they were staying in Kiryu. There was a young cadet pilot sitting in the carriage, and when I got on, he came up to me and saluted.

'Sir,' he said, 'may I ask you, what is your opinion about the surrender broadcast?'

I looked at him, and I remembered the officer who had come over from Atsugi on the day after the surrender to try to persuade us to fight on. Somehow I felt that this young man seemed the type who might be another military fanatic, so I thought that I had better choose my words carefully. I said:

'I don't believe that the broadcast reflected the real wishes of His Majesty. I believe that we can continue the fight.'

The cadet smiled enthusiastically. 'Precisely, Sir', he said, 'That is exactly my own view', and for about the next twenty minutes he went on and on about how we were developing all kinds of new weapons and how we could still drive back the Americans. At last, to my great relief, we got to my station, and, as the train began to slow down I said; 'You must excuse me, I have to get off here.'

Suddenly, the cadet pulled out a pistol from his holster.

'Look,' he said, 'it's loaded. I was very glad to find that you were on the right side. If you had been a defeatist, I would have shot you, Sir.'

Well, I got off the train and slammed the door, and it was only then that a sort of wave of emotion came over me as I realized what a narrow escape I'd had. I looked down at my hands and noticed that the palms were covered with sweat. I couldn't stop thinking how absurd it would have been to have survived the whole war only to be shot by an idiot like that.

A couple of days before Mutsuo left Honjō Air Base, the remaining pilots held a farewell party in the village hall where they had listened to the emperor's broadcast. They raided the squadron's kitchens for food, took the last bottles of *sake* from the store. Someone found a couple of horse troughs, rinsed them out and filled them with *sake*, which they scooped up by the cupful, like water from a spring.

We all ate and drank, and talked about what we were going to do next. I remember my friend Konno saying that he was going to go to Hokkaido and buy a farm and keep cows. I know that not one of us said then that we would go back to college, although in the end we mostly did. There were several lads in our squadron who came from Hiroshima, and they were all particularly worried, because they'd heard the rumours, and didn't know what they were going to find when they went home.

Well, while we were talking, all at once there was a great yell from the other end of the room. We all looked around, and there we saw this pilot called Noda – he'd pulled his dress sword out of its sheath and slashed another pilot right across the backside. Luckily, one of the people there was a man called Okada, who was an expert at *kendō* – in fact he's the chief *kendō* instructor to the Tokyo police force now – and he managed to get hold of Noda and restrain him.

It turned out that the trouble had started like this. Noda, you see, was a *nissei* [second-generation emigrant to America]. His parents were still in Hawaii, and I think he had dual nationality. So of course poor Noda was terrified that, having fought in the Japanese army and been defeated, he would now be executed as a traitor by the Americans. Apparently he'd started to talk about this, and one of his friends had tried to cheer him up and advise him what to do, but the more he tried to help, the more upset poor Noda became, until at last he pulled out his sword, shouting: 'You'll never be able to understand how I feel.'

I met Noda again a few years ago at one of our reunions. Someone there reminded him of that incident, and asked him why he had reacted that way, but Noda said that he couldn't understand it himself now. He said that he must have been in a very abnormal state of mind at the time. I suppose in a way we all were.

'One hundred million people in a state of trauma' *(ichi-oku sō-kyodatsu)* was the phrase that the Japanese press coined to describe those days. The people had been taught to believe – and most had accepted – that a Japanese defeat was impossible. Now that the impossible had happened all the rules and relationships which governed normal life became fragile – everything was possible and nothing certain.

The numbing sense of disorientation was heightened by the economic chaos which reigned in the wake of Japan's defeat. For the next few years, the majority of Japanese people experienced conditions of poverty which are now hard to imagine. In 1945 government rice stocks, from which rations were distributed, amounted to less than one quarter of the official target, and only swift action by the American occupation authorities prevented widespread famine. Food shortages and poor housing conditions caused by the effects of bombing led to severe epidemics. In 1946 there were over 30,000 reported cases of typhoid. For the first few months after the surrender regular, legitimate employment was almost impossible to find, and throngs of demobilized servicemen and workers dismissed from munitions factories struggled to make some kind of living on the black market. A little later, much publicity was to be given to the case of a judge, Mr Yamaguchi, who, believing that it was immoral for someone in his position to buy goods on the black market, resolved to live entirely on his official rations. Within a matter of months, he died from malnutrition.

Towards the end of August 1945 Saitō Mutsuo received his army
papers from the commanding officer at Honjō, and took them back
to Yamagata, the place where both his family register and his
military service record were kept. He stopped for a day to bathe at a
nearby hot spring, and then he went home to the small, overcrowded
house where his parents were staying with relatives of his mother.

I went in, and greeted my family, and then . . . nothing. My mind
was totally empty. When I looked at the future, all I could see was
a big void. There was nothing left, no factories, no jobs. The only
thing that you could do at that time was deal in the black market. I
know that some *tokkōtai* survivors who had sharp enough wits
made fortunes in the black market with their two-thousand-yen
pensions. Some people from Honjō even had the foresight to take
things like petrol and aviation fuel with them when they left the
base, but I didn't have any heart for that sort of thing then.
    I remember that a few days after I got home, I first saw the
occupation forces. It was strange. We had been fighting them, and
they had defeated us, but I had never actually seen them. And
then, there they were, in the hot afternoon: an American jeep, full
of soldiers, driving down the dusty road. I thought about how
we'd been trained in the army to go everywhere on foot, and carry
all our equipment with us. And I looked at those soldiers sitting in
the big powerful jeep. And I thought: 'No wonder we lost the
war!'

Mutsuo's father Kōsuke suggested that, to pick up the threads of
his life, he should go back for a while to its source, to the rural
north-western region of Yamagata from which the Saitō family had
originated and with which they still retained certain faint emotional
ties. Mutsuo took his advice and spent some weeks of the autumn in
the spa villages of the region, enjoying the stillness and the mountain
air, and steadily spending his way through his two- thousand-yen
pension.
    On 1 January 1946, the Emperor Hirohito, on the request of the
occupation authorities, issued what is known as the 'Human Being
Declaration' (*Ningen Sengen*). In it, he disavowed any claim to divine
origin and stated:

The ties between us and our people have always stood upon
mutual trust and affection. They do not depend upon mere

legends and myths. They are not predicated on the false conception that the Emperor is divine and that the Japanese people are superior to other races and fated to rule the world.

There were those in the Allied nations, and even some in Japan itself, who wished to see the emperor deposed and tried as a war criminal. But ultimately the American authorities concluded that it was best to retain the emperor, while reducing his role to a purely symbolic one within a democratic constitution. The 'Human Being Declaration' was a crucial step in the creation of the emperor's new image. MacArthur and his advisers, translating the language of Shintō mythology into that of Western monotheism, may also have imagined that the demotion of god to human status would be a dramatic event in Japanese history, but for most people Hirohito's declaration was a statement of the obvious.

When I heard about the 'Human Being Declaration', I thought: 'What on earth is he talking about? No one ever imagined that he wasn't a human being.'

As far as the emperor's responsibility for the war was concerned – well, yes, in a way I do feel now that he was responsible. You see, the people who want to justify the emperor's action say that he only had the power to make recommendations, that it was the government who took the final decisions, so whatever he thought, he couldn't have prevented the outbreak of war. But then they always go on to argue that it was the emperor who insisted on a surrender in August 1945, and how wise and enlightened it was of him to have stopped the war when many military leaders wanted to fight on. But I think, if he had the power to stop the war in 1945, why didn't he have the power to prevent it in 1941? In the end, everything that was done was done in his name, so from a commonsense point of view you have to say that he was responsible. I know it's perhaps unfair to make comparisons, but I can't help thinking that if he had been a really enlightened emperor like the Emperor Meiji, the war might never have started. There must have been things he could have done to prevent it. Why didn't he do more to encourage negotiations with the Americans? Why didn't he go to America to talk to Roosevelt? There must have been things he could have done.

Do I feel resentment towards him? Well, I should do, shouldn't I? After all, the best years of my life were darkened by him and his institution. So I really should feel resentful towards him. But do you know, the funny thing is that if I were ever to meet the emperor face to face, I would bow down to him. I know I would. That's the power of education for you.

By the spring of 1946 the Saitōs were weary of living as guests in another family's house, and Mutsuo was sent out to find a lodging, a room – anything, however small, that they would be able to call their own. He went to Honjō because it was near and because he had come to know the town well during his time at the air base there. In the past eighteen months, more than half the buildings in Tokyo had been destroyed. It was not easy to find a place to live in the spring of 1946. Mutsuo decided to try the red-light district of Honjō, for the brothels here were of the old-fashioned Japanese variety and, unlike the new establishments which had sprung up like mushrooms around the American army camps, they were suffering depressed trade. Here, surely, there would be some empty rooms.

At one house, the madam directed him to a small annex at the back of the building. On the first floor of the annex there were two rooms, each measuring six mats, which she agreed to let the Saitōs occupy for a moderate rent. A *tatami* mat is the normal standard of measurement for Japanese rooms, each mat representing approximately the space that one person needs to sleep. Until summer Mutsuo lived in those two six-mat rooms with his parents and a young lodger, the son of one of his father's former employees, who had turned up on the doorstep asking for help. This was a time when needy friends or acquaintances were not turned away. You knew that next week you might be the one asking for food or shelter.

In the summer they were joined by Haruko, her husband Hachirō and three of her husband's nephews, who had arrived back from Taiwan homeless and penniless. For some days they tried all living together – five people in one room, four in the other – but even by the standards of 1946 this was too much to bear. Eventually they persuaded the brothel's owner to allow them to rent a couple more rooms in the main building itself.

Food was very scarce then. For a while my parents went off to Yamagata, because they knew that, being farther away from Tokyo, there would be fewer shortages there, and father thought that some of his relatives or friends might be able to sell him rice. When my parents found rice to buy, they wrote to me to come and collect it. Then I would go and buy a black-market railway ticket and go to Yamagata to fetch the rice. You had to buy black-market tickets, because for ordinary tickets you needed to queue for days. The black marketeers would get waifs and strays to sit in the queue for them, and then they would sell the tickets at some vastly inflated price.

When I wasn't fetching rice from Yamagata, I had nothing to do at all. I didn't even bother to get up in the morning. When we woke up, the lodger and I would take out a *shōgi* [Japanese chess] board which we had, and lie in our eiderdowns on the matted floor playing *shōgi* until it was time to go to sleep again.

White rice was so precious in those days that, when my parents came back, we decided that we wouldn't eat the rice right away. We would keep it for special occasions. The rest of the time we lived on sweet potatoes, which were relatively plentiful around Honjō even then.

The collapse of the economy was accompanied by catastrophic inflation. In the first two-and-a-half months of 1946 the cost of living index for Tokyo (in which 100 represented average prices for the years 1934 to 1936) is estimated to have risen from around 700 to over 15,000. In response drastic measures were taken, freezing bank deposits and enforcing the issue of new currency notes. By summer, all of Mutsuo's once substantial army pension had disappeared. The family had no money, and (since most of their possessions had been destroyed with the Sendagaya house) few goods to exchange for food. Mutsuo went out into Honjō to look for work.

After some days of patient searching and enquiring, he managed to find himself a job in the accounts department of what was then a little local pharmaceuticals business called Eizai Ltd (it is now a large multinational corporation manufacturing such best-selling products as Vitamin E pills and anti-cholesterol drugs). But Mutsuo's High-School education in economics had not included the basic skill needed by all Japanese office clerks: the use of the abacus. The girls of the Eizai accounts department watched with giggling incredulity as he tried to calculate bonuses and tax deductions, not with a few flicks of the little ivory beads, but painstakingly and laboriously with pencil and paper. After a couple of weeks he was transferred to the welfare department, where his job was the more congenial one of setting up the firm's first baseball team.

Of course this was the time of the great post-war baseball boom, and most companies were starting their own teams. I enjoyed organizing the baseball club, but I really had very little work to do. By this time I'd managed to get our lodger a job in the company as well, and I'd also made friends with a young man there called Naitō, who'd been in the naval *tokkōtai*. The three of us used to have a good time together. Being a drugs company, Eizai had large supplies of pure alcohol, and we developed the art of turning this into our own special brand of 'whisky'. Then we used to get some pigs' trotters from one of the local farmers, and boil them up with soy sauce to make a kind of cocktail snack, and we'd sit around, drinking our 'whisky' and licking the pigs' trotters and chatting. It was a nice life, but I realized after a while that I could not go on like this for ever – organizing baseball teams and making illicit alcohol. The more I thought about it, the more I realized that I would never get anywhere unless I finished my education, so in the end I applied to go back to Keio. Naitō stayed on there, and now he's the president of the company.

In April 1947 Mutsuo, now twenty-four years old, enrolled as an economics student at Keio University. Among the staff at Keio, he found a number of familiar faces from what now seemed the very distant past. Professor Koizumi had retired, after being seriously injured during the bombing of Tokyo (later he was to be appointed official tutor to Crown Prince Akihito). But others were still there: Professor Ikeda, the teacher who had made them work hard at their English in order to 'understand the mind of the enemy'; and Professor Hanabusa, who at the height of the war had always turned up for classes in an immaculate suit and tie, and who now, when suits were all the rage, stubbornly insisted on arriving for lectures in ragged and worn out wartime 'citizens' dress'. Although education was being reshaped into the US model of Junior High School, High School, and University the content of the teaching was not greatly changed Now, as in 1942 and 1943, teaching was sporadic and interrupted, for although drill and labour service were things of the past many of the students had to work part-time to keep themselves alive, and often the teachers themselves would disappear into the countryside for days at a time, in search of rice or vegetables.

None of my close friends from High School was in my class at Keio now. Many of the students were young men who had been at army or naval cadets' colleges, and, when these were closed down at the end of the war, had transferred to ordinary universities. They were rather a cliquish lot. They tended to band together with their old friends from cadets' school, and on the whole I avoided them. I did notice, though, that amongst the students whom I had known in the early forties, it was often the ones who had been the most nationalistic and the most enthusiastic about military drill who were now the first to latch on to the new radical political ideas. It was understandable really: they were the ones who swam with the current, it was just that the current had suddenly begun to flow the other way.

As far as I was concerned, I suppose I would have classified myself as a moderate. I wasn't ever a very political person. Just after I went back to Keio the new Constitution was adopted, and we discussed that quite a bit, particularly as one of our teachers, Professor Asai, had been on the committee which was supposed to have been responsible for drawing up the Constitution. But I got the impression that Professor Asai was not very happy with the outcome, and that a lot of things had been more or less forced on them by MacArthur.

What I felt about the Constitution was that it was a beautiful idealistic document, but in the end it was, as they say, 'rice cakes painted in a picture'. Particularly I felt that way about Article 9. It is a splendid idea to renounce war and keep no armed forces, but unless you are surrounded by other peace-loving countries, it simply doesn't work out that way in practice.

The post-war Constitution, which came into force on 3 May 1947, stated that sovereignty rested not with the emperor but with the Japanese people, and that the highest organ of state was to be the bicameral parliament, or Diet, elected by all citizens over twenty years of age. The emperor was retained merely as a symbol of 'the unity of the people'. The most continuingly controversial clause of the document, however, is Article 9, which states:

Aspiring sincerely to an international peace based on justice and order, the Japanese people forever renounce war as a sovereign right of the nation and the threat or use of force as a means of settling international disputes.

In order to accomplish the aim of the preceding paragraph, land, sea, and air forces as well as other war potentials, will never be maintained. The right of belligerency of the state will not be recognized.

There is still some doubt as to who was responsible for the authorship of this clause, although it is generally accepted that the main provisions of the Constitution were drawn up by MacArthur's political advisers. But perhaps it is also right to point out the success of what some have called 'the translated Constitution': for it was to retain broad support from the great majority of Japanese people for the next several decades, and to acquire a position of such great symbolic importance in political life that, although Article 9 is constantly violated in practice, any talk of revising it still arouses intense passions in the 1980s.

Until his graduation in 1950 Mutsuo, like many other students of that age, had not only to study but also to earn enough money to keep himself and his parents.

My first idea was to sell things on the black market. It was fairly easy to get food in Honjō, you see, so every morning I would come into Tokyo with a rucksack filled with sweet potatoes and spring onions, and try selling them on the street. I didn't have much success, though. I had assumed that the best place to sell vegetables would be right in the centre of town, in places like Ginza, but after I'd spent several days squatting by the streets with my wares earning hardly anything, I gave it up as a bad job. It was only later that I understood what a naive and inexperienced black marketeer I had been – because of course places like Ginza had been so badly bombed that there was practically nothing there at all, and all the people who lived and worked there had acres and acres of open wasteland, on which they were busy growing their own vegetables.

Well, after that I kept going through the employment columns in the newspapers, until one day I saw an advertisement for someone to work as a salesman for a firm making billiard equipment. I went along to the office, and I got the job right away. As it turned out, it was the best job I could possibly have found. At that time, you see, the real way to make money was to work for the occupation forces, and this little company had got an exclusive contract to maintain and repair the billiard tables in the recreation clubs of every US base in or around Tokyo. They charged a standard fee: so much for mending cues, so much for repairing baize, and so on. But the fees were usually based on the cost of repairing the maximum possible damage, whereas in fact more often than not there was only a tiny tear in the baize or a little chip off the end of the cue. All the payments came from a special government supply office which paid for the expenses of the occupation forces, and they never questioned the bills they were sent, so in the end the whole business was really like dipping your hand into an ever-open till.

My job was quite simple. In the morning, an American jeep would arrive to collect me and a maintenance man from the company. All day we would drive around to the various US bases, and at each I had to speak a few sentences of pidgin English to the American soldiers in charge, and translate their instructions into Japanese for the maintenance man. Then, while the maintenance man did his job, I could hang around the base canteens, exchanging little jokes with the soldiers in a mixture of English, Japanese and sign-language, and enjoying all kinds of wonderful things that were quite unimaginable in the world outside: American cigarettes and cups of coffee and big, juicy hamburgers. It was the best of all possible lives, and I made so much money that I was able to buy all the furniture for our house which my parents were starting to rebuild at Sendagaya.

I never felt any hostility towards the Americans at the bases. After all, as I said, even during the war I'd never really hated the Americans. Only sometimes I couldn't help looking at them and thinking that if the emperor's broadcast had come a few weeks later, I might have flown my plane into one of their ships, and who knows which of them I might have killed.

While most of his fellow-students turned up for classes in their 'demob suits' – military uniforms stripped of their badges and insignia – Mutsuo, as one of the perks of his job, was able to dress entirely in clothes from the bases' PX stores. These were the days when it was the most fashionable thing in the world to be seen about town carrying a copy of *Reader's Digest*, and it was pleasing to be able to stroll around the Tokyo streets in American slacks and an American sweater, lighting Lucky Strike cigarettes with a Zip pocket lighter. It was, of course, strictly speaking illegal for Japanese civilians to buy PX goods, but at this time there were large areas of social existence to which the police were simply obliged to turn a blind eye. Only once Mutsuo was stopped and advised to dress 'a bit less conspicuously'.

Sometimes, though, it depressed me to walk around in Tokyo. Under every railway bridge and underpass there were rows of black-market stalls, and all the way from Kanda to Ginza the streets were lined with little illegal gambling booths. At night, you couldn't walk from Shimbashi Station to Ginza without passing a Pan-Pan Girl [prostitute] about every five metres. Those were the girls who, two years ago, had been called the 'flowers of Yamato', and now they were selling themselves on the street to keep from starving. After a while I started to avoid those areas at night if I possibly could. It made me sick to see it.

Already before the war the overcrowded Japanese cities had begun to expand downwards, creating 'underground cities' – the miles of subways and underpasses, maze-like arcades of shops, bars and restaurants whose surreal, sky-less perspectives still surprise and bewilder the stranger. But in the first post-war years the 'underground cities' served another purpose, providing a home for thousands of orphans and 'lumpen' (down-and-outs) who made their living by shining shoes, gathering and recycling cigarette stubs, or by other more shadowy and violent means. Every now and then their teeming, verminous communities would be raided by police, who would cart the children off to orphanages and the adults to welfare centres, but within a few weeks most would have filtered back again to resume their subterranean lives.

In 1947 the press reported one such raid which had netted an unexpected catch:

In the morning of 27th February, during a raid on the Minami-ku, Osaka, 'underground city' police discovered Tōjō Hichio (46), younger brother of the former General Tōjō Hideki . . . The younger Tōjō, with a grimy moustache which exactly resembled that of his brother, and with the collar of his tattered 'citizen's dress' turned up against the cold, was bundled into a truck with the other down-and-outs and removed to Osaka Welfare Centre, who later dispatched him to the nearby Kosai-in Hospital.[2]

The elder Tōjō was not so fortunate. When the occupation authorities arrived to arrest him after the surrender, he had attemp-

ted unsuccessfully to commit suicide. In 1946 he was put on trial for
war crimes, of which he was found guilty, and in December 1948 he
was executed, together with six other prominent political and
military leaders. (The great majority of executions for war crimes
took place not in Japan itself, but in the countries which Japan had
occupied. In all, over nine hundred convicted war criminals suffered
the death penalty.) At the time these sentences were carried out a
number of others who had been imprisoned as war crimes suspects,
but against whom insufficient evidence had been collected, were
released without further proceedings. The most notable of these was
Kishi Nobusuke, later to be prime minister of Japan from 1957 to
1960.

> In a way, I didn't like the outcome of the trials. It seemed to me
> wrong that people like Hirota[3] should be executed when others
> who must have done things that were just as bad were never tried
> at all.
> But about Tōjō I could feel only a kind of anger. I thought:
> 'Wasn't he the person who made a special book of military rules
> telling us that we must never be captured alive? Wasn't he the
> person who insisted on fighting to the last man, who urged us to
> crash our planes into enemy bombers? And then, when they came
> to arrest him, he couldn't even manage to shoot himself. He let
> himself become a prisoner.' I could never feel sorry for him.

During the final year at Keio University, the pressures of combin-
ing work and study intensified. Mutsuo would borrow notes from
fellow-students, and in return treated them to the expensive meals
which he could now afford with his large earnings from the billiard
company. In the last few weeks before his finals he took time off
work to concentrate on classes and revision, and in April 1950 he
received his degree in economics from Keio. By now the billiard
repair business was prospering so much that the company was
reluctant to let him leave, and so, somewhat against his will, he
agreed to stay on with them until autumn. But by the end of
September he felt that the time had come to find a permanent career.
The timing was fortunate, for less than three months earlier the
Korean War had broken out. To Korea, which had been spared
bombing raids during the Second World War, this violent manifes-
tation of the growing tensions between the capitalist and communist
superpowers brought appalling misery and destruction. But for the

Japanese economy it was, quite simply, an unexpected gift. Japan, as the industrialized area nearest to the war zone, was suddenly inundated with demands for vehicles, spare parts, clothing and a host of other items destined for the (mainly American) United Nations forces in Korea. Tokyo hotels, bars and nightclubs flourished as UN soldiers on rest and recreation leave poured into them seeking a momentary obliteration of the memories of war. Between 1950 and the signing of the Korean Armistice in 1953, war-related procurements in Japan are estimated to have amounted to just under one billion US dollars.

The outbreak of the Korean War had another important consequence for Japan: it sharpened the antagonisms of the Cold War, and so greatly speeded a change which had already begun to take place in the policies of the American occupation authorities. No longer was attention focused upon the destruction of militarism in Japan and the re-education of its citizens in the ideals of liberal democracy. Now, subtly and gradually, the emphasis was shifting to the creation of a Japan which would be powerful enough – both economically and politically – to provide a counterweight to the Communist Menace in Asia. From now on, American occupation policies were almost entirely directed towards the achievement of this new goal. The stringent reparations demands and rigorous anti-monopoly laws which had earlier been proposed were quietly abandoned. Businessmen, politicians and civil servants who had been purged because of their associations with wartime policies were allowed to filter back into public life.

Six weeks after the outbreak of the Korean War, GHQ authorized the setting up of a 75,000-man National Police Reserve (*Keisatsu Yobitai*). The name deceived no one for, although restricted in its functions and equipment, this was unmistakably a military force. The following year, a memorandum by the US National Security Council defined the United States' aims with respect to Japan pending the conclusion of a peace treaty as being to:

(1) Take such steps as will facilitate transition from occupation status to restoration of sovereignty.
(2) Assist Japan in organizing, training, and equipping the National Police Reserve and the Maritime Safety Patrol in order to facilitate formation of an effective military establishment.[4]

The experiment with total disarmament had lasted just five years.

Saitō Mutsuo's approach to job-hunting was straightforward. He went to the University's Careers Office and asked which companies paid the best salaries. The first name they gave him was that of a large securities firm, which turned out to be willing only to offer him a post in Hokkaido. Mutsuo, who did not wish to move so far from Tokyo, turned this down. Their next suggestion was a chemicals company named Kantō Denka, whose business was rapidly expanding as the Korean War boom took its hold on the Japanese economy. Mutsuo applied to them and was offered a job in their sales department. So, in the autumn of 1950, he began his life as a permanent managerial employee with the company – or rather, to use that most popular of Japanese borrowings from English, as a 'salaryman'.

When I joined Kantō Denka in 1950, I soon realized why the company paid such good salaries. You see, that was the height of the Korean War boom and, like most chemical companies, Kantō Denka was making so much money that they hardly knew what to do with it all. Their main product was magnesium soda, and at that time they were selling it at something like 150,000 yen a ton, which is an enormous price. Nowadays, even with money being worth so much less that it was then, it only sells for about 50,000 yen a ton.

But Kantō Denka was one of the companies which had been earmarked for possible requisition under the reparations scheme, and they didn't want to invest in diversifying and expanding the company, because they were still afraid that all their plant might be removed and taken off to the United States or somewhere as part of the war reparations payments. So that was why they gave such high wages and salaries, and even paid out dividends of 30 per cent which was almost unheard of for a Japanese company.

But by the time the Korean War boom was over it was evident that the reparations claim on the company was not going to be carried out, so then they started to develop new products. They diversified into chlorine production, and experimented with producing vinyl chloride for artificial leather goods. That wasn't very successful, though, so later they concentrated mainly on producing chlorine as an industrial cleaning agent, and also on developing the basic materials of caprolactan, for use in nylon production.

Japan, which before the war had been one of the world's biggest producers of cotton textiles, was now just beginning to develop production of the new, synthetic fabrics. Between 1955 and 1973 synthetic textile production was to increase roughly seventy-four-fold. For companies like Kantō Denka, business was booming. But Mutsuo at first did not find it easy to adapt to life in the organization.

I started off in the sales department. As far as I was concerned, that meant that my job was to sell the company's products as effectively as I could, and that's what I set about doing. Sometimes, if I thought it would help secure a sales contract, I would take potential customers out to expensive meals in high-class restaurants, and then I'd send the bill in to the accounts section. And it worked very well. I was a very successful salesman, and the company management recognized that. But unfortunately, they also felt that I was not good for the harmony of the company. You see, it wasn't really the done thing for a new junior recruit like me to go entertaining people in expensive restaurants. They felt that I was being too self-assertive. Later, I understood that that was the difference between life in the military and company life. As an army officer you were expected to assert yourself and use your own initiative, but in the company that sort of behaviour was felt to be disruptive.

In September 1951 the Treaty of Peace for Japan was signed in San Francisco, formally ending Japan's state of war with the Western Allies and with most of the Asian nations which she had fought or invaded (the Treaty was not signed by the Soviet Union, nor by the People's Republic of China, Taiwan, or the two Koreas). The signing of the Treaty of San Francisco ended the American occupation of Japan, but on the same day Japan and the United States also concluded a security agreement which provided for the retention of American military bases in Japan and so reinforced Japan's position as a cornerstone of US security arrangements in the Western Pacific.

By this time, despite conflicts of personality at work, Saitō Mutsuo's life had slipped into a smooth and peaceful routine. Every morning he took the rush-hour train from Sendagaya, where he still lived with his parents in their rebuilt house, to the office in central Tokyo. Every evening, at varying hours, he caught the train home again. The Sendagaya which had grown from the ashes of the bombing was not so very different from the area as he had known it before the war. The same small houses and shops crowded together on their little building plots; the same few square yards of garden were beginning to sprout the same arrangements of rocks and potted trees; the familiar bright colours of eiderdowns out to air adorned the balconies every morning. Only in a few places were the skeletal frameworks of the first three- and four-storey blocks of flats beginning to break up the low horizons of the city's residential areas.

When Mutsuo was not at work his greatest pleasure was to go by train out to the suburb of Urawa, where his sisters and their families were living. Here he had enrolled in a club to study *utai* – for he had inherited from his father a love for this music, whose slow, ancient chanting provided a welcome contrast to the frenetic world of the chemicals industry.

The *utai* club was organized by a history teacher from the local high school, a man with whom Mutsuo, despite the disparity in their ages, soon established a friendship. After some time, the history teacher suggested that a marriage might be arranged between Mutsuo and his daughter Yoriko. A formal meeting of the two took place, and both readily consented to the plan. Mutsuo was then twenty-nine, a graduade of a respected university, with the likelihood of a successful career ahead of him. The prospective bride was twenty-four, attractive, well-educated and of a good family. They had a number of further meetings, mostly at the Saitōs' house in Sendagaya, and in 1952 they were married. The following year their first child was born: a daughter, whom they named Chieko.

Soon after, the calm and predictable pattern of career and family life was shaken. Mutsuo's father, Saitō Kōsuke, had been suffering for some time from worsening bouts of bronchitis; in 1954 his heart gave out under the strain of illness and he died at the age of 69. A few months later, Mutsuo had a recurrence of tuberculosis. Fortunately it was not a very severe attack, but it was still necessary for him to take three months off work, and the treatment itself left him with slight but persistent ear trouble.

The illness itself was not so terrible. What really shocked me was that, after I returned to work, I was called in by the senior management and told:

'We think that you need a chance to recover your health completely, so how would you like a change of scene from Tokyo? We thought a spell working at our factory in Shibukawa [about a hundred miles west of the capital] might be just the thing for you.'

Of course I didn't have any choice. I had to go, but it came as a great blow, because I knew that managers or workers from the Shibukawa factory were sometimes promoted to the headquarters in Tokyo, but no one had ever been sent from headquarters to the factory before. It was a real mark of displeasure, and I felt very disheartened about it. However, I wasn't going to give up or resign, so we let the house in Sendagaya, and moved out to Shibukawa. We lived there for the next four years.

My first job at Shibukawa was a general managerial post, dealing with everything from insurance to the running of the canteen. It was a very easy life, but its easiness did not make me happy. I felt as though I was working in a kind of vacuum, where there was no response and no resistance. There was little to do, and it didn't seem to make any difference whether I tried hard or not. So naturally I ended up getting by with the minimum of effort.

Shibukawa means 'Bitter River'. There must have been times when it seemed an appropriate name. Their life there was not made easier by the fact that old Mrs Saitō, whom Mutsuo and his wife were expected by custom to look after, was beginning to grow frail and lose her memory.

However, even at Shibukawa, there were moments of happiness. One was the birth of a son, Tarō, in 1957. Another was the advent of television. For Mutsuo's children were to grow up in a world very different from that of his own childhood. The kites and spinning tops and bamboo stick swords which he had enjoyed had not disappeared, but were rapidly being supplemented by other playthings: plastic boats, buckets and spades, hoola hoops and toy telephones. And the vanished hero of *Bōken Dankichi* was soon to have worthy successors in the incorruptible cops of *Highway Patrol*, and in *Superman*, who strode weekly on to thousands of Japanese television screens accompanied by the immortal words: 'Faster than

211

a speeding bullet; more powerful than a locomotive; leaping over skyscrapers . . . Day and night he keeps up the fight for Freedom and Democracy!'

Mutsuo had grown up in an age when it was common for middle-class families to have a living-in servant. Now, as economic growth began to provide more attractive and better-paid jobs for young working women, the newspapers recorded the final demise of that era:

'Maids wanted', say the advertisements in seventeen Tokyo employment bureaux. But the bureaux are reported to be growing worried at the lack of applicants for the jobs. On 23rd April [1957], one Shibuya bureau organized a conference at which about twenty people – including housewives, daily helps and employment advisers – discussed the problem. Their conclusion was that 'the living-in maid is vanishing. From now on it will be the era of daily or part-time helps'. . . .

Shibuya employment bureau's own survey shows that, for a 9 a.m. to 6 p.m. day, the average [maid's] wage is 250 yen [about 5/– 25 pence – at 1957 values], plus travel expenses and lunch. Those who are unwilling to pay that much have no hope of finding domestic help.[5]

In practice, as the expansion of light industry, department stores, restaurants and hotels offered alternative employment to young women, the 150-yen-a-day domestic disappeared from all but a very few households – mostly those of foreign diplomats and business-men. She was replaced by what the media, with their talent for catch-phrases, instantly named 'the Three Sacred Objects', a term traditionally applied to the emperor's regalia of mirror, sword and jewel, but now transferred to the totemic symbols of the prosperous household: the washing machine, the refrigerator and the television set.

The great television boom of the mid-1950s was much encouraged by the rise of Rikidōzan, a Korean-Japanese wrestler who moved from a moderately successful career in *sumō* to a trememdously successful one in the professional wrestling ring. In 1954, at the peak of his career, the television companies put up sets outside every major Tokyo station, and crowds of thousands gathered in front of them to watch the unimaginable spectacle of the burly Japanese wrestler performing his characteristic *karate* chops upon his villainous American challengers, and winning. The newspapers rewrote their 1945 slogan – 'one hundred million people in a state of dementia'.

It was my sister Yasuko's family who got a television first. I watched it when I went to visit them, and was entranced. At that time, if you had a television, your house was more or less open to the public every evening – all the neighbours and friends would come into your sitting room to crowd round the set.

After I saw their television, I was longing to buy one for ourselves. They cost about 70,000 yen, which was quite a large sum of money in those days. But I thought about it for a while and then one day I just made up my mind and I went to the bank and took out 70,000 yen and went off to Akihabara [an area of Tokyo famous for its large numbers of shops selling cheap electrical appliances] where, even then, there were thousands of little electrical goods shops, all clustered together in a square mile or so of narrow streets. I found the set I wanted, and brought it home, and we became the very first family in the Shibukawa factory to have our own TV.

I'm not sure which year it was when we bought the television, but I know that we had it already when the Crown Prince got married. That was 1958, wasn't it? I remember seeing the wedding on television, particularly the part near the end where some youth threw stones at the parade.

After a couple of years at Shibukawa, Mutsuo was promoted to become warehouse manager (a key position, since Japanese management places great emphasis on maintaining a smooth flow of raw materials and finished products into and out of the plant). The challenge of the new post revived his interest in his work, and the next year he was awarded the company's special prize for good work.

It was a funny thing, but getting that prize made a big psychological difference to me. I started to feel that the people in the headquarters hadn't forgotten all about me after all. I felt that my work was being appreciated, and that made me try all the harder. And in fact, not long after, I was recalled to the Tokyo headquarters and put in charge of the share section.

It was 1959 when Mutsuo moved back to the capital. While he was in Shibukawa he had sold the family's old house in Sendagaya, and instead bought a plot of land at Urawa, near to the homes of his sisters. Now there was a certain pleasure and excitement in having to hurry round the offices of builders and architects, studying blueprints, looking at photographs, comparing prices, and planning, for the first time, a house of his very own. While the house was being built, Mutsuo left his family in Shibukawa and went to stay in a little traditional Japanese inn near the city centre.

Because of this he was in Tokyo in the summer of 1960, when the Security Treaty with the United States, which had been signed at the time of the San Francisco Peace Treaty, came up for renewal. The revised Security Treaty, reawakening memories of militarism and fears of war, evoked immense opposition in Japan. In June the streets of Tokyo were filled with the biggest political demonstrations the capital had ever witnessed, and the edifice of Japanese liberal democracy created by MacArthur's GHQ faced the severest test of its stability.

Both Tsutsumi Ayako and Iida Momo were, in their different ways, participants in the anti-Treaty demonstrations of 1960. But for Saitō Mutsuo the huge chanting crowds and the slogan-emblazoned banners were merely something that he watched on television or passed on his way to work, and observed with a distant and dispassionate eye.

My feeling about all those people who went on the demonstrations was that they were really opposing the Security Treaty for opposition's sake. Mind you, I'm not necessarily saying that I wholly agree with the Treaty. There may be things that are wrong with it, but I still believe that it's a necessary evil. After all, whatever you may say (and I know my children don't agree with me on this: they think I'm a right-wing old fogey) but whatever you may say, I think that a country needs some kind of defence, and if you don't have an effective defence force yourself, you at least need some form of guarantee.

On the other hand, I didn't have anything against people demonstrating, if that's how they felt about the matter. I thought they had a perfect right to do it if they wanted to. After all, that's what democracy is all about, isn't it?

10

Tsutsumi Ayako

After August 15th they stopped making weapons at the place where I worked in Inchon. In my last week there, the main thing we had to do was to go through all the papers in the office, and decide which ones should be burnt. The Korean workers there were not nasty to us in any way. In fact, the Korean woman who worked in the office gave me a present when I left. She had graduated from Girls' School, you see, and she had a whole collection of Japanese literature books from school. When I went home she gave them to me as a parting present.

I left on about 22nd August. There were four other girls from the office who lived in Kwangju, so we all travelled back together. The army sent one of the soldiers from the Inchon base to protect us, but I didn't see any signs of disturbances or trouble on my way home.

At home Ayako found her mother, together with her eldest sister, who had recently returned from Japan, and the two younger children. Her father was still away at a construction site in Chedjudo, and there were anxious weeks while they awaited his return. In those weeks they barricaded themselves inside their house, and might have starved but for the loyalty of their *omoni*, who continued to come to them, bringing food and news of the outside world.

For a couple of weeks we didn't hear any news of my father, and Mother was very frightened. Sometimes *Omoni* brought stories of robberies in the city, but at that time we didn't hear of any killings. Only later I had a letter from a girl who had been in the dormitory with me at Inchon. Her family had been living somewhere out in the country, and after the surrender the peasants there took her father and they buried him up to the neck in the earth and then cut his head off with a saw.

Mother was worried about going back to the Mainland as well.

215

We had heard the rumours that the occupation forces would rape all Japanese women, and Mother said to us: 'When we get back, we must cut our hair short, and make our faces black with charcoal. That way we may possibly be safe.'

But all the same, we still wanted to go back. We felt that in the Mainland people would be kind. It would be warm there. People would help one another. Somehow we couldn't stop ourselves from believing that, if we could only get back there, everything would work out all right.

In September their father at last returned unharmed, and immediately they began to make plans for their escape. The first to leave, sometimes on the large official refugee ships, sometimes on hastily acquired fishing or coastal vessels, were the Japanese police and prominent government officials, who had no illusions about the fate which awaited them if they remained. Ayako's father's tenant, the policeman from Kwangju Police Station, was among those who managed to obtain a place on one such boat, and he offered to escort the four children and their mother to Japan while their father remained in Kwangju to dispose of his houses and business.

We caught a train from Kwangju to a little port nearby. On the train I remember that there were two American soldiers, and we looked at them with great curiosity, as it was the first time we had seen any of the 'American and British Devils', but actually I didn't think they looked terrible at all – just rather smart and handsome.

When we got to the port, we found that there were five boats leaving at the same time. They were quite small. There were about ten families on each. I didn't feel at all frightened then, because most of the people on our boat were policemen's families, and the policemen all carried pistols. The governor of Kwangju and his family were on our boat too. The only problem was that, just before we were supposed to leave, my little brother couldn't be found. We hunted everywhere, and Mother started to get hysterical. At last we found him, waiting in a queue for the wrong boat.

We left at about midday, and we were supposed to reach Fukuoka [in southern Japan] the next day. But this was the typhoon season, and in the night we struck a huge typhoon. Everyone was lying down in the hold of the ship, being seasick.

216

The governor of Kwangju was lying next to me being terribly sick. But for some reason I didn't feel sick, so after a while I went up on to the deck of the boat. It was dark and the wind was howling and the rain and spray were blowing across the deck. Suddenly the boat started to list, and all sorts of things that were lying loose on the deck rolled over and over and fell into the sea. I managed to cling on to something to stop myself going too. But my mother, who was lying downstairs in the hold, could hear all these things rolling, koron-koron-koron, across the deck, and she was sure that I must have gone with them. Ever after that she used to have a recurring nightmare where she dreamed that I was rolling off the deck of a boat into the sea, and she would wake up with a start in the middle of the night screaming: 'Aré! Aré!' It even became a sort of family joke in the end. My brother and sister used to say: 'Oh no, Mother's started her 'Aré-ing again!'

I'm not really a religious person, but that night in the typhoon I was so frightened that I started to pray. I didn't pray to any particular god, just to Heaven. I prayed:

'Please don't let me die. If I survive this I shall devote all the rest of my life to helping mankind. Even if all the others die, please let me be saved. Or, if it is really my time to die, at least let me die on dry land, not here out at sea.'

The gale went on all the next day, but in the evening we managed to reach land at a small island off Nagasaki. We stayed there all the next night, sheltering in port from the typhoon. We slept in the boat, and the next day we went on to Fukuoka.

Of course, because of the storm, we had been separated from the other boats which left with us, but later on we found out what had happened to them. We were lucky to have arrived safely. One of the boats had capsized, and everyone aboard had been drowned, and another one had been blown back into a port in Korea, where all the passengers were robbed and sent back to sea with nothing but the clothes they stood up in.

So eventually we reached Fukuoka. But the typhoon was still blowing, and as we went to get off the boat one of the women was swept off the gangplank and into the sea. No one could help her, because the waves were so rough. We just all watched as she struggled in the sea. After a while she disappeared from sight. Then she reappeared again, but she wasn't struggling any more, so we knew that she was dead.

At Fukuoka they were taken to a reception camp where, first of all, they were sprayed from head to foot with DDT. For two or three days they remained in the camp, exchanging what possessions they had with them for food. Their intention was to make their way to their original home in Shikoku, where they hoped that relatives would give them shelter. But the typhoon had not yet abated: it was what is known as a 'typhoon sitting on a chair', a wind which remains in the same spot, viciously chasing its tail round and round until its energies are dissipated. The small boat which Ayako's family took to cross over to Shikoku was again blown off course, to the coast near Hiroshima, and there was another boat journey and then a further train journey before at last they reached their destination, the little town of Ikeda, deep in the hollow of a Shikoku mountain valley.

On the journey from Fukuoka to Ikeda I had my first sight of Japan (except, of course, that I must have seen it when I was a baby, but I couldn't remember that at all)'. I thought the scenery was very beautiful, particularly the mountains, which seemed so green after the bare Korean mountains.

But apart from that all my illusions were broken. Right from the start, we had to go around with our possessions, bargaining with farmers for a few bowls full of food. No one seemed kind or friendly, as we had imagined them. I kept remembering the woman struggling in the water at the harbour, and everyone blankly looking on. I thought, can this really be the place they called the Land of the Gods?

And the worst thing of all was to look out of the train windows and see poor, ragged-looking Japanese people; Japanese people pulling carts and digging ditches. I had never seen that in Korea, and I had never even dreamed of it before.

In Ikeda they found refuge with Ayako's uncle (her mother's elder brother), who had a modest job with a government-run monopoly company. He offered the family the use of the two upstairs rooms in his five-roomed house, and for a couple of days even shared his food with them, a generous act in the harsh circumstances of that time. But after that they had to fend for themselves, taking their few remaining possessions, one by one, up into the mountains to exchange for potatoes, or sometimes merely for the stems and leaves of the potato plants, which could be used to make a vegetable stew (it was now that the lessons in economical living which Ayako had

218

received at Kōshū Girls' School were put to good use). In November Ayako's father rejoined the family. He arrived back from Korea with a rucksack crammed with yen notes, and for a while the family's food problems seemed to be eased. But it soon became clear that in the winter of 1945 a few family heirlooms, a gold ring or two, would have been worth more than a sackful of paper money. Inflation was rampant, and the local farmers knew how to drive a shrewd bargain. No doubt the country people were quietly conscious of the irony of fate which had brought the once sophisticated city-folk flocking to their doors, haggling like market day housewives for a bunch of onions or a little bag of rice. This was a time when many farmhouses acquired their first battered radio or antique clock, and many farmers' wives obtained their first fine silk kimono.

We were so hungry that winter. I remember that there was a little sweet-shop at the corner of the street where we were staying, but the only sweets which they had to sell were something brown and quite disgusting. I don't know what they were made of. They looked and smelt like horse-manure, but, as there was nothing else to buy there, we bought them all the same.

But the hardest thing was the lack or rice. Sometimes I used to think that I would be happy to die if only I could eat a big bowl of white rice first. For a while my father went to his family, because they owned a farm, and when he came back he managed to bring us a bit of rice from their house, but we could only use it very sparingly. When I went to wash the rice before we cooked it, I was so desperate that I popped some of the raw grains in my mouth and started to chew them. There was a *kamidana* in that house, and whenever it was possible the family would put a little bowl of rice there as an offering. One day I was so hungry that I stole the bowl and ate all the rice myself. I felt bad about that afterwards, though.

Another time I remember waking up late at night and seeing my mother and father cooking some rice in a metal pan over the charcoal brazier which we used to heat the room. They were doing it quietly, while the rest of us were asleep. My father ate the rice straight out of the metal pan, and when he had eaten as much as he wanted, he gave what was left over to my mother.

The new Constitution which was at that time being prepared by the Japanese and American authorities was, in its final form, to state:

Marriage . . . shall be maintained through mutual co-operation with the equal rights of husband and wife as a basis. Laws shall be enacted considering choice of spouse, property rights, inheritance, choice of domicile, divorce and other matters pertaining to marriage and the family from the standpoint of individual dignity and the essential equality of the sexes.

Over the next couple of years, the laws were enacted: the extensive powers of the head of the family over the private lives of other household members were curtailed; the system by which the eldest son (rather than the widow) commonly inherited all the father's estate was abolished. But, while such reforms as coeducation and women's suffrage could be achieved instantly by legislation, the reform of family relationships was a far slower process. It is quite possible to reverse your feelings about an ideal, a moral value, a political institution; but to reverse your feelings about your husband or wife, your parents and yourself is much more difficult.

At this time I was no longer feeling that I ought to apologize to the emperor for not serving him well enough in the war. My feelings about the emperor were sort of numb. Soon after we came back to Japan, I saw the photograph of the emperor's meeting with General MacArthur: the emperor looking so small and stiff and the American general looking big and really like someone who had won. I felt sorry for the emperor when I saw that picture, but even more I felt that I didn't want to look at it, and I didn't want to talk about it. It was like something painful which is better not to touch.

I didn't think that the emperor was responsible for the war. My father blamed it all on General Tōjō. 'That Tōjō . . .' he used to mutter.

I didn't hate the Americans at all then. I could see that what we had been taught about them was quite untrue. In fact, I began to realize how easily people can be misled and brainwashed, the way we had been, and that made me think what fearful creatures human beings can be. Perhaps it was partly because of this feeling that I decided at this time that I would like to become a teacher. I thought I might apply to go to Nara Women's Teacher Training College. But I had no one to advise me about that sort of thing, so first of all I decided to write to Mr Niimi, who had been my favourite teacher at Kōshū Girls' School. (He was the one who taught us about the theory of the emperor as an organ of state.) He had come back to Japan and was living in Hiroshima now.

He wrote back to me straight away. It was a very kind letter, but what he said in it was: 'At an important time like this it is not good to leave your parents and spend your time following your own wishes. You would be better to remain under your parents' authority, and prepare yourself for marriage.' ('Train to be a flower-bride' was the expression he used.)

So after that I took his advice and abandoned my ideas of a teaching career.

Soon after returning from Korea, Ayako's father had begun to draw up plans for a business venture with his old friend the Kwangju policeman, who was now living nearby in Shikoku. The logic of his scheme was straightforward: since most Japanese city centres had been levelled by bombing, there would soon, surely, be a boom in the construction industry. He and his partner would therefore set up a little business digging out sand and gravel from local river beds and selling them to builders' merchants. They managed to put together the necessary capital, and were about to set up their company, but at that very time came the emergency economic measures of February 1946. The money which they had deposited in the bank was frozen, and the enterprise had to be abandoned.

It was clear, however, that the family could not remain as guests of the uncle in Ikeda for ever. The generosity which was so freely offered in the first moment of crisis began, if left indefinitely unrepaid, to create strains in the delicate balance of family relationships. To spread the weight of obligations more easily they decided to move to Kyushu, where another uncle lived. This time, however, they hoped to be able to find a house of their own so that, although they might initially need to ask for help, they would in the end be able to establish themselves as neighbours rather than dependants. (It should be mentioned that the *hikiagesha* – refugees – who often returned having found and lost their fortunes in Japan's overseas empire, encountered some hostility from the rest of Japanese society, partly because they represented a further burden on already impoverished communities, partly perhaps because they were an unwelcome reminder of vanished glories.)

In the meantime Ayako was sent to Kyushu in advance, to smooth the way for her parents' arrival by working as an almost unpaid assistant in Kyushu Uncle's business, a small shop selling cosmetics and miscellaneous household goods: everything from brooms to mouse-traps and *katori senkō* – the green, incense-scented coils which are burnt in Japanese houses during the summer to drive away mosquitoes.

My uncle's shop was just one room – about the size of the living room of my present house – and it was crammed full of shelves and boxes of goods. He sold them wholesale and retail.

When I first went to work there I was happy, because the food seemed very good compared to what we'd been eating for the past six months. But the work was hard. I had to get up early in the morning and spend all day serving in the shop, and then in the evening I had to work as a kind of maid, doing the cooking and cleaning for my uncle's family. I was still longing to be able to continue my education, and I once asked my uncle's family if I could have a few hours off each week to go to evening classes, but they made faces about it, so I let the subject drop.

I worked for my uncle for about a year. There is just one memory from that time which is strong in my mind. My uncle's shop was not right in the town centre, but a little way out, about two kilometres from the station. Almost everything between the shop and the station had been bombed, so it was possible to see a long way in that direction. It must have been one evening in summer. There was a very big red sun on the horizon, and from far away I could see a group of demobilized soldiers – about four or five of them – walking along the road away from the station. They were walking in step and, as they came nearer, I could see that they were dressed in rather shabby old uniforms, but their faces had an expression of happiness – I suppose they had just returned home from abroad – their expression seemed to say: 'now we are going to begin a new life'. I stood by the door of the shop, and as they came past, I bowed deeply to the soldiers. I bowed to them quite instinctively, as a sign of respect.

After Ayako had worked at the shop for several months, Kyushu Uncle made her family an offer: he would lend them the capital, and they would set up and run a branch of his business in a mountain village about two hours by bus from the town where he lived. The family gratefully accepted. They moved to Kyushu in the autumn of

1946, and the following year Ayako joined them in their new home in the village of Nojiri.

Life in Nojiri was hard. First there was the new shop to look after. This was mainly the responsibility of Ayako's elder sister, who, at twenty-four, should by now have been married, but for the circumstances of the war. Their mother did the housework, and also tended the family's quarter-acre plot of land, where they grew all their own vegetables. Their father, meanwhile, had returned to his dreams of turning gravel into gold, and set up yet another construction company. Ayako helped with all these activities, as well as struggling to keep up her interests in education and self-betterment in the unpromising surroundings of the Kyushu mountains.

For the 45 per cent of Japanese families who now earned their livings from farming or fishing, life had not greatly changed during the two decades since Ayako's father, Mr Hasebe, had abandoned his family's farm. Only the economic conditions of the late 1940s, in which the urban population was suddenly and drastically impoverished, gave them a certain illusion of comparative wealth. The Japanese government, on the insistence of GHQ, had now just embarked on a programme of land reform which was to provide a basis for a real improvement in the economic status of the mass of the rural population over the next decade. But in the meantime villages like Nojiri (whose very name, meaning 'Backside Field', suggests its poor environment) remained no more than a collection of mainly wood-and-thatch farmhouses, straggling from an unpaved main street among terraced fields towards the dense greenery of the higher mountain forests. There were no telephones; many houses were without electricity; and the only means of reaching the town was a two-hour bone-shaking journey on an infrequent bus.

At that time none of the children in Nojiri wore shoes. I heard that, during the war, there had been some evacuees staying in the village, and when the evacuee children went to school the local children threw stones at them because they were wearing shoes.

I used to go barefoot all the time. For some reason I specially remember standing barefoot in the village fishmonger's shop, queuing for sardines. Being up in the mountains, you see, it was hard to get fresh fish, and to buy four or five sardines was regarded as a real extravagance.

In Nojiri we didn't have a radio, and I missed that terribly. I would have given anything to have a radio, but in the end I had to wait two or three years before we could afford it. I think it was about 1950 that we eventually bought one, and the first time I turned it on I heard the voice of a well-known Japanese opera singer of that time, singing an aria, and it seemed like one of the best things I had ever heard.

Ayako's twentieth birthday passed. She was living in a time when all truths and values had been turned upside down, and like most people of her age group she was full of eagerness for new knowledge and new experiences. Life in Nojiri seemed restrictive and frustrating, but she did her best to make what she could of any available opportunities to expand her ideas and understanding of the world outside.

The main social event for the young people of Nojiri were the twice-monthly meetings organized by the House of Longevity (*Seichō no Ie*). The House of Longevity was a syncretic spiritual movement whose avowed aim was to seek the truth behind all world religions, but which also had right-wing political connections. It had been founded in the early years of Shōwa, but the intellectual curiosity and spiritual vacuum of the post-war years enabled it to expand rapidly, particularly in country areas which more established religious and philosophical currents failed to reach. In Nojiri the meeting of the House of Longevity took place in the village hall, where a preacher from the town would give a little sermon – perhaps on the nature of the universe, perhaps on the values of family life – and his young audience would then have a chance, in discussing his theme, to air their own views and seek guidance on their own problems. Ayako did not become a convert to the faith, but the meetings undoubtedly exercised their influence on her way of thinking.

The other thing that happened while I was at Nojiri was that the art teacher at the village school set up a record society. He would give a little talk about a piece of classical music, and then play us the record. Our music lessons at school hadn't been very good, so all this was new to me. I remember that at one of these meetings I first heard Beethoven's Fifth Symphony, and it moved me so much that I just sat there and listened as if I was rooted to the spot.

That art teacher was a very kind person. Sometimes I used to visit his house. He had rows and rows of lovely, illustrated art books on his shelves. I used to gaze at their covers, and I longed to be able to borrow them, but I didn't quite like to ask. One time, though, he suggested that I should do a picture for him. He asked me to draw a bamboo shoot, so I drew it as carefully as I could and showed the picture to him. I suppose it was from then that I started to think about becoming an artist.

Not only was post-war democracy bringing its gradual changes to the position of women in Japanese society, but also the experience of war itself had opened new areas of activity which had previously been closed to them. Wartime labour service had shown that women were capable of driving trucks and controlling railway points. The war, too, had left large numbers of young widows and of women whose chance of marriage had passed them by, and such people were to remain a significant element in the Japanese labour force for years to come. These influences wrought changes both in men's expectations of women and in women's expectations of themselves. In 1946, for example, women were admitted to the police force for the first time, and in later years some Japanese women were to reach pre-eminent positions in the world of education, journalism and literature. But the belief in marriage as the supreme goal of womanhood remained very strong, and many positions, particularly the most prized careers in the upper ranks of the civil service and big business, continued in practice to be accessible only to men.

Ayako was by nature a hard worker. She enjoyed helping her father on his construction sites, preparing the wages for the day labourers and even watching and learning the skills of the stone-mason as he chipped the blocks of stone into shape, fitting each into its place in a roadside embankment or the foundations of a house. The construction boom which her father had predicted was already taking place, and was to gather even greater momentum as the effects of the Korean War began to work their way through the economy. Everywhere prefectural governments and town councils embarked on programmes of reconstruction and public works. For Ayako, too, it was sometimes amusing to be the only woman in the masculine environment of the building site: one day she gave out a wage packet and was surprised when, in return, the young worker sheepishly pressed into her hand a crumpled and roughly-written love letter.

I got on so well with my work that Father once said to me: 'Nowadays women can even join the police, so I suppose there would be nothing funny about a woman running a construction company', and he suggested to me that if I wanted to, he might arrange for me to inherit the business.

But I wasn't interested. I enjoyed the work on the site, but what I didn't like was seeing Father going round from one local government officer to another, bowing and pleading for contracts or planning permission. I could never have done that.

In the spring of 1951, Ayako became engaged. It was an engagement by *omiai* – arranged meeting – the couple being brought together by the preacher from the House of Longevity, whose meetings Ayako had so faithfully attended for the past four years. Her future husband was a disciple of the religion, a twenty-eight-year-old primary school teacher named Kuriya Tadahiko.

I think that what attracted me to him was that, at our first meeting, he said: 'I have nothing to offer you. I have no money, and I must support my two sisters out of my small income' (his parents had died young, you see, so he was looking after his sisters).

It's a strange thing, but that appealed to me at the time. Because somehow, to be in love with someone makes me feel very guilty. If I eat good food or wear smart clothes or am happy it makes me feel guilty. I don't know why it is. Perhaps it's because of the war, because so many people from my generation died young. I feel that always I have to be working as hard as a carthorse pulling a cart.

I was in two minds about getting married. In a way I was afraid that I might remain isolated in the end of the world for ever, just being married and bringing up a family and dying. But then sometimes I hoped that getting married might be a way of escaping. I thought that perhaps it might mean that I could move away and meet new people and do different things.

Between their first meeting and their marriage in the autumn of that year, Ayako and Tadahiko met four or five times. Once they even went on a day's excursion together, to the small town of Aoshima, where the mountains of Kyushu plunge vertiginously into the Pacific Ocean. They travelled by bus and train, a journey which in those days took five hours each way. But, like most respectable engaged couples of that time, they did not hold hands or kiss as the train swept them past glimpses of glinting blue ocean horizons.

As preparations for the wedding progressed, Ayako's visions of escape faded. Her eldest sister was now married to a local journalist; her elder brother was still away at pharmacy college; and the two younger ones, who were at High School in the nearest large town, had found lodgings there to avoid the daily bus journey. Ayako's parents firmly refused to allow her to leave home as well, and stipulated that if she married, her husband should come to live with them at Nojiri. Soon her father began to build an annex to the family house, where Ayako and Tadahiko were to live, so that she might continue to help in the shop and the vegetable garden after her wedding.

The marriage ceremony of Tsutsumi Ayako and Kuriya Tadahiko took place in autumn 1951, in the town of Kobayashi, where the bridegroom worked. There were about thirty guests, most of whom were teacher friends of Tadahiko's. Ayako's guests were her parents and Kyushu Uncle. After the ceremony, since there was no money for a honeymoon, the couple returned to Tadahiko's old bachelor quarters in Kobayashi, where they spent the first night of the marriage, sharing one small bedroom with Tadahiko's two teenage sisters.

For about the first six months, things went well. I wasn't very happy; I wasn't very sad. I felt: 'This is what marriage is supposed to be like.'

We lived in our new wing of the house at Nojiri. I spent all day doing the housework or helping mother with the shop. Father was away at his construction sites most of the time, and my husband would get up early every morning to catch the bus to his school in Kobayashi.

But after about half a year I began to feel small doubts. Somehow, the very things which had attracted me to him in the first place became annoying after our marriage: the fact that he had no money, and no ambition. He used to say: 'I don't want to become a headmaster. I should rather leave all that and get a little hut in the mountains and spend my days burning charcoal.'

Before we got married that sounded very romantic, but afterwards I started to think, well, after all, it is better to have some money.

In the evenings, when he came back from work, we would sit silently in the house. He was always reading books on education – Pestalozzi and so on. I liked to read Western romantic novels. I read *Madame Bovary* and books by Romain Rolland and Hermann Hesse. Also I liked classical music: I wanted to listen to Beethoven and Schumann, but what he really liked best was to listen to Japanese children's nursery rhymes. He was a kind person, but very quiet. We could never really find anything to say to one another, and I don't remember once going out anywhere with him after our marriage.

But by the time these doubts reached the surface of her consciousness, Ayako was already expecting their first child. In December 1952 her baby was born at the family home in Nojiri, with a midwife in attendance. It was a boy, as Ayako had hoped, for, she would say, 'Boys are able to do what they want'.

Like most new parents, Ayako and Tadahiko drew up a careful list of possible names for their child, looking not just for a pleasant-sounding name, but also for one whose *kanji* characters would convey an auspicious meaning. In the end, they chose to call the baby 'Yūji'. The first syllable of his name is written with a character sometimes pronounced 'Hiro', meaning 'abundant'. This is also the first character of the name 'Hirohito'. The second syllable is written with a character meaning 'to rule'.

I thought of that name as a form of respect for the emperor. I believe that he is a good emperor. I didn't ever think that he was responsible for all the things which went wrong in the 1930s and 1940s. It was just that he had bad advisers.

I still say to my son sometimes: 'You have a noble name. Don't do anything to blemish it.'

Domesticity – 'a good wife and wise mother' (states the writer and critic Fukuhara Rintarō) has long been the ideal of woman, with her responsibility for all domestic matters . . .

Gods, as in the case of the Greeks, are numerous in Japan. Wives are also gods ('Mountain Gods' as they are playfully called) in this country. In the beginning there was the Sun-Goddess, whose descendants built up the country . . . .[1]

In pre-war years the 'Mountain Gods' may have privately mourned or occasionally rebelled against their fates. But to question it in public had been impossible. Women had been restrained from public self-expression even by their language – the Japanese spoken by women being so distinctly different from that used by men that until the 1920s or 1930s it was considered comical for a woman to write an article or letter in the blunt 'mannish' language of the newspapers and magazines. But by the 1950s coeducation and political emancipation were breaking down these barriers. Even the domestic deity could be doubted.

Happiness! [wrote a woman correspondent to the *Asahi Shimbun* in 1952]. Women search for this as though it is dropped at some street corner. And this is always [seen as being] tied to marriage. . . . Marriage is a sort of struggle between a man and a women, who have different backgrounds, environments and personalities. . . . I do not believe that women's happiness is found only in marriage.[2]

In 1953, Ayako had enrolled in an art correspondence course run by the Musashino Art College in Tokyo. In the mornings she prepared her husband's breakfast and saw him off to work. By day she suckled the baby, tended the family shop, prepared the evening meal. At night she studied. But family life in the house at Nojiri did not contain the space and privacy necessary for actual painting or drawing. All she could do was to leaf through the glossy brochures and to read and re-read the detailed instructions on the use of perspective, of light and shadow, which arrived in the bulky envelopes from Tokyo.

At about this time Ayako read a story. It is the story of a boy growing up in a small provincial town. His father is bullying and materialistic. Before he reaches his twenties he is already burdened with the responsibilities of the family, earning money to keep his father and educate his brothers. But the boy has a secret strength: a belief in his own genius. All around him the world is in turmoil, seething with a revolution of new ideas. In his twenties, now a young man, he suddenly abandons his town, his friends and family, and sets course for the great cultural centre of his time, Vienna. He writes: '*Courage!* In spite of all the weakness of the body, my genius will triumph. . . . Twenty-five years! See, they have arrived! I have them. . . . This very year the man must be revealed in his entirety!'[3]

229

The story is that of the early life of Beethoven as described in the pages of Ayako's favourite writer, Romain Rolland.

If you want a pretty, poetic explanation for why I decided to run away from my family, you could say it was because I read that story.

But really, underneath everything, the reason was different: it was the feeling of frustration which I had inside myself. I had wanted the baby because I thought that having a child would fill up the empty space in my life. But it didn't work that way. The empty space grew larger. The pressures of the family, of continuing the family line, seemed to grow heavier rather than lighter. And there also grew the fear that nothing would ever change: I would be here, as I was, for ever.

So I decided that, whatever happened, I was going to go to Tokyo and study art. Although my husband and I had seemed to grow apart rather than together since our marriage, I did not leave in order to get away from him. I thought that if he would agree to move to Tokyo we would go together, and that would be all right. But if he refused to come with me, I would go alone, and that would be all right too.

However, when I talked about my idea, not only my husband but also my parents and all the neighbours thought that I had gone quite mad. My husband was totally against my going to Tokyo, but, being a quiet person, he did not argue in a forceful way. My father, though, was bitter and angry, and my parents threatened that if I left they would have nothing more to do with me.

At that time there was a fortune-diviner who was famous in our part of Kyushu. He lived among the mountains near the coast at Aoshima, the place where my husband and I had gone for our courting when we were first engaged. Before I finally made up my mind to leave home, in the autumn of 1953, I went to see the fortune-diviner. I didn't really believe in that kind of thing, but still I went. And the strange thing was, as I walked up the path through the mountains towards his hut – the mountain-slopes were all covered with fallen autumn leaves at that time of year – I really began to imagine some feeling of sacredness in the air of that place. The fortune-diviner was an oldish man, I suppose about in his sixties. I told him that my mind was uncertain: I wanted to go away and start a career, but I did not know whether I could leave my family. The old man drew me into the room and made me stand in front of his God Shelf. He asked me the date of my birth, and what Chinese characters I used to write my name. He studied the lines on my hand, and peered at my face for a moment or two. Then, quite roughly and rudely, he shouted: 'Get away! Go wherever you want to go! A person like you has no business staying anywhere!'

So that was that. I paid him one hundred yen, and I had my decision. Before I left he muttered something about my suffering from illness: he said I would have trouble with my hips (I think he said hips, or it might have been eyes) and he pushed a little paper packet into my hands, saying that this was a potion which would cure me when I became ill.

On my way home down the mountain I opened the packet. All there was inside was a handful of dry autumn leaves. That made me laugh, and then I felt suddenly very happy. I had my decision, and everything was light and clear.

In establishing a new life outside her family, there was only one group of people whom Ayako knew to approach for help: her childhood friends from the Kōshū Girls' School – now living scattered throughout Japan, some working, others married with young families of their own. During her marooned years in Nojiri Ayako had begun an old-girls' newsletter, little by little gathering addresses and fragments of news from the dispersed remnants of the Japanese community of Kwangju. Now these addresses became her life-line to the world outside: she wrote to one to ask for a night's lodging on her way to Tokyo, to another for advice in finding accommodation and work once she arrived in the city. Meanwhile, her father ranted with helpless rage at her insane determination, while her husband quietly woke every dawn to spend the first hour of the day kneeling in front of the family's *butsudan*, reading aloud from the prayers of the House of Longevity.

The first person I wrote to in Tokyo was Atsumi-san. She was the girl from my class who had gone to medical school during the war, but after that she had changed to doing some other university course, and as far as I remember at that time she had just graduated. I wrote to her and explained my situation, and asked whether she would help me to find a place to live in Tokyo.

But when she wrote back, she said that I was completely wrong to think of leaving my family. She said that if I came to Tokyo I would be putting my feet on a slippery slope and as likely as not I would end up polluting the Tokyo water supply. These last words were a reference to the writer Dazai's suicide.[4] You see, ever since Dazai had killed himself by jumping into the Tamagawa reservoir, it had become almost a fashion for people to commit suicide in that way. And that was what Atsumi-san thought would become of me if I left home and went to Tokyo alone.

Well, after that I wrote to another girl for help. She was a girl who had been in a different class at my school, and I hardly knew her at all. I didn't tell her anything about my circumstances. I simply said that I was moving to Tokyo from the country, and asked if she would advise me how to find accommodation, and she wrote back and said that she would.

One day, very early in the spring of 1954, Ayako brought a packet of sweets from the family shop and gave it to her son Yūji, who was now just able to walk by himself. Then she wrapped him up warmly and sent him next-door to share his unexpected treat with the neighbour's children. As soon as he had gone, she took her suitcase and walked to the bus stop. Her husband followed her, but only to say 'Goodbye. Have a safe journey.'

With an old umbrella strapped to her bulging black bag, she seemed unmistakably an *O-nobori-san* ('Going-up-person') – a country woman going up to the city to seek her fortune.

It's strange, but in spite of the dreams I had had since the war about the Imperial Palace, I wasn't particularly interested in seeing the real thing. Once I started work in Tokyo I must have passed the Palace moat quite often on the bus, but it didn't make any particular impression on me. It was only much later, when my family came to Tokyo, that I actually went there for sightseeing.

The first thing I did after finding a place to live in Tokyo was to look for Musashino Art College. I didn't know my way around at all, so I stopped a passer-by in the street and asked him the way. To begin with he looked puzzled, but after a while he said: 'Oh, you want the College do you?' and he gave me some directions. Well, when I got there I was quite surprised to find a very large and grand building with students hurrying about in all directions. I walked around for a while – and then I realized my mistake: the

232

place I had come to was not an art college at all, but Tokyo Women's University.

It took me a very long time to find the real Musashino Art College, and when I did I had a different kind of surprise. It was such a small and poor and decayed-looking building, standing in the middle of fields on the outskirts of town. Later I found that people nicknamed it 'the Ragged Art School'.

I went into the office and enquired about becoming a full-time student, but from what they told me I understood that I could not hope to pay the fees and support myself with the savings which I had brought from Nojiri. First it would be necessary to take a job and save more money.

'Next year', I thought, 'I will go to art school. . . .'

The job which Ayako found was with Yasuda Life Insurance, one of the largest Japanese insurance companies and an offshoot of the great pre-war Yasuda *Zaibatsu*. But Ayako's position was at the very bottom of the Yasuda employment pyramid, far removed from the ranks of the lifetime company employees – the regular office clerks and managers, with their substantial salaries, bonuses, and fringe benefits. Ayako was employed as a door-to-door insurance sales-woman. As such, her income was derived mainly from her tiny percentage share of each new contribution that she managed to collect. After a couple of days' training the saleswomen (they were all women) were sent out in groups to work through an area of town, street by street. They were accompanied by a male supervisor, who carried the company flag and shepherded them from one street corner to the next. His task was to ensure that they did not succumb to despair at the hopelessness of the job, and run away.

With the help of her contact from Kōshū Girls' School, Ayako had found a small four-and-a-half mat room in a suburban house which was occupied also by the landlord's family and another lodger. Her room had no cooking facilities and, like many less well-to-do city-dwellers, she went to bathe in the steamy heat of the local communal bath-house. But her earnings from the Yasuda Insurance Company did not even stretch far enough to cover the modest rent, her ten-yen train fare to the city centre and the thirty-five yen bowls of noodle soup which she bought from a stall in front of the station. Within a few months the life's savings which she had hoped to invest in an art diploma had dwindled almost to nothing.

233

The other lodger in the house where I lived was a young student. He had the bedroom next to mine, and the two rooms were only separated by a thin sliding screen. At first this made me very nervous and at night I was afraid to take my clothes off when I went to bed. However, the landlord assured me that he had nailed the screen tightly shut, so there was no fear of the student wandering into my room.

But later that spring I woke up suddenly in the middle of the night. It was quite dark and the student was kneeling beside my bed, whispering my name. Then he began to make suggestions, saying: 'Shall we do this and that' . . . you can imagine what sort of things he said. I sat up in bed and began to scold him very firmly, and told him to go back to his own room at once. And, in fact, he went.

He was only a young man, and his intentions were not very bad. Later, because he knew that I wanted to be an artist, he asked me to paint a portrait of his mother. He brought me a photograph of her, and asked me to copy from it. But the photo was so tiny and faded that I could hardly make out the face at all.

At about this time I went to visit a friend from school who was living in the Shinkuku district. While we were chatting I mentioned the student and his photograph, and said that I didn't know what to do, because the photograph was so small that I could not possibly paint a portrait from it. But my friend had an idea. She said: 'Go to the front of Isetan Department Store in the evening. There are always street artists hanging around there. One of them will draw a portrait for you.'

So that evening I went to look for Isetan Department Store. Although it is such a big building, it was not easy to find it that first time. I didn't know my way around Shinjuku in those days. In some places there were still patches of overgrown wasteland left from the wartime bombing. In other places there were streets being dug up, and new buildings under construction. At last I reached Isetan, and, sure enough, on the pavement in front of the shop I found a rather large, tall man with a beret pulled down on one side of his head, drawing portraits at one hundred yen a time.

I showed him the student's photograph but he, too, said that it was far too small to copy. However, he said, since I had come all that way, why didn't I let him draw my portrait instead? So I gave him one hundred yen, and he drew a picture of me. While he sketched, he asked me questions – where did I come from; what was I doing in Tokyo? When I told him that I wanted to be an artist, he said: 'That's easy. If you want to draw pictures, just come and join us any evening'. As simple as that. So I did.

After dark Mr Enomoto, the man with the beret, was the king of the few square yards of pavement in front of the closed and shuttered department store. A survivor of the wartime imperial navy, and a former male model for art-school life-drawing classes, he had a reputation formidable enough to keep his territory relatively free from the depredations of the gangs which controlled most of the Shinjuku night life. Apart from Ayako, four other pavement artists worked under the protection and control of Mr Enomoto: a middle-aged pair who were addressed by all as Auntie and Uncle, a man named Mr Koda, and another who (because of his foppish attire) was generally known as 'The Bow-Tie'.

Soon after the shops had closed, they would set up their equipment along the edge of the street. Each artist displayed a couple of carefully drawn samples copied from magazine illustrations of famous filmstars – Gérard Philipe, Humphrey Bogart, Ava Gardner. They worked until one or two in the morning, most of their trade coming in the late hours from the patrons who staggered, laughing and open-handed, out of the bars and brothels and mahjong parlours of the neighbouring red-light districts. Sometimes they attracted the custom of passing GIs, pointing to the pastel glamour of their sample portraits and calling out: 'Hey Mister, one hundred yen'.

All through the autumn and winter of 1954, and through most of 1955, Ayako spent her evenings drawing portraits in the street and her days sitting in the public library, keeping warm and reading the Japanese translation of Proust's *A la Recherche du Temps Perdu*.

Most evenings, she earned about five hundred yen. She had started, out of honesty, by admitting to her customers that she was only a beginner, and charging them half-price, but she soon discovered that this confession touched a soft spot in their sentiments, so that often she ended up earning twice as much as her fellow-artists. Soon after joining Mr Enomoto and his street artists, Ayako moved to Shinjuku to be nearer her work. She rented a room in a building filled with cheap bed-sitters whose other residents were all *yoru-no-onna* (ladies of the night): bar girls and hostesses and prostitutes.

The place where we worked was just near the Red Line and the Blue Line. [The Red Line and the Blue Line were the licensed and unlicensed prostitution areas.] I remember that I hadn't been there very long when, one day, a whole gang of workmen came along and began to put up corrugated iron fencing all along one of the streets. At first I couldn't imagine what was going on, but later it turned out that the Crown Prince was going to drive in some sort of procession down Yasukuni Street, and the iron fence was to prevent him from having to see the red-light areas as he drove through.

In Nojiri, two-and-a-half-year-old Yūji was being looked after by his grandmother. In 1955 Ayako received a letter to say that her mother had suffered a stroke. Now there was no one to take care of the child, and Tadahiko's younger sister had had to be summoned from town to act as a temporary nursemaid. Ayako debated in her mind whether to stay or to return home. Again she consulted a fortune-teller, this time one of the more secular variety, who earned a living beside her on the Shinjuku pavement, shaking a box of fortune-sticks for credulous passers-by. The fortune-teller (with a fortune-teller's instinct for reading the hopes of his subjects) told her that her mother would recover, and that she had no need to return home. So she stayed. Then came an urgent, pleading telegram, begging her to come at once, and she relented and agreed to return for just one month.

I hardly had any money at that time, so all I could buy to take back to my son were two toys: a toy gun and a toy sword. I went by train to Miyazaki and then by bus to Nojiri. When I said hello to my son and gave him the presents, he seemed frightened. He didn't seem to recognize me. After a day or two he became used to having me around, but when I left again at the end of my month's stay he didn't cry or show any emotion at all.

While she was in Nojiri, the go-between who had arranged her marriage (and who remained theoretically responsible for its success or failure) came to speak to Ayako and her husband. He asked them whether they had any intention of seeking reconciliation, and told them that, if they did not, they should terminate their relationship officially with a divorce.

A Japanese divorce by mutual consent is the simplest thing in the world to obtain: it requires no court proceedings, no questions of innocence or guilt. But the power of social pressure is far greater than the sanction of the law, and Japan continues to have one of the lowest divorce rates in the industrialized world. For Kuriya Tadahiko and Tsutsumi Ayako, however, the social constraints were not so strong: they were in any case newcomers to the village, and Ayako's family, as returned emigrants – *hikiagesha* – had always been looked on with that quiet but profound suspicion which village people reserve for outsiders.

Before Ayako returned to Tokyo, therefore, she and her husband went to the local government office, signed the papers stating that they agreed to the divorce, and sealed them with their name- seals. When that was accomplished, it was necessary to find a new foster-mother for little Yūji, for Ayako's own mother was still too frail to look after him. To leave the child with someone totally unconnected to the Hasebe–Tsutsumi family would have been considered most irregular. So Ayako now entrusted her son to a middle-aged woman whom her father had first met during their more prosperous years in Korea, and who had been his mistress ever since. After their return to Japan Mr Hasebe had set up his mistress in a house in Miyazaki, not far from his family's home. Here the child was to live for the next three years, while Ayako returned to Tokyo to resume her life as a pavement portrait artist.

After I went back from my visit to Nojiri, though, I started to grow tired of being a street artist. After all, I couldn't help feeling that it was some kind of cheat really. Most of the customers were drunk, and in the poor light of the street lamps they could hardly see what their hundred-yen portraits were like. But sometimes I used to worry about how they must feel when they woke up the next morning and examined my drawings in the light of day. There was a little mystery which had intrigued me for some time. Every now and then, while we were working, a smartly-dressed, rich-looking man used to call on the person we called The Bow-Tie. Every time he came he would bring a packet and an envelope full of money, and as soon as he had left, The Bow-Tie would always start to sigh and pull a long face. I was so curious about it that one day I said to The Bow-Tie: 'Who is that grand-looking gentleman who's always coming to visit you?' The Bow-Tie grimaced and said: 'Oh, that's my other boss. That man runs a doll-making company, and I do a bit of part-time work for him, painting faces for the dolls. It pays quite well, but it's horrible fiddly work. I'm thinking of giving it up soon.'

So I suggested to him: 'Why don't you pass your job on to me? I'd like to have a go at it.' He agreed quite willingly. He gave me the address of the company manager, and I went along to the office, pretending that I was a graduate from a famous art school. They let me have the job right away.

Painting smiling faces on dolls seemed at first to be an even greater mockery of her artistic ideals than sketching portraits of the flotsam of Shinjuku night life. The monotonous work strained the eyes and stretched the nerves. But it brought in money; and little by little Ayako began to realize that by working during the evenings and weekends at this travesty of her ambition she might in fact be able to support herself through a genuine art school education.

In the spring of 1957, with a loan from her old classmate Atsumi-san to help towards her first year's fees, she enrolled at last as a full-time student of oil-painting at Musashino Art College. There was nothing to spare for luxuries, but at least she had bought her share of the dreamed-of freedom of student life. She took a flat with a girlfriend; had a couple of innocent flirtations with her male classmates. When she could not afford a new pair of shoes, it did not matter: she went to college without shoes and earned the nickname of 'The Barefoot Contessa' (after the popular Hollywood movie of that name). It did not greatly worry her that she was ten years older than her fellow-students. All distinctions of age and background were submerged in the common struggle to pay the rent, to get to morning classes on time, and to refine one's emotions into shapes to fit the squares of canvas on the classroom easels.

In autumn, when the College held its annual arts festival, the students' paintings were hung in displays around the walls, and Ayako and her friends could mingle with the guests who came to view the exhibition, comparing each other's works with a mixture of envy, flattery and quiet pride. On that day the rule of the College was that all established orders should be overturned. The teachers became servants, and the professor of oil-painting donned a chef's hat and set up a stall in the classroom, where he served his students with bowls of boiled vegetables and cups of *sake*.

It was Ayako's final year at college when the students of Tokyo turned out in force to demonstrate against the Mutual Security Treaty with the United States, and Ayako went with them.

'I didn't go on the demonstrations for political reasons. I wasn't at all interested in politics. But what happened was this: during one of the biggest demonstrations a classmate of mine was arrested. As soon as we heard the news, the students were summoned to an Emergency General Meeting. Usually student meetings were about very frivolous subjects, and everyone would be in a light-hearted mood, but this meeting was quite different. The chairman of the students' council made a speech saying that we must demand our friend's release at once. Some people were crying. The atmosphere in the meeting became full of a very powerful feeling. It was just like during the war.

After that we all made banners and went off to protest outside the Diet buildings. Actually, looking back on it, I think all those demonstrations were a waste of time. Five million people turned out on the streets, and what did they achieve? Nothing.

But I must say that I did enjoy marching down the middle of the street, holding hands, blocking the traffic and being followed by all the television cameras. That was a nice sensation.

11

Iida Momo

From the big house in Fujisawa which Iida Toshifumi had bought during the war, and which his son has now inherited, it is only ten miles to Atsugi Air Base, where General Douglas MacArthur first set foot on Japanese soil.

Since we were near to Atsugi, where the most fanatical of the military's 'no surrender' faction had been based, for a day or two after the emperor's surrender broadcast we saw figures in uniform standing in the town centre handing out leaflets. The leaflets said that the broadcast was a lie, and that the Imperial Headquarters was being moved to the mountains to continue the fight. I saw people take the sheets of paper from the soldiers and read them, but there was never any reaction at all. Everyone was too tired and confused. They simply didn't want to know.

I suppose the Americans must have discovered from their intelligence sources that Atsugi was likely to be the centre of any resistance to the surrender. That must have been why MacArthur chose to land there: to demonstrate his power. In any case, being near to Atsugi meant that we were among the first people to see the Americans when they arrived.

The very first time I saw American soldiers was just a few days later, in the road in front of Fujisawa Station. Nowadays, of course, it's a proper town high street, but in those days it was just a bumpy, unpaved cart track. I had gone into Fujisawa by bicycle to do some shopping, and I'd bought a big bag full of mandarin oranges and was carrying them home on the handlebars of my bike. Well, at that time, you know, English had been banned from the curricula of most schools, and all the English words which used to be used in ordinary conversation had been replaced by Japanese expressions, and there were very few people around who remembered any English, but somehow I just couldn't wait to show off the little bits that I knew from my classes at Ichi-chū. So when I saw these two American soldiers walking down the road towards me, as I didn't know the English word for mandarin oranges, I called out to them: 'Hey you, small orange!' and I threw them an orange each out of my bag.

For a second they started, as if I'd tossed a hand grenade at them, but then they saw what it was and caught the oranges and smiled and waved at me. They looked really pleased.

There's another incident I remember, which happened about a couple of months later. At that time, all the trains in and out of Tokyo were unbelievably crowded – there were people who'd been evacuated to the country going back to find out what had happened to their houses; and there were city people going out to the country to try to buy food; and of course there were the black marketeers. They were mostly old people, often old ladies. Their sons or husbands would set up a stall somewhere in the city centre, and the old ladies would be sent out to the country to buy goods for the stall. The black marketeers were the real experts: they brought ropes with them, so that they could tie themselves on to the trains. Other people just used to hang out of the doors and windows by their arms. Often the trains were so crowded that people fell out and were killed.

Well, one day I was going into Tokyo and I happened to be lucky, because I actually managed to get inside the carriage instead of having to clutch on to the door. But once I got inside, I realized that something strange was happening. Most of the carriage was packed solid with people, but in one corner there was an empty space, surrounded by a sort of wall of staring people. I squeezed through towards that corner and I saw that in the middle of the space there was one, lone American GI. Normally, of course, the American soldiers travelled in their own special coaches at the front of the train, but this poor lad must have got on the wrong coach by accident. He was very young, just a teenager, and he looked like a nice guy. He was squatting in the middle of this circle of onlookers, and I think he must have been really frightened, because he kept glancing around with a strange, fixed smile on his face. All the other passengers were discussing him.

One kind-looking granny with a big black-market bundle on her back was saying:

'He must be going to Yokosuka [a large naval base]. But if he's going there, he needs to change at the next station. So you think he knows? How can we explain to him?'

So I elbowed my way right into the space where the American was squatting, and I asked him in English: 'Where are you going?'

That seemed to alarm him even more. He turned his fixed, nervous smile to me. 'Yokosuka', he said. So I said: 'For Yokosuka, you must change trains at the next station.'

Well, he got off at the right stop, but he was still looking around anxiously as if he wasn't quite sure that he hadn't been tricked in some way. But if he was surprised, the other people in the carriage were even more amazed, because I had spoken to him in English – I actually knew how to communicate with the Americans. All the rest of the way into Tokyo they gazed at me with a kind of silent awe.

The great experiment that the American occupation authorities were conducting in Japan involved not only the reform of laws and institutions, but also the attempt to transmit an entire new political culture to their defeated enemy.

The Japanese people [it was decreed] shall be afforded the opportunity and encouraged to become familiar with the history, institutions, culture and accomplishments of the United States and the other democracies. Association of personnel of the occupation forces with the Japanese population should be controlled only to the extent necessary to further the policies and objectives of the occupation.[1]

For those on the receiving end the experiment was sometimes bewildering, far from wholly successful, but nevertheless of profound and lasting significance. On 15 September 1945 an enterprising Japanese publisher produced a *Handbook of Japanese–American Conversation*. Within weeks, four million copies had been sold.

Not all the acts of GHQ, however, reflected its proclaimed 'desire for individual liberties and democratic processes'. On the day after US troops first entered Tokyo censorship of radio broadcasts was imposed, and a month later newspapers and magazines were also subjected to the scrutiny of the Supreme Command's official censor. Articles which criticized or embarrassed the occupation authorities were strictly controlled. But in other respects, the media were left free to express the explosion of new and diverse ideas, the clamour of previously unheard voices, which the surrender had suddenly released. There were voices which for years had been suppressed by the old order; voices of those looking for new ideals to replace the shattered certainties of the past; voices seeking to distil art or meaning from the unfathomable sufferings of the last three years. In 1946 alone more than sixty new Japanese magazines began publication. Many lasted only for a few issues, but even some of the more short-lived exerted their influence on the intellectual ferment of the times.

My first feeling after the war was simply: 'I've survived!'

There was an expression which was popular in the press at that time: 'A hundred million people in a state of trauma'. That was how Japan was said to be in those days, but I didn't feel that way at all. On the contrary, mentally and spiritually at least, I felt full of strength and energy. There were so many things that I wanted to do.

In practice, one of the first things I did was to get involved in the setting up of the magazine *Sedai* ['Generation']. The idea of this magazine was that it would be something quite new: a serious, national magazine, produced by students and for students. It was also intended to bridge the gap between literature and the social sciences. We thought that, by bringing together the literary currents which had been suppressed during the war and the concepts of social science – which at that time hardly existed at all in Japan – we could build the foundations for a new cultural movement.

Our generation of students, you see, mistrusted our elders, because we had seen during the war how hollow their values were. Of course there were some young people who had accepted these values. For them, the older generation provided a convenient scapegoat, which they could blame for their own mistakes. But at least as far as most of my friends were concerned, we had never accepted what the authorities had told us. Now, when everyone else seemed blank and confused, we felt that it was a time when we had to do something.

In autumn, normal teaching was resumed at Tokyo University. Momo re-enrolled, but from then until his graduation in 1947 he attended scarcely any classes. For the first year-and-a-half after the surrender all his energies were channelled into the newly-opened worlds of literature and politics.

One of the first acts of the American occupation authorities had been to release all political prisoners held under the repressive 'Peace Preservation' laws of the 1920s and 1930s. Out into the light of day came half-forgotten faces from history – men like Tokuda Kyūichi, one of the founders of the Japanese Communist Party, who had been imprisoned for the past eighteen years. Tokuda and a handful of other communist leaders were among the very few Japanese political figures who had rejected all compromise with the militarist ideology of the last decade. Now, on their release, they welcomed the American forces as liberators, and in accordance with the still-predominant communist ideal of a 'united anti-Fascist front', they lent their enthusiastic support to GHQ's democratic reforms. In October 1945 the Japanese Communist Party became the first political party to re-establish itself in post-war Japan. In the three months from December 1945 to the beginning of March 1946, its membership grew from 1800 to almost 7000.

One of my friends went along to the big rally which was held on 10 October to welcome the communist leaders who had been released from prison. But he came back feeling a bit disturbed at the whole thing. You see, most of the people who were there were old left-wingers who had recanted their views during the 1930s and 1940s. Some of them had maybe been imprisoned and tortured, and some no doubt had just recanted because it made life easier for them. And now suddenly they were confronted with these men who had stood firm in spite of torture and years of imprisonment. Some of the people in the crowd were weeping, and others even bowed down and prostrated themselves on the floor. It was as though Tokuda and the rest had become gods, and these people were confessing their sins and asking their absolution.

In January I went to a rally which was addressed by Nosaka Sanzō [later chairman of the Japanese Communist Party], who had just come back from sixteen years of exile in China. But I kept wanting to shout out: 'No, no, that's not how you should say it.' It wasn't just that he spoke in this strange, old-fashioned way, not at all like ordinary day-to-day language; he also actually spoke with a funny, sing-song intonation, like a foreigner speaking Japanese.

It couldn't be helped, of course. What could you expect after all those years of isolation? But right from the beginning I felt that there was a kind of dilemma about those leaders. In a way you had to respect anyone who could hold on to their beliefs for eighteen years in prison or sixteen years in exile. In a way you did feel they were like gods. And yet at the same time, in a sense, they were living ghosts. The very strength of their beliefs had arisen because they had refused to change with the times. And now they were trying to rebuild and lead the Communist Party of the 1920s. Only we weren't in the 1920s any more. Such a lot had happened while they had been in prison or in exile, but that they just couldn't understand.

In spite of his doubts about the quality of the Party leadership Momo was eager to involve himself in the resurgent politics of the left, and in 1946 he was given an opportunity to do so: a friend invited him to help in the setting up of a national trade-union movement, to be called the All-Japan Congress of Industrial Unions (*Zen-Nihon Sangyō-Betsu Rōdō Kumiai Kaigi*, or *Sanbetsu* for short). The Japanese union movement, after making some progress in the 1920s, had been first controlled and then extinguished by the authorities, from the start of the China War onwards. But the removal of restrictions on organized labour in the autumn of 1945 produced a sudden and spontaneous outburst of industrial action by workers all over the country.

As an American observer described it:

In the first year and a half after the war union membership leaped to nearly five million, more than ten times the prewar peak, and organized labour had become a force to be reckoned with in politics.

One factor in the extraordinary rebirth of the labour movement was a sense of liberation and hope for a better life in new Japan, evident in the dazed but happy faces of the marchers on Japan's first post-war May Day. A year earlier such a demonstration would have met with machine guns. Another factor was a surge of long-repressed and angry protests against injustice and hardship. There was also an element of conformity and social compulsion, unions were now correct and backed by the voice of authority . . . only the voice was now MacArthur's.[2]

By the end of 1946 there were over 17,000 unions, and in that year two national trade union federations were established: the Japanese Federation of Labour (*Sōdōmei*), which was closely associated with the Japanese Socialist Party, and the largely communist-dominated *Sanbetsu*. Momo's role in the organization of *Sanbetsu* was a modest one: he earned a few yen in weekly pocket money by working part-time in a room of the Congress's makeshift headquarters, helping to proof-read and print their newsletter, *Sanbetsu Information*. But the position gave him the opportunity to observe the comings and goings of everyone from stevedores and coal miners to street entertainers with their hand-carts and brightly coloured *kamishibai*, all seeking advice on the techniques of political activism.

The first *Sanbetsu* headquarters were in what we used to call the Electricity Union Building. Actually it had belonged to one of the electricity generating companies, but after the surrender it was taken over by the workers, and they allowed us to use a few rooms in it. The building was next to the bridge at Sukiyabashi [near the Ginza entertainment district of Tokyo] – there used to be a river with a bridge across it at Sukiyabashi in those days. Of course it's all been concreted over now. For some reason the Electricity Union Building had survived the bombing. It was about the only building still standing in that district.

There are little things I remember which bring back the atmosphere of the *Sanbetsu* headquarters in 1946. For example, one image that sticks in my mind is of a dumpy, round-faced middle-aged lady, suddenly wandering into the office and announcing that she was the delegate from the *kamishibai* Workers' Democratic League. I was the only person who wasn't busy at that moment, so I talked to her for a while, and gave her some of our pamphlets and so on. Then, after she'd gone, I noticed this rather battered paper umbrella lying on the office floor, and I thought: 'Oh dear, the *kamishibai* lady's left her umbrella behind. I bet she'll be in a state when she notices that she's lost it'.

At that time, of course, everything was so scarce and everyone was so poor, that losing something like an umbrella was a real disaster. Sure enough, about ten minutes later the *kamishibai* lady came rushing back into the office, out of breath and looking quite pale. But when she saw her umbrella she cheered up again, and she went out clutching it to herself like a lost child.

The loss of an umbrella in 1946, when many people were unable even to afford a bowl of rice, was really no laughing matter. A census in April of that year had found that some six million Japanese workers were unemployed. On 19 May 1946 250,000 people took part in a massive 'food demonstration' to demand improved distribution of rations.

The circumstances of the times fuelled the militancy of workers movements and left-wing political parties, and these in turn caused growing alarm both amongst the American occupation authorities and amongst sections of the Japanese public. In April 1946, in the first general election to be held under universal suffrage in Japan, left-wing candidates had achieved some successes; but a substantial majority had been gained by the right-wing Liberal and Progressive Parties. During the year there were also some counter-offensives by employers in firms where workers had taken over control of production. One popular technique (successfully used in the case of labour disputes at Yomiuri Newspapers and the Tōshiba Electrical Company) was the creation of relatively docile 'company unions' to divert support from the more militant nationally organized craft unions. In the spring of 1947 the confrontation between left and right reached a crisis point in the event – or, more accurately, the non-event – which became known in Japanese history as the 2.1 *Zenesto* (February 1st General Strike).

When the right to strike had been reintroduced towards the end of 1945, one group of workers who had expressly been denied this right were government employees. (This restriction remains in force to the present day, although it is frequently ignored.) At the beginning of 1947, Japanese government employees planned a strike which would at once support their claims for higher pay and assert their right to withdraw their labour. The plan received support from other unions and from *Sanbetsu* itself, and was gradually expanded to a more ambitious scheme for a General Strike, whose objectives would include the establishment of a national mimimum wage and the creation of a new popular government. It was undoubtedly these political objectives which caused so much concern to the government and the American authorities. The General Strike was due to begin on 1 February 1947. On 31 January, after unsuccessful attempts by GHQ to persuade union leaders to abandon their plan, MacArthur announced that the strike was prohibited. At that time, with hundreds of thousands of US troops stationed in Japan, and the psychological impact of defeat still fresh in everyone's mind, the unions did not feel able to defy GHQ's orders, and in an emotional broadcast speech the chairman of the strike committee, Ii Yashiro, announced: 'In the light of the strict orders of the Supreme Commander for the Allied Powers, we have no option but to abandon the strike . . . I can only recall the saying: "one step back, two steps forward". Workers and peasants, banzai! Let us remain united.'

The banning of the 1st February General Strike was to be seen in retrospect as one of the first signs of the 'reverse course' which would be pursued by the occupation authorities in the late 1940s and early 1950s. In the world outside the battle-lines of the Cold War were emerging. In Japan, GHQ began increasingly to turn its attention from the dismantling of the wartime power structures to the containment of the enemy on the Left. At the same time, the Japanese Communist Party itself adopted a more and more hostile approach to the policies of GHQ, and the unity of the left-wing labour movement began to crumble. After the collapse of the 1st February strike movement non-communist sections of *Sanbetsu* split off to form a separate union organization, and by 1950 the radical *Sanbetsu* had lost its influence and a new, much more moderate body, the General Council of Trade Unions (*Sōhyō*) assumed the centre stage of the Japanese union movement.

By then, however, Iida Momo was no longer actively involved. Just a week before the split of *Sanbetsu* he suffered an attack of tuberculosis, provoked in part by the hard work and poor diet of the past year-and-a-half. In one respect Momo was fortunate. At that time tuberculosis, whose only cure was months of rest and nourishing food, was commonly nicknamed 'the luxury disease'. In a period when all were hungry and most were overworked, tuberculosis patients were not always treated with the care and sympathy which was necessary for their cure. But Momo's father had suffered from tuberculosis himself in his early twenties. For months, while Momo lay, bored and helpless, in his bedroom at Fujisawa, Iida Toshifumi devoted himself to saving his son's life. By the autumn of 1947 Momo seemed well enough to take his final examinations at Tokyo University, and, in spite of his lack of study, he achieved outstanding results. There is a tradition that the best students from the Law Faculty of Tokyo University should enter careers in the Finance Ministry and the Bank of Japan. In 1947 Momo's contemporary, the novelist Mishima, entered the Finance Ministry, and Momo applied for, and was offered, a position in the Bank of Japan.

Of course I didn't really want to join the Bank of Japan. What I wanted to do was to go with the things I had been involved in before my graduation: literature and communism. But my father had been very unhappy about what I was doing. He kept saying: 'Your ideas are getting bad.' It seemed that almost everything I wanted to do annoyed my father. However, he was just willing to put up with it while I was a student on condition that I got a 'proper job' when I graduated.

My father's idea of a 'proper job' was working for some kind of government organization. I think he felt that way partly because of his experiences during the war. For years he had been bossed around by the military or by government officials, and he felt that they were the people who had the real power and influence. Well, now there were no military left, so what he wanted me to do was to become a government official, and he saw a good post in the Bank of Japan as answering that description. The thing that he least wanted me to do was to become a writer, because Father really despised and mistrusted all kinds of literati and journalists and so on. 'Gangsters in smart suits', that's what he used to call them.

It's funny, I remember a while ago reading an interview with a famous writer. The interviewer asked him what he attributed his achievements to, and he answered: 'My obedience to the wishes of my parents'. When I think about it, all my achievements seem to be based on my disobedience to the wishes of my parents. I sometimes think that in fact all of modern Japanese history and culture is like that: made from the struggle between parents and children. At any rate I know that I was a most un-filial son.

But at the same time I couldn't help realizing that I had been extremely lucky to get such a good education, particularly at that time, when relatively few people went to university. I knew that my father, who'd never even completed primary school himself, had sacrificed a lot to send me to Tokyo University. For the last twenty-two years, as they say, I'd been 'eating without repaying', and I felt that to go on insisting on doing what I wanted would be – well, it might be acceptable in places like America – but somehow I felt then that it was not what I ought to do. So I applied for a job in the Bank of Japan.

Momo was accepted by the Bank of Japan towards the end of 1947, but he did not complete as much as a single day's work there. Before starting work he was asked to collect his academic records from Tokyo University, and, on his way to the University registrar's office, he collapsed with a second and severe attack of tuberculosis.

When you have TB, before an attack of coughing comes on, you often have this strange feeling of tension. I remember that feeling very clearly. I was walking down the main street of Hongō towards the university with a friend, a girl student from Tokyo Women's University. Up until then I had been feeling fine. The worries and arguments about the job were settled, and physically I felt better than I had done for months. But then, as I was walking along the road, suddenly this terrible feeling came over me. I thought: 'This is it', and I began to cough blood.

My friend took me in to some place along the road, which looked like an inn. Then she must have rushed off and telephoned for help. At any rate, some time later my father arrived in a taxi. I was too ill to be taken back to Fujisawa, so instead he took me to his office building in Shiba. He had a bed made up for me on the top floor of the building, and I stayed there for more than a month.

If Momo had not been too ill to move, he might have looked out of the windows of the room where he lay, and seen the landscape of his childhood, now a wilderness of ashes from which the first new buildings were just beginning to arise. In the spring of 1948 he was taken back to Fujisawa, where he remained for the next year, waiting for a bed to become available in one of Tokyo's desperately overcrowded and understaffed hospitals.

All the time I was in bed in Fujisawa, I could do nothing at all. I couldn't read books or look at a newspaper or listen to the radio. The slightest thing might bring on an attack of coughing. For a year I just lay there and stared at the ceiling. Some people couldn't manage doing that. They got too restless and impatient, but if you did that, you died. I think somehow that what helped me was my experiences during the war. Having survived the war, I was determined not to die now.

My father was really alarmed, because all the time I kept coughing so much blood. I think that he believed I was dying, and he went to the very best experts on TB that he could find. But the experts said that we shouldn't be frightened. Apparently, it didn't matter how much blood you coughed. The important thing was to remain mentally calm. It was only when people began to panic at the sight of their own blood, and tried to prevent themselves from coughing, that there was a danger of choking and dying.

In 1949 I finally managed to get a place in Tokyo Dai-Ichi Hospital, where I was looked after by a Dr Mikami. I stayed there for about a year and a half. Of course, the doctor and the nurses at Dai-Ichi Hospital were marvellous, and I feel very grateful to them, but the thing which actually saved my life was streptomycin. It was just at that time that streptomycin began to be available in Japan. I had two courses of treatment with the drug, and after that I slowly began to get better.

As the treatment started to take effect, Momo gradually emerged from the cocoon of illness to resume his interest in the world outside. Already, in the hospital refectory, staff were going round with petitions saying: 'We refuse to become front-line nurses again!' For by now the Korean War had broken out, and Japan had become a crucial staging-post and source of supplies for the United Nations forces fighting on the Korean Peninsula. The Cold War in the wider world was reflected in a hardening of political divisions within Japan. In his Constitution Day speech in May 1950, MacArthur had denounced the Japanese Communist Party as the 'agents of aggression'. In the year that followed, thousands of communists and left-wing sympathizers were dismissed from 'sensitive' positions in government employment or in companies which had supply contracts with the American forces. The communists themselves were divided over the correct response to the situation. The Japanese Party had recently been subjected to heavy criticism from both Russia and China for their excessively conciliatory line towards the American occupation authorities. In February 1951, at the Fourth Party Congress in Tokyo, it was decided that existing policies should be reversed, and a strategy of 'armed struggle' against the existing order should be pursued. A number of leading communists fled to China, and the remainder set about re-creating the network of underground cells which had formed the basis of the Party's organization during the pre-war years of repression.

In the autumn of 1950, Momo was moved from Tokyo Dai-Ichi Hospital to a government-run sanatorium in a village on the east coast of Japan. Although he was now able to take an interest in politics, his health was shattered by the effects of tuberculosis, and he was to remain in the sanatorium for more than three years. There could be no question now of resuming his planned career in the Bank of Japan or, for the time being, of finding any other normal employment. He had nothing to lose, and nothing to prevent him from following his own artistic and political inclinations. Shortly after entering the Muromatsu Sanatorium he began work on his first full-length novel, and, at about the same time, he joined the underground Japanese Communist Party.

One of Momo's first discoveries at the Sanatorium was that almost half the women patients were divorced. For this there were two reasons: some had simply been discarded by their husbands when illness made them valueless as housekeepers or rearers of children; but many more had conducted divorces of convenience, because government welfare payments were not available to them as long as any member of their household was a wage-earner. To many thousands of sufferers, tuberculosis brought not only pain, enfeeblement and the likelihood of death – it was still the most common cause of death in Japan until 1951 – but also great financial hardship. Deprivation, as so often, created its own vicious circle. If you were poor and undernourished, you were more likely to contract the disease; if you contracted the disease, years of enforced unemployment made you poorer still; the further you sank into the abyss of poverty, the less likely you were to be able to afford the rest and nourishing diet which were essential elements in the process of recovery. For those who qualified for it, the government welfare payment was adequate as long as they were receiving free board and medical care in a hospital or sanatorium, but if they left before they were fully cured the impossibility of surviving on the meagre government allowance would soon drive them back to work, and so to almost certain relapse and probably death.

Since 1949 the Japanese government, on the advice of American financial experts, had been pursuing an economic reconstruction policy which involved tight control on government expenditure, and when a new scheme was announced for 'reviewing the criteria on which patients were admitted to and discharged from hospital', the reaction from Japanese tuberculosis sufferers was immediate. For as they understood it, this 'review' was in fact a plan to reduce the government's health spending by turning them out of their hospitals and sanatoria earlier than ever, sending them home to fend for themselves or become a burden to their relatives. And in the 1950s even the seriously ill knew how to use the techniques of post-war democracy to good effect.

Autonomous unions of patients were set up in every hospital and sanatorium, and a national-level organization, called the Japan Patients' League [*Nihon Kanja Dōmei*] was created. We were one of the most powerful union movements in the early fifties, not because we had any financial strength, but because our struggle was genuinely a matter of life or death to us. We began at Prefectural level. All the local patients who were able to move converged on the Prefectural Government offices. We would occupy the offices and stage sit-ins until the local officials signed statements agreeing not to revise their policies on discharging patients. It was immensely successful, because almost everywhere we had the support of public sympathy and the mass media behind us. In most Prefectures, the local government gave in quite quickly.

Events came to a head in the summer of 1954, by which time Momo had been elected chairman of the Central Committee of the Japan Patients' League. Anxious to press their advantage after these successes at local level, his Central Committee demanded a mass meeting of League members with the minister of welfare in Tokyo. (The mass meeting of union members with management, or of protestors with government officials, has been a common and effective instrument of political action in post-war Japan. The psychological advantage conferred by sheer weight of numbers more than makes up for the disadvantages of social deference or lack of negotiating skills amongst those with grievances to air.) In preparation for the final confrontation, big demonstrations were staged in Tokyo in July. From all over the country came groups of protesters: emaciated, prematurely aged, some unsteady on their feet, some with the unnatural animation of illness. Their gaunt ranks and painted banners filled the pavements outside government offices throughout the capital.

And then, within a matter of days, the wave of protest which had built up over the past year broke and receded. The summer of that year was an exceptionally hot one, and on 27 July one young woman protestor suffered sunstroke, collapsed and died. And instantly, the

253

public voices which had supported the cause turned against them. Their aims were good, it was argued, but their methods were too extreme. Abruptly deprived of sympathy and momentum, the movement collapsed, and Momo had no choice but to order a retreat.

Immediately after the collapse of the Japan Patients' League, he himself was discharged from the sanatorium. His father, who had been informed of the date of Momo's release, was waiting eagerly to welcome his son home after almost five years of absence. But just before Momo left Muramatsu Sanatorium, a message arrived from the Party. Like all Party directives of that time, it was written in code and on very thin paper, so that it could be swallowed in case of emergency. It gave details of the underground bureau to which Momo had been appointed. He was to report there directly upon his release. In Fujisawa Iida Toshifumi went on waiting, but his son had already vanished into a world which was beyond his reach or comprehension.

The way the Party organization worked was like this. Each Prefecture was divided into so many Areas. In Ibaragi Prefecture, where I worked, there were four Areas, and each had an Area Bureau consisting of usually, two or three Party cadres. I was assigned to one of the four Ibaragi Area Bureaux, and my Bureau had two other members, one of whom had been a Communist MP for a short while after the war. In practice, our main job was to go around the local villages, passing on Party directives to the various cells and generally organizing the farmers' movement. Our Bureau reported to the Ibaragi Prefectural Bureau, which reported to the Kantō Regional Bureau, which in turn kept in touch with the upper reaches of the Party hierarchy, all the way up to General Secretary Tokuda, who was in exile in China.

As party officials, we were theoretically supposed to receive money from Party funds. But actually no money ever came. In practice, you just had to find your own way of feeding yourself and your own place to sleep. In a way, it was like a beggar's life. If you didn't have the support of the people, you were dead.

When Momo began full-time work for the Party, it was not easy to be a professional revolutionary in rural Japan. Seven years ago, the situation in the countryside had been very different: then, more than

60 per cent of farmers were tenants, renting all or part of the land they worked. Most were extremely poor, and the disparity between their way of life and that of the large landlords was glaringly visible. Besides, land rents were so high that the tenant farmer's profits were pared to the point where he could no longer farm efficiently. In this situation, demands for radical land reform received widespread support. By 1947 the militant Japan Peasants' Union (*Nichinō*), in which the Communist Party had considerable influence, had more than a million members.

But the potential for the rural-based revolutionary movement in Japan was evident not only to the Communist Party, but also to MacArthur's GHQ. As they saw it, the unequal distribution of land and inefficiency of farming techniques had distorted Japan's economic development, contributed to the rise of nationalism and militarism, and was likely to undermine the political stability of post-war Japan. Soon after the beginning of the occupation, GHQ ordered the Japanese government to 'break the economic bondage which has enslaved Japanese farmers through centuries of feudal oppression'. In December 1945 the government produced its own proposals for land reform, but these were dismissed by GHQ as being too cautious and too favourable to the landowners. So the following year a new, more radical, Second Land Reform was introduced. The essential provisions of this reform were that absentee landlords lost all their land; landlords living in the community could keep approximately two-and-a-half acres, or, if they were farming the land themselves, up to ten acres. The remaining land was redistributed to tenants, who bought it at a nominal price. The reform applied only to farmland: the mountain forests which cover two-thirds of the country remained in the hands of private landlords, and this was of some importance, for the forests were a source not only of firewood but also of all kinds of delicacies – mountain potatoes and edible bracken, pine-tree mushrooms and fiery green horse-radishes – which could be sold at enormous prices to the epicures of the city.

But still the Land Reform Act of 1946, as it was gradually put into force over the next four years, brought an unquestionable improvement to the prosperity and status of Japanese peasant-farmers. By 1950 more than 70 per cent of farmers owned all their land (while many more owned some land but continued to rent an additional field or two), and it is no great exaggeration to claim, as one authority does, that the Second Land Reform was of all the post-war reforms, the one which brought about the greatest change in Japan's economy and society, and moreover, the most successful of all the land reform measures carried out in a large number of countries in the period immediately after the second World War.[3]

For a while, many small farmers retained an affectionate feeling of gratitude towards the radicals of the Communist Party or the Japan Peasants' Union, whom they remembered as lobbying hard for land reform, and as helping in some areas to organize tenants' representation on the land committees which ensured that the reforms were fully implemented. But with time, inevitably, the political interest aroused by the issue of land reform faded, and the farmers' concerns returned to the price of rice, the supply of water to their flooded fields, the improvement of the main road to their village – subjects on which Marxism–Leninism seemed to have little to say.

Somewhere in most Japanese villages you may find by the roadside a small, comfortable stone figure with a benign and weather-worn face. Often in front of him will be a cup of water, a few sticks of incense or a bunch of crumpled flowers. The figure is a *Jizō*, a representation of a friendly spirit to whom people will offer thanks for averted disasters or unexpected blessings.

I heard that, a few years earlier in Ibaragi, when the land reform was at its height, the villagers had even said that they would make *Jizō* statues of the Party organizers, so that they could show their gratitude to them. But by the time I started working there, we were gods who had fallen from heaven. They would offer us a cup of tea, because still they had a vague feeling that after all, they owed us something, but that was all. By then their interests were in drainage and water rights, and they knew that they could get more out of local conservative politicians from the Liberal Party or the Democratic Party, who had direct access to people in power.

Later on it got worse still. Fewer and fewer farmers would even offer us tea. They were becoming more prosperous, you see, but there we were, still going around in shabby clothes. I remember that at that time I was still wearing the cast-off army uniform that I had been given in the sanatorium. I would walk down the main street of some respectable country town, and I didn't realize until afterwards that I was starting to look odd, because everyone else was now so much more smartly dressed. I suppose it wasn't really surprising that the farmers began to regard us as if we were wandering beggar-priests, and didn't want to let us in the house.

In the Communist Party, opinion was divided on the best method of dealing with the challenge presented by the Land Reform. The official line was that, as long as the mountain forests remained in the lands of big landlords, the process of land reform was incomplete and Japanese feudalism remained intact. Occupy the forests, ran the theory of the Party's chief agricultural expert Itō Ritsu, and the Japanese power structure will begin to crumble about your ears. The principal instrument for the execution of this policy were the Mountain Village Guerrillas (*Sanson Kōsakutai*), armed brigades recruited mainly from the ranks of the young and idealistic urban intellectuals, many of them students who had dropped out of courses in politics or economics, turning their text-book knowledge of the injustices of the system into a total commitment to the life of a revolutionary outlaw. In some areas, they occupied forests and forced landowners to extend the local farmers' rights to gather firewood, hunt game and collect the wild fruits of the mountain. Elsewhere, in places where forest landlords were reaping the first profits of Japan's economic recovery – selling land to the government for roads, reservoirs, railway tunnels – they engaged in sporadic bloody battles with construction workers. But the Mountain Village Guerrillas were poorly armed and their actions were uncoordinated: in the end, their scant numbers were simply swallowed up by the vastness of the Japanese forests into which they vanished in pursuit of an elusive and ultimately illusory feudal enemy.

In Ibaragi, which lies in the flat Kantō plain, there was in any case little prospect of stirring up excitement about the ownership of mountain forests. So Momo and his colleagues looked for other ways to reawaken the radical sentiment of the local farmers.

As far as we were concerned, it was all very well for city academics like Itō Ritsu to sit there in Tokyo telling us to attack the landlords, but you only had to put a foot into an Ibaragi village to realize that in fact there simply were no landlords any more. So one of the local cadres, Yamaguchi Takahide, who was an ex-Communist MP, had developed his own agricultural theory, which was that the principal enemy was no longer the landlords but monopoly capital, and that if you wanted to organize the farmers, who were now in effect all small-scale private producers,

the target which you should concentrate on were the big monopolistic enterprises.

For example, in Ibaragi many of the farmers grew sweet
potatoes, and sold a large share of their crop to big food
companies to be turned into starch or sugar. The companies
which bought the potatoes were so large and powerful that they
could virtually set their own prices. So one of our aims was to
encourage farmers to work co-operatively to raise the price of
their crops. In some places local starch factories were surrounded, and if the company refused to pay the price demanded by
the farmers, they would seize the sweet potatoes from the trucks
going into the factory, and take them away and bury them in the
ground.

Another thing that we tried to do was to organize the second
and third sons of farming families.

You see, in spite of the reforms of family law and the
inheritance system, most second and third sons didn't in practice
inherit any land because the farms were two small to be subdivided. Often, the younger sons would help on the farm during
the busy times of the year, and in the slack times would go off to
the towns to work as seasonal labourers. They worked mostly in
heavy industry. As industrial workers, they were right at the
bottom of the heap: they were poorly paid and non-unionized,
and usually the companies didn't bother to insure them so they
could get no compensation for industrial accidents.

We had some success in winning support from the younger
sons, but with the rest of the farming community in the end I
have to say we failed. In that sense you can say GHQ's policy
worked as they intended it to. The problem from our point of
view was that even when the younger sons of farm families did
give us their support, they had no money and no power in the
household. They couldn't invite us in for meals or ask us to stay
the night, because the head of the household generally didn't
want anything to do with Communist Party members any more.

I have vivid memories of one village where we ended up
having to hold cell meetings in the graveyard, standing among
the hummocks of graves on freezing dark winter's nights, trying
to hold serious political discussions while all the time you had to
stamp your feet and slap your sides to stop yourself from
catching chilblains.

By 1954 the strategy of armed struggle, which had been adopted at the height of the Korean War, had become so out of joint with political reality in Japan that it created situations which hovered between the tragic and the absurd.

At that time the Party had a military wing and a political wing, which had quite separate chains of command. In my area of Ibaragi there were two underground military bases, but since I belonged to the political wing I didn't have much to do with them. However, I did visit each of them once to pass on various Party directives.

Now, when I talk about military bases you mustn't imagine that I'm talking about a regiment of soldiers, or even a small unit. In fact, our two military bases each consisted of a solitary individual, one stationed in Fukawa Town, and one in Sakura Village.

When I went to visit the 'military base' in Fukawa Town, the first thing I noticed was a plain-clothes detective waiting for me on the platform as I got off the train. I recognized him at once – he was wearing the unmistakable uniform of plain-clothes detectives – and sure enough, as I started to walk down the road, I could see that he was trailing along behind me. I was quite often followed by the police in those days, but they never arrested me. I think that was part of a deliberate policy of leaving the Party in a sort of shadowy world where it was not quite illegal and not quite legal, not really alive and not really dead.

But it certainly made it obvious that, whatever we might choose to pretend, our underground organization was in fact pretty transparent.

Anyway, I started to walk down the road from the station to the house where our military commando lived. It was evening and all of a sudden I saw, coming down the road towards me, a figure which looked for all the world like something out of some old fairy story. It was a little thin young man with a typical young peasant's face, and he was bent almost double under a huge pile of brushwood which rose from his back as high as a two-storey house. I watched him come nearer, and then I realized that this was our 'military base'.

It turned out that the only family in the neighbourhood which had been willing to harbour someone from the military wing of the Communist Party was a *burakumin* family who were one of the

259

poorest households in the whole village. Because they were so poor, although they offered this young man a bed, they couldn't afford to feed him free of charge as well. So from morning to night he had to work as a kind of servant to the family, collecting their firewood and so forth. And all they could give him in return was the same food that the family ate: nothing but noodles with water and soy sauce on them. Of course there were no newspapers and no radio.

I was rather taken aback to discover that this military cadre, who was supposed to be at the forefront of political agitation in the area, had not even heard that there had been an armistice in Korea.

Well, I passed on the Party directives to him, and he just nodded in vague, weary sort of way. I couldn't help remembering Mao's theory that a revolutionary should be able to live amongst the people like a fish in water. It seemed to me that this poor boy had gone one stage further: he'd become part of the water itself.

A bit later I went to visit the other 'military base' at Sakura Village. He was not an outsider, like the young man at Fukawa, but a nice, middle-aged farmer who had lived in the village all his life, except for a spell of military service in China.

But when I went to see him I had an odd, uneasy kind of feeling, because as soon as I had explained the Party's message to him, he started smiling in a funny, furtive way and whispering:

'Oh yes, it's quite all right. Everything's going to be quite safe here. You see, I've got a tank out there. I've buried it in the fields and when the time comes I'm going to bring out my tank and drive it through the streets.'

Well, as I say, the military and political wings had quite separate structures, and I didn't really know what weapons were available, but it did seem to me most improbable that this middle-aged farmer had a tank buried in his fields. However, I thought it was none of my business, so I didn't say anything about it.

The next news I heard of that farmer was that he had committed suicide. Apparently, he had seen someone who was a stranger to the village walking near his house, and he'd started crying: 'This is the end. They've come to get me.' And he went right home and killed himself.

I could see it all then: there was this farmer, for years on end fighting an invisible mirage war all on his own in the village, and gradually his nerves must have become overstretched. I suppose it started with him comforting himself with stories about imaginary tanks, and ended up at the point where the sight of a stranger was enough to push him over the brink.

For the Party, the apathy and disarray of the military wing might not have been so serious if the policy of underground struggle, coming just at the time when most Japanese people were experiencing the first real improvement in their living standards for many years, had not robbed the Communists of much of their popular support. In the general election of 1949 the Party had obtained almost 10 per cent of the popular vote: in the 1952 election, when the Party, though operating underground, continued to put up candidates, they did not win a single seat, and in the election of February 1955 they managed to regain just two. At the same time the Japanese Socialist Party, whose share of the vote in 1949 had been only slightly higher than that of the Communists, won 156 seats in the 1955 election, while the two conservative parties continued to consolidate their dominance of Japanese politics, a dominance which was soon to be greatly increased when they united to form a single Liberal Democratic Party (LDP), which has been in power ever since.

On 29 July 1955, the Japanese Communist Party held its Sixth Party Congress in Tokyo. At this Congress it was decided that

> the tendencies of ultra-left adventurism and sectarianism which appeared during the period of dissension should be officially repudiated, and 'the whole Party should be armed with the theories of Marxism–Leninism'.[4]

What this meant in practice was another abrupt switch of direction, this time from the strategies of underground organization and armed struggle to a policy of winning public support through the establishment of an open, above-ground party operating within the existing political system. *'Aisareru Kyōsantō'* – 'A lovable Communist Party' – was the image into which the movement was to form itself.

For some, particularly members of the military wing of the Party or the Mountain Village Guerrillas, the pronouncement came as a shattering blow. Those of them (and there were a substantial number) who had committed illegal acts during the years of underground struggle now found themselves at once outlaws from the rest of society and condemned by their own Party for 'ultra-left adventurism'. But for Momo the change of direction was both welcome and expected.

To my mind, the whole problem of Communist Party policy in the early 1950s was that it started from a misunderstanding about the meaning of the Korean War for Japan. What the Party leaders thought was that the Korean War was a crucial battle with American imperialism, which might extend to engulf Japan itself. They saw it as a time of revolution and counter-revolution. But what they totally failed to see was that the Korean War was economically beneficial to Japan, and that it had started Japan on a track which was to lead to the period of high economic growth. That misunderstanding made a gap between Party policy and reality which grew and grew until it came to a head at the Sixth Party Conference.

For me, the decision of that Conference was something inevitable, just like the end of the Pacific War. It was simply a matter of waiting until the Party leaders in exile in Peking came to grips with what was actually going on back home.

Ten days after the Japanese Communist Party's Sixth Party Congress, on 8 August 1955, one of the first Japanese versions of a wonderful new gadget was put on sale by a tiny company called Tokyo Communications Industry: it was a radio so small and light that you could actually carry it around in one hand, and it was known by an imported English word, 'transistor'. Soon after, the company replaced its rather cumbersome title with a name which, it was hoped, would give the new product a more jazzy, Western appeal. They renamed the firm 'Sony'.

After the Sixth Party Congress, Momo was promoted to become chairman of Ibaragi Prefecture's Western Division Bureau. But neither the elevation of status nor the reversal of Party policy brought any great change to his everyday life.

Even after the Sixth Party Congress, I still didn't actually get paid any money. We all had our own ways of supporting ourselves. Some of the time I lived off the donations of Party supporters;

sometimes I used other ways of raising funds which were, well, a bit less respectable.

One of my sources of money was the conservative mayor of Shimodate, which was the place where I was living at that time. I would go along to the mayor's office and start to make a nuisance of myself, and if I kept it up long enough, he was sure to call me in and give me 'money for the taxi fare home' – except that what he gave me was usually enough for quite a few taxi fares.

Mayor Kikuchi – he became a Liberal Democratic Party MP later on, but he's dead now – he seemed to me to typify a certain kind of post-war conservative politician. Right after the war he'd got together a group of young people who'd lost practically everything, and he put them to work in the black market. Then, after the economy picked up, he wanted to become respectable, so he turned his black-market operation into a power-base, and went into politics.

The funny thing was that after a while Mayor Kikuchi and I grew quite fond of each other. He even once suggested that he should arrange for me to marry his daughter. You see, he was, you might say, an old outlaw who had made good, and I think he saw me as perhaps a new sort of outlaw. Maybe he even suspected that the future might lie with people like me, and he wanted to hedge his bets just in case.

Around the outskirts of Shimodate lay some of the last visible relics of the Korean War boom: the empty shells of factories which had flourished on war procurement orders, but had failed to adapt to the slower, steadier economic growth of the mid-1950s. Now their deserted buildings stood, crumbling and sprouting weeds, awaiting the fat years of the sixties which would fill them with new tenants, or level them to make way for bigger workshops and taller smokestacks. In the midst of this landscape stood a line of factory workers' houses, many of them still occupied by men who had refused to leave when their company went bankrupt and they were made redundant. Here Momo found a temporary home.

One fact that I quite pride myself on is that, since the end of the Pacific War, I have never once paid rent. I got by most of the time by squatting: that's something which is quite common in England, isn't it? But I don't think there can be many Japanese people who are quite as expert at it as I became in those years.

While I was living in Shimodate, most of the workers in the other houses found temporary employment digging pebbles out of the river. It worked like this:

One day, out of the blue, a construction company appeared and set up camp on the bank of the river. They brought their own itinerant labourers, who lived in the camp, but they also employed quite a few local people while they were there. It's a terrible thing if you think about it: here was some little businessman who'd set up his company, and somehow managed to pull a few strings and get permission from the local government to dig pebbles out of the river. He probably hadn't even had to pay a thing for that permission. So he came along with his workers, dug out all the river bed, and then moved on to the next place, leaving the river completely stripped of its fish and plant life, looking like a muddy ditch.

The workers who were employed to dig up the pebbles wore rubber suits and worked standing chest-deep in water, even in the middle of winter. Many of them got terrible rheumatism later as a result of that work.

Then one day, just like that, I walked past the construction company's camp and saw everyone packing up.

'What's going on?' I asked.

'Oh, we've finished with this river', they said, 'Now we're off to Hokkaido.'

At the time, the whole thing puzzled me. I thought: 'Why are they going round the country digging up all these pebbles?' But looking back on it, I can see how it all fits in. Of course that was the beginning of high economic growth, and all the piles of pebbles out of the bed of the river were on their way to build the foundations of the economic miracle.

Soon Momo, too, was moving on, up the ladder of the Party organization, to the city of Mito, where he became head of Ibaragi Prefectural Bureau. But now already certain currents were emerging which were to lead both to the reshaping of the Japanese political left and to his personal fall from grace. One of the currents flowed from the Sixth Party Conference, which had disillusioned many militant left-wing Party members. Another, more significant, current had its origin in the criticism of Stalin initiated by Khrushchev in the following year of 1956. Although the Japanese Communist leadership had accepted and concurred with Khrushchev's statements, many Party members and sympathizers believed that the issue had been dealt with in a superficial and perfunctory way and that the problems posed by Stalinism and its aftermath were far more profound and lasting than had been officially admitted.

From this time I began to feel that there were two principal problems to be faced. The first was to understand how Japan's rapid economic growth fitted into the context of modern capitalism, and the second was to understand in practice what would happen to socialism after de-Stalinization. In order to deal with these two problems I felt that we had to come to terms with certain facts: namely, that it was not possible to understand the rapid growth which was taking place in Japan by using the old Stalinist type of Marxism, and also that the capitalist system which we were analysing was one that had been reorganized in the framework of American neo-imperialism.

Of course now all this is taken for granted, but at the time it was very new, and we had to develop our own way of analysis from scratch by ourselves.

It was the search for solutions to these problems which towards the end of the 1950s triggered a chain reaction of fissions within Japanese Marxism, spawning the swarms of factions, tendencies and alliances which later acquired the generic name of the New Left. To detail the creation and division of each of these groups would in itself fill volumes, and only the briefest sketch of their genealogy can be given here.

Both the main breeding-ground and the main battle-ground of the new ideologies was provided by the university campuses – above all by the powerful students' movement *Zengakuren*, which at its inception in 1948, had been dominated by the Communist Party, but which by 1960 was largely controlled by dissident Marxism elements. *Zengakuren* was the training school for the leaders of the new revolutionary splinter groups – *Bundo* (the League of Communists), *Kakukyōdō* (the Revolutionary League of Communists) and others – which combined their condemnation of capitalism with a fierce rejection of bureaucratic fossilization of the Japanese Communist Party. And from these groups came yet others: the closely similar but violently antagonistic *Chūkaku* (Core Faction) and *Kakumaru* (Revolutionary Marxist League); and later the Japanese Red Army, which was to seize the international headlines in the 1970s, and its *alter ego* the United Red Army, which was to be the subject of one of the longest-lasting murder trials in Japanese history. Some of these groups were minuscule and short-lived; a few allowed their momentum to run dry in the arid wastes of undirected violence. But, taken as a whole, they were to have a substantial influence on the political and intellectual life of Japan over the next two decades.

There are times in history when processes which have been at work under the surface suddenly erupt, and directions which have been determined by years of slow change are for a moment clearly illuminated. In Japan one of those times was the year 1960. In the spring of that year, perhaps the most crucial of post-war industrial disputes began in the coal mines of Kyushu. As part of its high-growth strategy, the government was now encouraging a switch from home-produced coal to cheaper and more efficient imported oil as the main source of the nation's energy supplies. At the end of 1959 one of the largest Japanese coal mines announced plans for 1200 redundancies, provoking a prolonged and bitter strike which involved many vicious confrontations between pro- and anti-company workers, and between strikers, police and hired *yakuza*, brought in by the company to quell resistance.

But by early summer an even greater political crisis was taking shape: the renewal of the Security Treaty with the United States (the 'Ampo Treaty', as it was known in its Japanese abbreviation).

From the beginning, there had been many people in Japan who disliked the Ampo Treaty. The dislike operated on several levels. On the political level, the Treaty was criticized for enmeshing Japan in the enmities and strategies of the Cold War, and for providing a cover for Japan's own rearmament. On a more fundamental and emotional level, hostility to the Treaty was also bound up with the issue of American bases in Japan. In the first phases of the occupation, the overwhelming feeling had been one of awe at the superiority of the conqueror, and of relief that the terms of the conquest were so much less terrible than expected. But once the occupation was over and economic recovery had begun, the continued presence of large numbers of US servicemen in Japan began to be a source of some humiliation and resentment. If the American GI's had turned out to be far from the wartime caricature of 'American and British Devils', they also sometimes failed to be the walking advertisements for democracy envisaged by GHQ. There were some reports of rape and other serious crimes by soldiers from the bases and, since those involved could not be tried under Japanese law, there was a feeling, too, that the culprits were rarely adequately punished. Other smaller things also rankled. In the mid- 1950s, for no obvious reason, it became a fashionable pastime among US servicemen on leave in Tokyo to seize suitably small Japanese passers-by and throw them into the Imperial Palace moat. There was little that the victims could do to resist or retaliate. On a more serious plane there was the question of Okinawa, which had not been returned to Japan in 1951, but remained under American administration and was later to be a major base for US bombing raids on Vietnam. The effect of all this was not to produce a reversion towards the simple anti-Americanism so prevalent in the Japanese media in the late 1930s, but rather to give a further twist to what was now an intense and convoluted relationship.

Under the 1951 Treaty Japan had been largely a passive party to the relationship, merely entrusting the task of its defence to the United States, but the revised Treaty included in its title the word 'Mutual'. Although it did not commit Japan to assist America in case of war, it spoke in broad and vague terms of consultation whenever 'international peace and security in the Far East is threatened', and this, together with that troubling word 'Mutual', increased the fear that the Treaty might bring new risks of undesirable military involvement in an area where Cold War tensions were at their greatest. But opposition to the 1960 Treaty was particularly heightened by Prime Minister Kishi's determination to push ratification through the Diet at all costs. Kishi Nobusuke was in any case a rather unpopular politician, both because of his abrasive manner and because of rumours about his suspect activities in Manchuria during the war. His handling of the Security Treaty crisis both antagonized many who were not normally on the left of the Japanese political spectrum and presented a critical test of the strength of Japan's post-war political system.

The crisis began on 19 May when the ruling Liberal Democratic Party, which had been prevented by the opposition from completing the debate on the ratification of the Treaty during the normal Diet session, tried to force an extension. The proposal to extend the Diet session caused uproar, and the day's proceedings ended with Socialist Diet members staging a mass sit-down outside the office of the House of Representatives Speaker Kiyose, in order physically to prevent him from returning to the House to open a new session. In response, Kiyose called in the police to remove the blockade of protesting Socialists. (Only once before in Japanese history had the police been allowed to enter the Diet chamber.) In the absence of the Socialist Diet members, a motion to extend the session was hastily passed. Immediately after midnight Kiyose announced the opening of the new session, and a few minutes later, with the opposition still absent, a vote was taken on the ratification of the Security Treaty. It was unanimously approved. Under the provisions of 1947 Constitution this meant that, even if the upper house of the Diet failed to vote on ratification, the Treaty would automatically come into force within thirty days.

Later that year a prominent Japanese academic wrote:

> May 19, 1960, along with December 8, 1941, will become an unforgettable date for the nation. It is well known that on December 8, 1941, the surprise attack against Pearl Harbor touched off the Pacific War which cost the lives of 1,200,000 of our countrymen, but May 19, 1960, was the day when the government, under Kishi Nobusuke, who had been involved in planning the surprise attack, delivered a surprise political attack against the nation and against democracy.[5]

This was not the end of the story. The opposition parties and most newspapers condemned the passing of the Treaty as undemocratic and unconstitutional. The wave of public discontent grew. On 28 May Kishi denounced his critics, claiming that he had 'the support of the silent majority'. A few days later a new anti-Treaty movement was formed, calling itself 'The Silent Majority Against the Security Treaty'. On 4 June an estimated five million people demonstrated against the Treaty in cities throughout Japan, while twenty thousand shops were closed, and a strike by railway workers brought all trains to a halt. On 15 June a second massive demonstration was staged, and four thousand students from the radical *Zengakuren* attempted to storm the Diet Building. This action led to a clash with police which left one thousand people injured, and one student – Kamba Michiko, the daughter of a university professor – dead. This was the point at which public feeling against the Treaty reached its most explosive.

At the time of the anti-Treaty demonstrations, I became chairman of the Ibaragi Prefecture Anti-Treaty People's Congress. This was made up of members from the Communist Party, the Socialist Party and the local trade-union movement. Our main task was to mobilize people and organize transport for demonstrators going to Tokyo. Most days we sent at least four coach-loads of people to Tokyo, and at the very peak of the demonstrations we were sending as many as fifteen coach-loads in one day.

I didn't really believe that this was the beginning of a revolution. It was not a revolutionary type of mobilization. But I did think that it was extremely important to show that even during a period of high economic growth there could be great struggles against the system on specific issues.

It was at this time that I began to be really critical of the Party leadership. Until I joined the Prefectural Bureau I suppose that I had still tended to look up to the Party leaders, but now that I was nearer to them in rank I had plenty of opportunities to go to the headquarters in Tokyo and see them in action, and, well, I couldn't help feeling that they were a pretty stupid lot.

What particularly struck me was the pathetic way they reacted when the girl student Kamba Michiko was killed in the demonstration outside the Diet. There was a story going around in the Party at the time that, later that day, Miyamoto Kenji [the Communist Party Secretary General] and some of his henchmen drove around the Diet building in their big limousine, and Miyamoto remarked: 'It's only one dead student. What's all the fuss about?'

I thought: 'How on earth can they be so insensitive? Don't they understand the terrific impact that the girl's death is having on public opinion?' and I felt that anyone who could make a remark like that clearly had not got the faintest idea of what it means to be a revolutionary.

In Ibaragi we had thousands of leaflets printed and distributed, saying 'Follow Kamba Michiko', and one of my friends had a huge placard put up on a local station, with big characters painted on it saying 'We deplore the death of Kamba Michiko'.

But the Party headquarters disapproved, because you see Kamba Michiko hadn't been a Party member. So a few days later this man from the headquarters turned up in our office. He didn't say that he'd been sent to question us: he just appeared, as if he'd dropped in for a visit. But we could soon tell from the drift of his conversation what he had come for.

In those days, of course, the Party was supposed to be strongly pro-China and pro-Mao Tse-Tung. So when this man from the headquarters started asking questions about our behaviour, I just said to him: 'I see from the papers that Chairman Mao has described Kamba Michiko as "a heroine of the Japanese people". What is the Party headquarters' opinion of that statement?'

That really confused him. He didn't answer the question, he just got up and left in a hurry.

But many of those who had themselves opposed the Treaty or disapproved of the conduct of the government in the earlier stages were becoming alarmed at the forces which the protest had released. This alarm was most clearly illustrated by the behaviour of the press. On 17 June the seven major national newspapers, all of whom had shown varying degrees of sympathy towards the protestors, issued a joint statement, published on every front page, which emphasized the need to defend democracy without violence, and called for restraint on all sides. By then it was becoming apparent that nothing short of a total overthrow of the government could prevent the Treaty from being ratified. On the night of 19 June thousands of demonstrators gathered round the empty Diet building, but this time no attempt was made to break in. The protestors sat on the pavements and in the roadways in a symbolic all-night vigil. At midnight, many of the crowd began to weep openly as the Treaty of Mutual Co-operation and Security passed silently into Japanese law.

Those were hectic days in the summer of 1960. Being in the Prefectural Bureau, I at least had an office by then, but I still didn't have anywhere to live. Some nights I slept in the office, on the table or the floor, and other nights I spent in the headquarters of the local Teachers' Union, but there I didn't even have room to stretch out fully, and I just used to go sleep sitting on a chair.

In our office, from morning to night, there was a constant stream of people, holding meetings, painting placards, making telephone calls. We always had a big pan of rice and a big pan of miso soup on the burner in the office, and when anyone felt hungry they would pop down to the nearest shop and buy some onions or maybe a bit of plaice, which we'd grill to make a meal. There was never enough money. All the money we had went into mobilization. We rarely had any time to go out for a drink in the evenings. Often we worked all night.

The height of the struggle came in the middle of the rainy season, and our office in Mito had a leak in the roof. We tried mending the leak by pinning a bit of plastic sheeting to the ceiling, but of course every time it rained the plastic sheet would just sag in the middle and start to fill up with water. How many times I remember lying in that office after an exhausting day, staring up at the ceiling, watching the rain gradually dropping into the bulging plastic, and thinking: 'Bother that leak'.

On 23 June Prime Minister Kishi, criticized from within his own party and from outside for his conduct of the Security Treaty issue, resigned. But his resignation was far from being a defeat for his policies. The Treaty on which he had staked his political career formally came into force on the day of his resignation, and he himself was to remain an influential if shadowy force within the Liberal Democratic Party for years to come.

Early in September the coal miners' union accepted a settlement which in effect opened the way to widespread pit closures. The defeat of their struggle is seen by many people both as crucial victory for the Japanese government's high-growth strategy and as a major blow to radical unionism in Japan.

On 20 November, Kishi's successor Ikeda Hayato went to the polls campaigning with a promise to 'double the national income' within the next ten years. He won a landslide victory, the LDP taking 296 seats, while the Socialist Party took 145 and the Communists, accused by some supporters of having had a half-hearted attitude to the anti-Treaty struggle, won just three.

Ikeda Hayato's electoral pledge proved to have been a cautious one. In fact, between 1960 and 1970, the Japanese national income almost trebled.

PART IV

Reaching Destinations –
1960 –

. . . and keep pace with the progress of the world.
(Emperor Hirohito's surrender broadcast, August 1945)

12

Saitō Mutsuo

When I became head of the company's share section, Kantō
Denka was not yet quoted on the stock market. So although I was
pleased at the promotion, I found myself back again with precious
little to do. Almost the only thing my section was responsible for
was altering the names on share certificates when they changed
hands, and any of the clerks could manage that.

Meanwhile, I stayed at my inn in central Tokyo, and at night I
sat up late playing mahjong with the assistants from my section. In
the morning, the maids in the inn didn't usually come round to
open the blinds, and it was so dark in my room that I often slept
until midday. Then, when I woke up, I'd ring up one of the clerks
in the office and ask what was going on there. Quite often the
answer would be:

'There's nothing on today that we can't handle. You stay where
you are, and we'll come round to see you at 5 p.m.'

So at five o'clock all three of my staff would turn up at the inn,
and we'd eat dinner together and then start another session of
mahjong.

However, one day one of my superiors called me in and said:
'We realize that you don't have a great deal of work in your
section, but it doesn't really do to have people in your position
turning up for work at all times of the day. It makes a bad
impression, you know. So we're going to move your section to the
eighth floor. That way at least your behaviour won't be quite so
noticeable.'

So up we all went to the eighth floor, which was the top storey
of the building, where there was nothing apart from our office and
a few store-rooms. Then I had a new idea. You see, this was just
the time when instant coffee first came out. So I sent one of the
clerks down to buy a big jar of instant coffee, and then I had a

275

circular sent round the company saying: 'Coffee is served on the eighth floor – 20 yen a cup'. Soon everyone was coming up to my office for coffee. They nicknamed it 'Saitō's coffee shop'. Even the men on the board of directors dropped in now and then for a cup, but of course I couldn't really charge them 20 yen, so in the end we just left a box in an obvious place by the door and let people put money if they felt like it. But in fact we did collect quite a bit of money that way – enough to take the section out to the occasional meal or excursion to the cinema.

In Urawa, meanwhile, the little two-storey house was rapidly taking shape: first the wooden frame, then the walls and tiled roof, the sliding screens, the polished wooden boards of the kitchen floor and the brocade-edged *tatami* with their sharp scent of newly-cut straw. And then it was time for Saitōs to move in: Mutsuo and Yoriko; the now ill and rapidly weakening elder Mrs Saitō; Chieko, who had just started primary school; and Tarō, then a sturdy three-year-old infant.

For me, those years at Urawa were among the most satisfying, at least as far as my work was concerned. For the rest of the family I think it may have been different.

In the company, you see, nobody really knew anything about stocks and shares. All they expected me to do was to keep the share section going the way it had always gone before. But after a while I became convinced that, from the point of view of the company's long-term development it was essential to get our shares quoted on the stock market. I went to the senior management with my idea, but they weren't enthusiastic about it. They said that other people had tried to do it in the past but they'd never succeeded. Of course the Tokyo stock market has very strict rules for accepting companies – the company had to have more than a certain number of shareholders, so many thousand shares had to be exchanged every week, and so forth. But in any case I persisted with my idea, and in the end I was told: 'Very well, if you want to give it a try you may, but it's your own responsibility.'

So after that I had everything to do. I had to draw up a plan and execute it entirely by myself, with just my small staff to help. That was the end of my lazy life. For the next couple of years, I was up every day around seven, and usually didn't have time for anything more than a cup of tea before I dashed out to work. My wife would call a taxi to take me to the station, otherwise I would never have managed to catch my train. I would go by train to Tokyo station, usually standing all the way, although my train wasn't as crowded as the ones earlier in the morning. From Tokyo station I walked to the office in Marunouchi, and normally got there around 9.30. Then, first of all, I had to ring round all the major stockbrokers to find out how dealing in our shares was going, and after that I would make my own estimate of the shares' current values. Next there were meetings with potential share buyers, and meetings with people from the media. At that time the Japan Short-Wave Broadcasting Service was running a programme for investors, so I would get in touch with the producer to encourage him to mention our company.

Almost every evening I was out entertaining reporters from the financial weeklies, or sometimes from the financial pages of the daily newspapers.

I hardly had any time to spend with the family in those years. Even at weekends I was often away playing golf with important business contacts. That was when I took up golf for the first time. For my wife particularly I think it must have been hard. Also at that time Mother was becoming very senile. It was a sad, hopeless, long decline, and my wife had to spend a great deal of time looking after her.

However, in the end I did succeed. In 1962 our shares were first quoted on the Tokyo Exchange Second List, and two years later we moved on to the First List. If I think about the footprints which I have left on the history of Kantō Denka, that must be the most important, because it was something that I genuinely planned and carried out myself. And I think that, if I hadn't done it then, the moment might have passed us by, because that, as it turned out, was the very peak in the boom of share prices. In 1964, because of a government credit squeeze, prices crashed and stricter regulations on share dealings were introduced. After that it would have been much harder for our company to have gone public.

But the credit restrictions and associated bursting of the stock market bubble caused no more than a momentary quaver in the sharply upward-sloping line of Japan's economic growth. The years from 1955 to 1957 they had called 'the Jimmu Boom', because the country, it was said, was more prosperous than it had ever been since the days of the mythical Emperor Jimmu. But the years from 1959 to 1961 outshone even the Jimmu Boom, and the makers of memorable phrases were sent scurrying in search of still greater superlatives. The expression they produced was *'Iwato Keiki'* – 'the Rock Door Boom' – Japan had seen nothing like it since the Sun Goddess Amaterasu Ōmikami peered round the rock door of her cave, bringing dawn to the world. From then until the early 1970s the Japan's GNP grew at an average rate of more than 11 per cent a year.

Everywhere across Japan shining new heavy industrial estates – *kombināto* – were beginning to point their red-and-white-striped chimneys to the sky. Kantō Denka, too, was soon planning a major expansion at a *kombināto* in western Japan. When the first of these estates had gone into operation in 1959, sightseers from all over Japan had come to gaze at the sparkle of its lights in the night-time sky – a 'million dollar night view'.[1] (It was only later, as the first sense of wonder faded, that the chimneys which sparkled with lights at night were found by day to block the sun with clouds of asthma-inducing smog.)

In 1963, Japan acquired its first satellite television link with the United States. A grand media extravaganza was planned to celebrate the inauguration of the link, but on the appointed night Japanese viewers switched on their sets to find that the satellite brought them something different: the news of the assassination of John F. Kennedy.

The following year the Tokyo Olympics, which were to have taken place in 1940 and had been postponed because of historical circumstances for twenty-four years, were finally opened. The event became, in the hands of the government, a massive exercise in presenting the image of the new Japan, not only to the world, but also to Japan itself. £900 million was spent on preparations for the event – only a fraction of it on the ultra-modern silver tent-like structures which formed the centrepiece of the Olympic Village itself; much more on resurfacing roads and constructing new expressways, and above all on the Shinkansen Railway, which was opened ten days before the Olympics themselves, after the luxurious 150-mile-an-hour bullet trains had first been shunted into place by humble steam engines.

Already, the young clerks and secretaries in Mutsuo's office were of a generation for whom the Pacific War was only a vague childhood memory.

After I became share manager, I started to notice little differences between my own attitudes and those of the younger assistants in my section. It seemed to me that the younger generation acted far more coolly and rationally than people of my age-group, and that they always liked to eliminate risk before they attempted anything. That sort of attitude seems to me to have both a good side and a bad side to it. For example, with the business of getting our company quoted on the stock exchange, the younger men in my section were very cautious and pessimistic – they said it had been tried before and failed, so what was the point? But I felt that, well, I had nothing to lose, so why not at least attempt it? I'm not saying that my generation's approach to things is necessarily good, because – I suppose as a result of the way we've been trained – we'll attempt things even if they are one hundred per cent hopeless, and only find out after a lot of wasted time and effort that we've been, as they say, flogging a dead horse.

People of my generation tend to commit themselves to things very wholeheartedly. For example, if I had a boss who treated me well, I would feel a sense of commitment [*on*] to him, and if that boss later got into difficulties I would do my best to fulfil my commitment by helping him out, even if it damaged my own career. But on the other hand, with the assistants in my own section, I've always tried to treat them as well as I possibly could, but once they move on, as far as they're concerned, that's the end of the relationship between us. We might perhaps exchange New Year cards, but that's about it. I don't blame them for it. They have their own lives to live. It's just the difference between their age-group and mine.

In 1964 Japan was admitted to the Organization for Economic Co-operation and Development and joined the richer nations of the West in subscribing to Article 8 of the International Monetary Fund's constitution. Just as clearly as the status of the prosperous household was made visible in the washing machine, the refrigerator and the TV (of the latter there were now over ten million in Japan, almost one to every two families), so the country's status as a developed nation was symbolized by these two steps. In Japan, the term 'post-war' (*sengo*) has a rather more restricted meaning than the

English word, implying strictly 'the aftermath of war', and in 1956 the government Economic White Paper had already stated: 'Now the post-war period is over'. Now, at last, it was beginning to be possible to come to terms with the receding memories of militarism, defeat and hunger.

We started having ex-servicemen's reunions a year or so before I joined Kantō Denka. Various groups established themselves: there was a group of the people from Morioka, one of people from Honjō, one of people from Yōkaichi and so on. I don't bother much about the Morioka reunions, but the one which I most like to attend is the reunion of my old friends from Yōkaichi. The people that I got to know in the war are still really the closest friends that I have. The group from Yōkaichi has a meeting every year in December. We meet in a good Tokyo restaurant, and there are about twenty regulars who are always sure to turn up. If any of them is missing, you know that it can only be for one of two reasons: either they've been sent abroad on business, or they've died.

At our very first reunion, it was as if some kind of floodgate had broken. We all wanted to pour out our stories about how we'd survived and what we'd done since the war. But gradually things changed. We've mostly done quite well in our careers, and now we're people with responsible positions and lives which are full of hard work and stress, and our reunion is a day when we go back to our youth and all that stress is somehow momentarily released. Every year we repeat the same stories and laugh at the same jokes. It's strange, the way memory works. When you remember what you suffered, little by little the pain seems to get refined out of it, and in the end the worst experiences make the best memories.

In 1965, the year when Japan's foreign trade balance went into the black for the first time since the war, Mutsuo became head of the Nagoya branch of the Kantō Denka Chemical Company. In 1967, when Japan's GNP caught up with that of West Germany, he became head of the company's Osaka office. In 1975 he was appointed to the Board of Directors. By that year the Japanese government was predicting that the country's *per capita* GNP would surpass the 1975 level of the United States ($6,600) within five years.

It was the classic pattern of the upward path of a successful business career. The pressures of work were great. There were frequent moves from one city to another, causing temporary separations from the family. But there was also the satisfaction of being a participant in a period of history when Japanese industry experienced its most spectacular growth and faced some of its most challenging problems.

For companies such as Kantō Denka, the 1960s were the golden years. Japan's policy of heavy-industry-led high economic growth was at its peak. Between 1960 and 1971 the output of Japan's chemical industry increased at an average rate of 12.2 per cent a year. For a time, it almost seemed as though nothing could go wrong.

At the Nagoya office our main job was to sell the company's products to the various subsidiaries and sub-contractors of Toyota, because of course Toyota dominates the economy of the town. I'd been successful with the difficult business of the share issue, and so now I had a new feeling of self-confidence. I really sensed that I could make a go of things if I tried.

And then again, I was the head of the branch, and I was in my early forties. The conditions were perfect for becoming what they used to call a *mōretsu sha-in* – a dedicated company man. The work at Nagoya was extremely interesting and rewarding. When I arrived there the branch's sales were in the region of seven million yen a month. By the time I left, two years later, they had risen to about thirty million.

In Nagoya I found a flat for the family right in the centre of town, just a few minute's walk from the office. It was the most convenient place you can imagine. There was a hospital right next-door, a public baths at the back, and an undertaker's opposite. There were noodle shops and Western restaurants, coffee shops and bookshops and sweet-shops, all within a few hundred yards of the flat. It was the first time I had ever lived right in the middle of a big, bustling city. It was a very exciting and enjoyable experience.

At first, however, Mutsuo had the new flat to himself. In the highly competitive atmosphere of Japan's post-war education system it was above all important that the children's education should not be interrupted, so the rest of the family remained in Tokyo until the end of the school year.

I suppose I'm a pretty typical Japanese father. I'm not a very domestic person, but then I don't think that the average Japanese father is very domestic.

I couldn't help being aware, though, that the education my children were receiving was totally different from what we had been taught in my childhood. Things like mathematics and English were quite different – of course, we weren't taught proper English pronounciation at all. But the worst gap came in social sciences. The values they learnt were virtually the opposite of what we were taught. For example nowadays, if you so much as dare mention the word 'patriotism', they instantly label you a reactionary.

I find that my children are instilled with a terrible sense of guilt about the things that Japan did during the war. Particularly they have been taught in great detail about things like the atrocities of Nanking, and they feel immensely guilty about it. So if I maybe mention something about the need to defend the nation, they will at once say: 'Those sort of ideas were the cause of what happened during the war'.

I don't argue with them. It's no use. Any time that I've tried to argue, I've found that our minds are running on different tracks, and our words don't connect.

When we have our reunions of pilots from the *tokkōtai*, it seems that everyone has the same problem with their children. They're all taught to believe that it was people like us who were responsible for the war. But, I don't know, was it really our fault?

At least it's consoling to be able to talk it over with other people who have the same difficulties . . .

The next step up the corporate mountain came quickly: promotion to Osaka, the second largest city in Japan, and the centre of Kantō Denka's plans for expansion in the western region. From supervising a staff of eight, Mutsuo moved to heading a staff of twenty-five. From an office handling thirty million yen's worth of sales, he went to one handling 400 million.

Again he went alone, this time staying in a hotel until his family joined him later in the year. By the time the Saitōs arrived in Osaka, the city was in the grip of Expo fever. The vast suburban site which had been chosen to house Japan's World Exhibition on the theme of 'Human Progress and Co-operation' was already being levelled into a bulldozed mire on which the maze of exhibition halls would soon take shape.

As 1970, the year of the Expo, approached, Mutsuo's office became his company's Osaka 'embassy', dealing with a constant flow of important visitors from other parts of the country. Often, too, he travelled down to the huge new industrial estate of Mizushima, on the shores of the Inland Sea, to visit Kantō Denka's latest and largest factory, which had recently been constructed there. The expansion of output which came with the opening of the new factory created increased pressures on Mutsuo and his staff in the Osaka office, for it was they who had the main responsibility for finding sales outlets for its products. It was decided that a sub-branch should be established at Hiroshima, and for many months the organization and opening of the new office absorbed much of Mutsuo's time and energy.

In March 1970 the Osaka Expo, in which seventy-seven nations participated, was opened by the emperor and Crown Prince Akihito.

The emperor . . . rose in the royal box and delivered opening greetings, expressing his great pleasure that the Japan World Exposition had been organized with the co-operation of so many countries in the world and offering his sincere hopes for its success. Instantly, the '21st Century Fanfare' sounded sonorously, while a ten-gun salute boomed out from beside an artificial lake adjacent to the Festival Plaza, reverberating through the Senri Hills.

Then the moment Crown Prince Akihito pressed a button of a device installed in the plaza, six giant congratulatory paper balls, suspended from the roof of the plaza, split open, showering 30,000 paper cranes and 10,000 pieces of coloured confetti on the spectators. To the tune of electronic music, more than a thousand lights flashed on and off, while 30,000 multicoloured balloons rose into the sky; a graceful jet of water sprayed forth in the artificial lake and fireworks crackled overhead. Thus amid such a symphony of sounds and lights, the ceremony came to its climax.

At that instant, a gargantuan robot standing in a corner of the plaza – 14 metres tall and 50 tons in weight – came to life, emitting lights and scented mists from its body. Speaking in a mechanical voice, the robot shouted: 'My nickname is Deme (Pop-Eyes)! Welcome to EXPO '70!'[2]

The Expo, like the Tokyo Olympics six years earlier, symbolized a further stage in the metamorphosis of Japan's international image. A survey of the attitudes of foreign visitors to the exhibition showed that over 60 per cent associated the word 'Japan' with 'an industrial nation' or 'an economically developed country'. Only 6 per cent mentioned that Japan had been the first country to suffer atomic bomb attacks.[3] But the new image, too, had its darker side. Abroad, Japan's increasing economic power and growing inroads into foreign markets were beginning to cause concern amongst business and political leaders. At home, the campuses of Japan's universities were still littered with the debris of two years of violent protest, as the young rebelled against the new capitalist colossus which was emerging to replace the military monolith of the 1930s. And two months after the Osaka Expo's triumphant finale, even the abortive 'Shōwa Restoration' of 1936 was to be echoed in a bizarre black comedy, when the author Mishima Yukio and a group of supporters staged an attempted military *coup d'état* which ended in their ritual suicide.

Even before the Osaka Expo, I felt as though Japan had reached some sort of peak. The Expo, I suppose, symbolized that peak.

But then, just after the time of the Expo, came the dramatic suicide of Mishima Yukio. That made a great impact.

Without any real reason, I somehow had the feeling that there was a kind of pattern in the deaths of Japan's famous writers. Akutagawa Ryunosuke committed suicide just at the beginning of the economic crisis of the 1920s. Dazai killed himself during the terrible hardships of the post-war years. And now Mishima. I know that there is no obvious relationship between their deaths. But all the same, it seemed to me almost as though Mishima, as a writer, had some special sensitivity to the trend of the times, as if he had sensed a crisis coming.

The first of the series of shocks which were to jolt Japan's economic advance into a new direction took place the following year. In July 1971 US President Nixon announced his decision to visit China. The Japanese government had not been consulted on or warned of this decision, and it came as a considerable blow to their pride. Japan, after all, not only had close historical ties with China but had also paid a high economic price, in terms of lost trade, for following the American line of hostility towards the People's Republic.

But an even greater blow was to follow. Exactly one month later, Nixon announced America's 'new economic policy', including a 10 per cent surcharge on imports and suspension of the dollar's convertibility into gold. This led to panic selling of dollars on the Tokyo market and a massive drop in Japanese share prices. Eighteen months later the dollar was devalued and the yen floated. The government of Prime Minister Tanaka, fearing the effects of the yen's rising value on Japanese exports, began to pursue an expansionary economic policy which resulted in soaring inflation.

The effect of the 'Nixon shocks' was psychological as well as economic. Amongst liberal Japanese opinion there was an intense sense of disappointment with the actions of their American ally. A Tokyo University economist wrote, in 1971:

> The Nixon speech shows fully how deep is the moral, spiritual and intellectual decline of American society . . . There is no trace in it of the lofty spirit of liberty and equality of the American Revolution. Gone, too, are the anguish and wisdom which produced the New Deal policies. There could hardly be anything more hollow-sounding than President Nixon's statement that 'America's best days are yet to come . . .'[4]

At that time we were starting to have trouble with our factory at Mizushima. One of the processes that we employed there for the production of soda involved the use of mercury. There began to be suspicions that mercury from the plant was polluting the seawater, and the environment minister himself issued guidelines requesting us to convert to a different production process. Our company argued that we couldn't afford to invest in a completely new method of production. But just then came the Oil Shock, and the problems at Mizushima were dwarfed by new and much more important matters.

For the Japanese economy had not fully adjusted to the consequences of 1971 when it was plunged into further turmoil by the oil crisis. The OPEC oil embargoes and price rises of 1973–74 were particularly critical for Japan because of the Japanese government's deliberate policy of basing the country's energy upon imported oil. In 1950, oil had accounted only for 20 per cent of Japan's energy needs. By 1974 it accounted for 70 per cent. Doubling and quadrupling oil prices pushed inflation higher and higher. People began panic buying. Companies started to hoard goods. Essential items such as toilet paper and soap powder disappeared from the shops. In

1974 the Japanese economy registered negative growth for the first time since 1945.

But, not for the first time, an apparent disaster turned paradoxically into a new source of advantage for Japanese industry.

The motto of businessmen suddenly became '*Uri-oshimi, kai-dame*' [Don't sell – buy and hoard']. Every company wanted to hang on to its products because they knew that in a few months prices would have risen.

There was a lot of publicity that year about the chairman of a certain oil company who wrote an internal company circular saying that 'the oil crisis is the chance of a lifetime'. The circular was leaked to the public, and the chairman was severely criticized for it. But, to be completely honest, what he said was quite true. At least as far as our company and most other manufacturers were concerned, the oil crisis *was* the chance of a lifetime.

It was like the Korean War boom all over again. Sales were no problem at all. Instead of having to go out and look for customers, we could sit in the office and wait for buyers to come flocking to us, begging for goods. We made very large profits in 1973–74.

There were not only short-term, windfall gains to be made out of the oil crisis. The threat of disappearing oil imports, by dramatically revealing the weakness of Japan's industrial structure, also gave new impetus to much more important long-term developments.

For several years it had been clear to many businessmen and politicians that a new industrial strategy was needed. Wages were rising; environmental pollution was spreading; Japan's exports were facing growing competition from the emerging industries of countries such as South Korea and Taiwan. In 1970 the government's Financial White Paper had spoken of the need for Japan to 'give thought to the remodelling of her industrial structure to suit the new age'. But it was the 'Oil Shock' which provided the mood of urgency necessary to turn the vaguely-worded blueprints for a new society into practicable plans of action. A leading article from a financial newspaper indicated the speed with which large corporations reacted to the events of autumn 1973:

One of their major moves in recent weeks is the successive establishment of 'comprehensive countermeasures committees' led by top management at various enterprises. Many of these committees are designed not merely to take urgent measures to meet the reduction in the oil supply, but also to grapple with more basic problems, such as the switchover to production processes that will make more efficient use of energy, adoption of substitute forms of energy, development of energy-saving products, and reforms of the research and development structure for these purposes.[5]

All over Japan, companies engaged in basic heavy industry – steel, chemicals, oil-refining – were embarking upon a search for new technologies and new products. The Kobe Steel Company began research into the manufacture of robots. Chemical companies like Ajinomoto (the maker of a well-known brand of artificial food flavouring) diversified into medical research and genetic engineering. Soap and toothpaste manufacturers turned their attention to the development of non-petroleum energy sources. 'Knowledge-intensive industry' replaced 'heavy and chemical industry' as the magical formula to be repeated in the hundreds of government documents, businessmen's speeches and company annual reports throughout the 1970s. In the new and altered economic environment of Japan after Nixon and OPEC some companies thrived – the makers of computers, of microelectronic gadgets and industrial ceramics. Other companies, including Kantō Denka, fared less well.

After the Oil Shock we tried to diversify from industrial chemicals to consumer products. We made a tie-up with the Canada Dry company to manufacture their products in Japan. Virtually all our gains from the 1973–74 price rises were ploughed into the new project, but it was a big failure. From being a company which made substantial profits, we went to being one which could hardly pay dividends on its shares. We are still recovering from the mistakes of those years even now.

While the economy was in the throes of this reshaping, the political world was shaken by scandal. In 1972 Tanaka Kakuei, a self-made millionaire, became prime minister. His appointment received great public support. Not only was he (at 54) Japan's youngest post-war prime minister, but also, as a man who had risen from poverty to great wealth in the rugged world of the construction business, his background was in somewhat romantic contrast to the drab ascent from bureaucracy to politics which provides the normal career path for aspirants to this office. Some saw Tanaka as the model for a new breed of politician to suit the economic and political challenges of the 1970s. The press labelled him a 'folk hero'.

In 1974 the impact of the American Watergate Case turned the attentions of the Japanese press and public to the question of corruption at home. 'While the American press was reporting resolutely on Watergate', recalls one journalist, 'Japanese newspaper readers often asked us a question: could Japanese newspapermen expose a Japanese political scandal of equal magnitude as daringly and penetratingly?'[6] The answer, as it emerged, was that they could, and that they did not need to look far to find one. Awareness of the 'black mist' (*kuroi kiri*) of corruption surrounding Japanese politics was widespread, and the activities of Tanaka, the outsider who had thrust his way into the establishment, were particularly vulnerable to scrutiny. In autumn 1974 the popular press began to publish details of Tanaka's suspect business dealings. Much emphasis was placed on the prime minister's lavish dispensing of funds in the pre-election period, and on his acquisition of four private residences which together were valued at almost 10 million US dollars. Tanaka resigned shortly afterwards.

Less than two years later, as the fall-out from the Lockheed Affair in the United States reached Japan, Tanaka and several of his associates were arrested and put on trial, charged with having accepted bribes in return for assuring the purchase of Lockheed aircraft by Japan's domestic airline. The political system founded on the ideals of MacArthur's GHQ in 1947 had, perhaps surprisingly, developed sufficient stability to withstand even the revolts of the 1960s and the scandals of the 1970s. But it had done nothing to overcome a profound public scepticism about the motives of politicians. An opinion survey on the Lockheed Affair found that 73 per cent of those questioned agreed that 'a scandal was bound to occur as a result of Japan's political make-up'.[7]

Although I'm a businessman, I personally tend to support the Socialist Party. Of course I know that there are many things wrong with the Socialist Party, but still, I don't like to see the Liberal Democratic Party having an easy win at elections.

Since I was appointed to the Board of Directors, I've had to handle wage negotiations with the company union. It sometimes amuses me, because I suspect that the union leaders in our company, however militant they may sound when they're talking about wage rises, probably go off and vote for the Liberal Democrats in elections, while I'm voting for the Socialists.

What I can't stand about the Liberal Democratic Party is all this corruption. I know that politics is a dirty business. Of course they're all corrupt to some extent. But to my mind the LDP just goes too far.

In 1972, my daughter Chieko graduated from High School. She wanted to go to University, but I thought it wasn't a good idea. It would have been all right if she'd had some clear aim in her studies, like, say, becoming a doctor. But as she didn't, I felt that it would be better for her to do a two-year Women's College course.

However, Chieko was determined to take the entrance examination for Sophia University [a prestigious private university in Tokyo]. Well, I thought she hadn't the slightest hope of passing, so I said to her: 'All right, if that's really what you want, you may take the examination.' Unfortunately, she passed. There was nothing much I could do about it then. So she went off to Sophia University to study sociology.

Next, Tarō left. He tried to get into Keio University and failed, so he went to study at a crammer's in Tokyo for a year. After they had both gone, it seemed that, whatever my wife was doing, her mind was always fixed on the children in Tokyo. After all, for a mother, the children are the most important thing in life. So, a little later, she went to Tokyo and took a flat so that they could all be together.

For a short while, Mutsuo enjoyed a sudden reversion to bachelor life. He found a comfortable apartment in his childhood home, Kyoto, and commuted from there to work each day. But in 1975 he was summoned back to the company's Tokyo headquarters to become head of the Purchasing Section.

Several times while I'd been in Osaka I'd been offered a chance to return to Tokyo, but I'd always turned it down. I enjoyed life in Osaka. I felt that the Osaka office was something that I had put all my best efforts into. I took a kind of personal pride in it.

But I couldn't refuse the promotion which I was offered in

1975. And besides, all my family was in Tokyo now. So I decided to go back.

We had let our house in Urawa, so for a while I lived with my wife and children in a flat in central Tokyo. Then, after the tenants had moved out, we all settled in to our own old home again.

Soon after, Mutsuo was appointed head of the Tokyo office, and in 1980 he became managing director of the company's sales subsidiary. The advance was more one of status than of wealth. His income is not greatly above the average for managerial employees. His house is still the modest wooden suburban one he built twenty years ago. He has returned to the routine of catching the 8.49 from Urawa station to Marunouchi, although now, unlike his hectic days in the share section, he can usually be home by six, in time to watch the baseball game on television.

The children are no longer children. Chieko works in a government research office. Tarō is a post-graduate, keeping up the family tradition by studying at Keio. Often they are away from home pursuing their own lives, into which their parents do not enquire too closely. At weekends, therefore, there is quiet in the house, and Mutsuo can practise the chanting of *utai*, or do a little more of the intricate and satisfying work on the traditional paper screen that he is making in his spare time.

In August comes *o-bon*, the festival of the dead spirits, and, in the same month, the anniversary of Japan's surrender. Around this time Mutsuo and the other survivors from the second intake of special pilot trainees go to the Yasukuni Shrine to remember the ones who died. Afterwards, they gather – to talk things over and renew old friendships – at a nearby hotel whose manager is also a former army pilot. Each summer a special memorial for the dead from Yōkaichi Air Base is held in one of the ancient temples in the mountain forests of Nikkō. The chief monk of the temple, too, is a survivor of the *tokkōtai*.

It is very hard for me to say whether all those deaths were in vain, but deep inside me I have to believe that they had some meaning. Of course the strategy of sending people to suicidal deaths was an evil way to fight a war. But still I think that in a few decades from now, when all my generation have died away, then people will be able to look at the Pacific War in a calm and reasoned way, and

290

perhaps then it will be possible to make sense of things; to understand why those young people had to die. And I believe that such understanding will be worth looking for.

In 1980 Mutsuo and a few of his closest friends from his army days pooled their money to hire a Cessna plane for a private flight above Tokyo. For an hour or so they circled round the city, looking down to pick out familiar landmarks – one friend's house, another's office; the grey tower of Keio University; the white dome of the Diet building; to the left, the Olympic sports tracks and, beyond, the Meiji park; ahead, the green expanse of the Imperial Palace gardens, now overshadowed by sharp glossy pinnacles – the earthquake-proof skyscrapers of central Tokyo.

On the whole I am satisfied with things that I have achieved in my life so far, though some things I regret a little. For example, sometimes I think that I should have chosen a career in a different kind of company. I should have liked to have worked in a company making electrical goods. I really didn't know a lot about chemicals and, to tell the truth, when I applied for the job at Kantō Denka I had some idea that it was an electrical goods firm. It was only later that I found out what they made.

Sometimes I look back and imagine that the nicest thing of all would have been to apprentice myself to a master of traditional music, and to have trained to be a teacher of *utai*.

I think that I have been quite successful in my career. But then I cannot help wondering, did my success come from my own ability, or was I just part of my company's success, even of the success of the whole economy? If I were free to do anything I like with my future, what I should do would be to try something by myself, to work on my own, and see if I could build something by myself, from nothing. But I suppose that will remain only a dream.

13

Tsutsumi Ayako

Long before the day of her graduation from Musashino College had arrived, Ayako's vision of a free, artistic existence had once more, tantalizingly, receded into the distance. While she was still a student, a letter had arrived from her father: her mother was again seriously ill, and the arrangements for looking after the child were not proving satisfactory. Ayako realized that she could no longer evade the burden of responsibility for her family.

I remember that I got that letter in the post just as I was setting off to deliver a completed consignment of dolls' faces to the company office. When I read the letter, I simply didn't know what to do. All day I wandered around Shinjuku in a kind of daze. My mind was completely blank. Everything looked quite hopeless.

However, at that very time the doll company started up a new line of business. They started running correspondence courses for people who wanted to make dolls as a hobby at home. The company would send out doll-making kits, and instructions on how to put them together. This was tremendously successful, and soon they were asking me to paint more and more dolls' faces for their mail-order kits. This didn't leave me very much time for studying art, but at least it meant that I could afford to support my mother and son, and after I graduated from college I didn't need to look for a job. I just went on painting dolls' faces all day and every day.

My father sold the shop in Nojiri and went to live with his mistress, and my mother and son came to live with me in Tokyo. Also we were joined by my younger brother, who had dropped out of university and was doing odd jobs like delivering newspapers and working on building sites. I rented a house for us in the Kōenji district.

Sometimes it was a struggle to make ends meet, particularly in the early years. I remember one day going out to buy food for the family's main meal. I had only one ten-yen coin in my purse, and even in those days there was practically nothing that you could buy with ten yen. I went to the local shopping area and searched and searched for something that I could afford. In the end all I got was a bag of beansprouts, and I took them home and boiled them, and we ate them with soy sauce for our supper.

But after I graduated from college things got busier and busier and more and more money came in. Our lives just went up on the escalator of high economic growth.

The 'economic miracle' of the 1960s is most commonly thought of in association with the rise to international prominence of giant Japanese manufacturing firms: the Sonys, the Toyotas, the Japan Steels. But an important share of the impetus to higher economic growth came also from the less visible activities of the masses of tiny urban workshops which formed the bottom end of long chains of subsidiaries and subcontractors. At the beginning of the 1960s 43 per cent of Japanese workers were employed in plants with fewer than fifty workers, and 15 per cent in plants with fewer than ten (the comparable figures for the United States were 14 per cent and 4 per cent).[1] It was in these workshops – often owned and managed by small family firms – rather than on the modern assembly lines of the big companies, that one could find the instances of low wages and long hours of work which gave rise to the enduring image of the Japanese 'workaholic'.

Two years after her graduation Ayako entered the ranks of the miniature entrepreneurs, turning her workshop into a registered company with the imposing title of the Tsutsumi Doll Research Centre. In the beginning she had been painting fifty dolls' faces a day. Now the number had risen to over five hundred, and she found it necessary to take on part-time workers to help her fulfil the insatiable demands of the doll company's headquarters. Within a few years output had risen again to more than a thousand faces a day.

I used to get up in the morning and start work, and by the time I stopped, it would already be midnight again. I worked every day of the week, as I had done in the army supply depot – 'Monday, Monday, Tuesday, Wednesday, Thursday, Friday, Friday'. There was no time for any entertainment or relaxation. My only treat in those days was to have a little cup of *sake* each night before I went to sleep. The Tokyo Olympics took place while I was running the doll workshop. The marathon track passed quite near our house, but I never had time to see anything. Sometimes I used to think that I would end up like Kiguchi Kohei in the story: I would die on my feet with my paintbrush in my hand.

After a while the doll-painting business grew too large for the house where we lived, so I rented an office nearby. I persuaded my brother to help me run the company. Then we thought that we could earn a better profit by expanding the business to make, not just dolls' faces, but also bodies and clothes as well. By this time we were sometimes employing as many as forty workers, including part-timers. Then quite suddenly it seemed, I had a fair amount of money saved up. I had been putting a bit by every now and then, and with all the hard work of the past few years, I'd never had time to spend any. A friend of mine suggested that we should pool our savings and buy a bit of land outside Tokyo, and build our own painting studio, so that's what we did.

By the mid-1960s many people in Japan were discovering, with the same sense of wonderment, that they had attained a previously unimagined level of affluence. There was a new mood of confidence about. One group of eminent economists was predicting that, by 1985, 80 per cent of Japanese households would own cars, average *per capita* food consumption would have risen to 3000 calories, and *per capita* income would have reached the then-current level of the United States – $2000.

Ayako was now spending less time on the endless, intricate crimsoning of lips and dotting of eyes, and more on running the financial affairs of the Tsutsumi Doll Research Centre. And, at last, she was able to take time off at weekends to travel out to her studio to paint, not dolls' faces, but her own oil compositions.

And that was the time when she finally discovered that she was never going to be a painter.

Once I began to try to paint seriously, I found that I just had to accept the fact that I really had a very poor sense of colour.

And then, at almost the same time, another thing happened. Shapes started to become blurred. When I woke in the morning, my eyelids always seemed to be gummed together. When I walked in the street, I would see six ghostly traffic signs, where there was really only one.

I went to one doctor, and he told me that it was eye-strain, and that I had to avoid doing any work which would tire my eyes. I didn't want to believe him, so I went to another doctor, and then another, but they all said the same thing.

Soon after this discovery, Ayako went into a bookshop on an errand for a friend. Browsing among the shelves, she happened to pick up a book by Hermann Hesse, and there, in the pages of another of her beloved Western novelists, she chanced upon a philosophy to fit the new direction of her life.

The ideal person [writes Hesse] would sometimes write poetry, sometimes compose music. . . . And, best of all, this ideal person would not resist so bitterly and bloodily as we poor fellows do a change in himself when some new demand of the ideal required it of him, but would be in absolute harmony with himself, with the ideal, with fate; he would change easily, he would die easily.[2]

It was not, therefore, too late to change, to abandon her dreams of painting, to take up the challenge of a new craft, where the sensitivity of her eyes and her lack of colour-sense would cease to be of importance. Shortly before her fortieth birthday Ayako left the doll-making business in the hands of her brother, placed her son in boarding school, and moved out to the little pottery village of Kasama to begin a career as a maker of *Jōmon*-style earthenware.

The myths of her childhood had taught that the islands of Japan were born from the womb of the primal creatress and peopled with descendants of the gods of sun and storm.

The history books of today's children teach that the archipelago was formed by the melting of the last great ice-age, and first inhabited by a hunting people to whose culture archaeologists have given the name *Jōmon*.

Very little is known about the people of the *Jōmon* age. The single archaeological label perhaps covers a multitude of different tribes and ways of life. Our knowledge of them is derived from ashes of fires and fragments of bone. All that remains to suggest lost identities and imaginations is their pottery: crude at first – tall, irregular jars criss-crossed by rope-like patterns – but, over thousands of years, blossoming into wonderful profusions of furled and scrolled and ornamented shapes; extraordinary shapes, full of an exuberant energy quite unlike the restrained delicacy so typical of later Japanese art.

The rich clay deposits which gave the *Jōmon* potters the materials for their craft are still worked today. Their clay is sold to neighbouring villages which have become specialized centres of the art of pottery. One of those villages is Kasama.

Ayako first went to Kasama in 1966. At this time, growing disillusioned with her attempts at oil-painting, she had joined a pottery class in Tokyo. One weekend, the class went to visit a museum in a small town outside Tokyo. After looking around the museum they caught a taxi to the station, but as there was still an hour or so to go before their train was due, on the spur of the moment someone said to the driver: 'Take us to a place where they make pottery'.

So they drove out into the countryside, along rutted roads between the stubbly rice-fields, and into the narrow main street of Kasama village, where the taxi drew up outside the house of Fukuda, the most famous of the community's potters. With the others, Ayako walked from room to room of the potter's workshops. She observed the silent intensity of Fukuda's apprentices and assistants as they shaped the clay on their wheels, or dipped the finished pots in vats of glaze, hardly lifting their eyes from their work to meet the inquisitive gazes of the intruding visitors. She saw the row upon row of bowls and cups and *sake* jugs stacked in the kilns for firing, and smelt the pervasive smell of damp earth and clay dust. And she was entranced.

From that day on, every spare weekend was spent in Kasama, learning the potter's art from Mr Fukuda. But it was only the following year that, inspired by the sentiments of Hermann Hesse, she found the courage to abandon her city existence and settle in Kasama.

I bought one hundred *tsubo* of land near Fukuda's pottery, and I decided to build my own house and kiln there. The land cost me 5000 yen a *tsubo* [about 3.3 square metres] – it seems very little compared with land prices today, but it was hard for me to raise the money then. The house cost two million yen, and the kiln about another million. I would never have been able to afford it if it hadn't been for the help of my friends. One friend paid for half the cost of the kiln, and the people who worked with me in the doll-making business lent me money too.

I decided that my aim would be to make pottery in the style of the *Jōmon* age, but using modern technology. Once I had made up my mind, I had no anxiety about my new career. I still kept my financial interest in the doll-making business, so I had some assured income from that source. But in any case, I did not think for one moment that I would fail as a potter. I felt quite confident about my new life. I suppose that's just my nature. . . .

From the day she moved to Kasama there began the most satisfying period of Ayako's life. The work was almost as hard as it had been in the doll-making business. But no longer was she tied to the anonymous production of multitudes of identical rosebud faces. Now, all day, there was the feel of clay in her hands, and the delight of shaping it as she wished, pressing the soft reddish earth into the patterns of her imagination. The strong, solid shapes of her *Jōmon* - style earthenware did not strain her weakening eyesight; her lack of colour-sense no longer mattered, for the earth provided colours of its own.

Little by little, her fingers acquired greater skill. Her workshop gained its place in the pottery community of Kasama. She hired an assistant, then two. She began to exhibit her work, to accumulate a little hoard of savings. By 1970 she could afford the first holiday of her working life. She went on a package tour of Korea.

My Korean friend from Girls' School, Kanemoto-san – she's called Kim now – she and I had exchanged letters ever since we left school. I wrote and told her that I was coming to Korea on holiday and when I arrived at the airport, there she was waiting for me with a big bunch of flowers. I felt as if I had come home. I went round all the museums and art galleries in Seoul, and out to other towns, to look at all these magnificent old temples. But I didn't go to Kwangju. I can't say why, but somehow I just didn't want to see the place where I used to live.

In spite of growing success and prosperity, release from financial worries remained a retreating illusion, for success and prosperity themselves created new reasons to spend.

As far as money problems are concerned, this is the most difficult time I've known since I started the doll-painting business. You see, about two years ago I decided to build a second house. That way I can expand the pottery and take on new assistants. But raising the money to buy more land and build the new house has been a terrible worry.

My son went to college to train as a merchant seaman. He was lucky, and managed to get a good job as soon as he graduated. Now he's off at sea most of the time. He travels all round the world, you know. The trouble is that, while he's at sea, his company keeps sending most of his pay to me to look after, and, to tell the truth, I had to borrow two million yen of it to help pay for the new house. I haven't told my son about that yet, and I don't know what he'll think of it when he comes home. However, I suppose I'll get through this problem too in the end.

By now her pottery is exhibited not only in little local galleries, but in the chic department stores of central Tokyo. Introducing her exhibition for the New Year of 1980, Ayako wrote:

I am full of gratitude to have clay in my hands again this year. The primitive spirit of Jōmon seems to be binding itself around me more powerfully year by year, so that somehow it is impossible for me to separate myself from it. Will is stronger than ability. Again on this occasion my exhibition reflects the progress of my work, though it shames me that this progress still proceeds at a snail's pace. . . .

If you ask me if I've had a happy life, I should say, yes, you can call me happy.

Looking back, it seems that my fate was decided by tiny trivial actions. Little things that I did to help other people led to big changes which affected my life in a good way. For example, when the student next door asked me to make a portrait of his mother, that led to my becoming a street artist, and eventually going to art college. And then, when I went to buy a book for a friend, I discovered the words of Hesse which gave me the determination to start a new career as a potter. Through a whole series of chances I seem to have been guided towards some kind of destiny. When you think about it, it's almost frightening.

The first assistant who came to work for me here at Kasama later married a Spaniard called Antonio, and went to live in Spain. When their first baby was born, they invited me over to stay with them for a holiday, and I went. That was my first visit to Europe. While I was in Spain I went to see lots of art collections – the Prado and all those other lovely museums. In the museums I saw cases and cases full of Chinese pottery, but never saw any Japanese pottery. I thought that was a shame. After all, Japan sends so many cars and televisions and so on abroad. Why not art as well? So I had this fantasy that some day the museums I saw would have cases full of my *Jōmon*-style pottery.

I don't feel as though I've fulfilled my aims in life yet. Instead, I feel that the best and most successful time is just beginning. This is my ambition: that after cars and televisions, the next thing to come from Japan will be my pottery.

After all, if you're going to have ambitions, they may as well be big ones.

14

Iida Momo

Iida Momo was expelled from the Japanese Communist Party in 1964. The parting of ways had been a gradual and painful process.

The early 1960s were a period of particularly deep dissension within the Japanese communist movement. At home, rapid economic growth was creating circumstances which were unprecedented in Japanese history – circumstances, therefore, which demanded new strategies and new analyses. Abroad, the Sino–Soviet split was widening, creating delicate problems of international diplomacy for the Japanese Communist Party.

In 1961, at its Eighth Conference, the Party had adopted a new manifesto which represented a further shift from the revolutionary radicalism of the early 1950s towards a strategy of widening its appeal to an increasingly affluent Japanese electorate. 'At present', stated the new manifesto, 'Japan is basically dominated by American imperialism and Japanese monopolistic capital, itself ultimately subservient to American imperialism.' Our country, although a highly developed capitalistic nation, is, in reality, a vassal state half-occupied by American imperialism. Consequently, the argument ran, a two-stage revolution was necessary. First Japan must achieve 'independence and self-determination' by peaceful means, and only then could the transition to socialism take place. As a strategy for regaining electoral respectability, this new manifesto had some success. In the elections of 1963 and 1967 the Communist Party's share of the poll rose to 4.5 per cent, and the Party won five seats in the Lower House. In the 1970s its share rose far higher, reaching a peak in the 1972 general election, which gave the JCP thirty-eight Lower House seats.

But the electoral successes were achieved at the cost of a loss of the Party's radical impetus to the groupings of the New Left, and of a decline of its credibility amongst the influential circles of Japan's left-wing intellectuals. The new manifesto had provoked fierce debate within the Party, where a substantial minority, including the members of the Ibaragi Prefectural Bureau, regarded it as a retreat from revolution into a cheapened anti-American nationalism. But, with skilful manoeuvring, the Party headquarters managed little by little to undermine the position of the manifesto's opponents. On the very eve of the Eighth Conference, several of the regional bureaux which had been most outspoken in their opposition suddenly announced a change of heart. Those who persisted in opposing the new policies were either expelled from the Party or, as in Momo's case, stripped of their political offices.

Even though the whole Party throughout Japan had fallen under the control of the pro-Manifesto faction, I didn't leave the Party. I still wanted to keep on fighting within the organization for the things I believed in. But it was very hard. I had been purged from the central nervous system of the Party, and so I had no base now for political activity.

Suddenly, it seemed, I had gone into the shadows of history. I felt immensely isolated. The people who had left the Party earlier, around the time of the anti-Treaty demonstrations, had already built up their own new organizations such as *Bundo* [The League of Communists] and *Kakukyōdō* [the Revolutionary League of Communists]. But all my life and all my achievements had gone into my work for the Party. Now I had nothing. I had to start again, in the dark and on my own.

In this political vacuum, deprived both of activity and of the little financial support which his position as a Party cadre had provided, Momo returned to his other passion – literature. His first novel, *Monomi-Yo Yo Wa Nao Nagakiya* ('Watchman, How Fares the Night?') had been published in 1960, and had received considerable critical acclaim. Now he channelled his energies into writing essays and articles on political and social issues, and into starting a new full-length work to be entitled *Amerika No Eiyū* ('An American Hero').

I had written my first novel years earlier, while I was still in the TB sanatorium. I had written it as though it was my will, knowing that soon I would disappear underground to work for the Party. When I became a Party activist, I left the manuscript of the book in the hands of a friend. He circulated it privately, and after the Sixth Party Congress it was seen by the Kadokawa publishing company, who offered to publish it.

Of course in a way it was nice that the critics praised my novel. But in another sense I felt that their praise did not touch me. After all, I had written the book eight years earlier. By 1960 I had lost interest in it, and felt that it was hardly connected with me any more. It doesn't make much sense to have your work applauded after an interval of eight years.

For Momo writing was not an alternative to, or an escape from, politics, but rather a new foundation upon which to begin the rebuilding of his career as a revolutionary. He became an active member of the New Left literary circles which were acquiring a rapidly growing influence on Japanese intellectual life: he joined the New Japan Literature Group (*Shin Nihon Bungaku-Kai*) and the Science of Ideas Research Group (*Shisō no Kagaku Kenkyūkai*). With the eminent writer and critic Umemoto Katsumi, he founded the Japan Dialectic Materialist Research Group (*Nihon Yūbutsuron Kenkyūkai*). In the Tokyo meeting-places of these groups of radical writers he developed and argued his ideas as once he had done in the cramped, chaotic atmosphere of the Communist Party's provincial offices.

This was the time of Prime Minister Ikeda's Income Doubling Plan. The Communist Party did not believe that the plan could be successful, and the major New Left groups like *Bundo* also ridiculed Ikeda's policy. But they were wrong. The speed of Japan's economic growth was simply beyond their imagination. Unfortunately, this is a situation that you can see repeated again and again in the development of communism. Theory is constantly being overtaken by changes in the economic structure. Communism is very good at analysing what has happened in the past, but sometimes we are not very good at foreseeing the future.

Looking back on it, one can understand that it all began in 1960, with the defeat of the Mitsui-Miike miners' strike, and the shift from coal to oil as the source of energy for Japan's industrial growth. Basing his policy on the conversion from coal to oil, Ikeda quite easily managed to double Japanese people's pay packets, but at the same time he subordinated the country to the power of the multinational oil majors.

302

High economic growth, however, was not producing the social stability which Japan's conservative government had expected and desire By the mid-1960s there were gathering waves of protest against the normalization of relations with South Korea and against American involvement in Vietnam. A new generation was entering the factories and the universities. This generation had been reared on the ideals of the post-war Constitution, with its promise of democracy and individual liberty, and its renunciation of war. Now, as young adults, they were for the first time discovering the gap between these ideals and the reality of a Japan where political power had fallen under the control of a seemingly unshakable alliance of the right-wing Liberal Democratic Party and big-business interests; a Japan which had disbanded its armed forces only to replace them with 'Self-Defence Forces', and which by now was rated among the ten largest military powers in the world. The outlines of a new protest movement, whose scale would exceed even the demonstrations of 1960, were beginning to take shape.

In April 1967, during the annual 'Spring Struggle' in which Japanese management and workers hammers out the guidelines for the year's pay rises, the major trade-union federations called for a national one-day strike. At this time the Communist Party's secretary-general, Miyamoto, was away in China. In his absence, the remaining leaders rashly attempted to undermine the position of non-communist trade-union leadership by opposing the stoppage and instructing Party members to disrupt the strike action.

The whole union movement was plunged in chaos. Not only did the Communist Party HQ order members to act as blacklegs, they even encouraged them to destroy the strike's effectiveness by underhand means. In response, the unions started to demote any officials who were Communist Party members.

This created a situation which should never have to occur: a situation where one was faced with a choice between working for the interests of the proletariat or obeying the commands of the Party. Of course I wholeheartedly supported the strike, and co-operated with the union leaders who were organizing strike action in my home area of Mito.

Then Secretary-General Miyamoto returned from China, to find the Japanese communist movement in disarray. The only thing he could do was reluctantly to reserve the orders which had been given in his absence, and place the Party's support behind the strike. You might think that this change of policy justified the stand I had taken, but it didn't work that way. The Central Committee members who had tried to break the strike were forced to make self-criticisms, but all the same, I was still expelled from the Party for having disobeyed their orders.

Before his expulsion from the Party Momo had been invited to give a lecture to the members of the Free Theatre, a left-wing Tokyo theatrical company which specialized in performing the works of such *avant-garde* writers as Samuel Beckett and Arnold Wesker. The next production was to be a stage version of the famous director Ōshima Nagisa's film *Japan's Night and Mist*, which deals with the emergence of the Japanese Communist Party from underground in 1955, and this was the subject on which Momo was to speak. Amongst his audience was Sekiguchi Reiko, the actress who had the leading female role in the play. After the lecture she and Momo met again several times, and soon they fell in love.

In 1965 they were married. Reiko abandoned her acting career and went to Mito where, not long after, a son, Kyū, was born.

For the first years of their marriage, Momo and his wife occupied a flat in a council apartment-block typical of the thousands which had been built in the 1950s and 1960s in response to Japan's chronic housing shortage. The flat was what is known in Japan as a '2D-K' – two small matted rooms which serve as living rooms by day and bedrooms at night, and a wood-floored kitchen just large enough to double as a dining room.

Despite the good reviews, the royalties from Momo's novels were small, and he supported his family in the early days by means of a more mundane literary activity – writing articles for a publicity magazine produced by the Suntory Whisky Company. *Western Alcohol Paradise* (as the magazine was called) paid so well that with four days' work a month Momo could earn enough to live on, and have twenty-seven days free for revolutionary politics.

In 1965 the American bombing of North Vietnam began, and Momo went to Tokyo to take part in a sit-down demonstration in front of the US Embassy. Vietnam became the rallying point which could unite even the deeply divided forces of the Japanese Left. The newly-created Citizens' Cultural United Front for Peace in Vietnam (*Beheiren*) became the first major post-war political movement to escape domination by any single party or faction, and within its ranks Marxists like Momo worked side by side with social democrats such as the novelist Oda Makoto, who condemned the Vietnam War above all as a betrayal of the American Dream.

In 1967 the undercurrents of unrest at last broke through the glittering surface of Japan's prosperity. At first events seemed to occur at random, without pattern or connection. In February, students at Chūo University staged a protest against the raising of tuition fees. In May allegations of financial misappropriations at Nihon University, the largest Japanese private university, led to sit-ins and demonstrations. In June students of Kyushu University went on strike after an American military aircraft had crashed in the college grounds. In August there was a train crash in Tokyo involving a US air force fuel tanker, and residents of the areas close to the railway demand that the line should cease to carry supplies to American bases.

But Momo saw in these events the signs of a long-awaited coming.

By 1967 my friends and I knew that what was happening was the beginning of something which would go far beyond the level of 1960. So, at this time, we decided to form our own party, which we called the Communist Workers' Party (*Kyōsanshugi Rōdōsha-tō*]. To start with we had about one hundred members, though we could rely on the active support of two or three hundred more, and at the height of the struggle we could mobilize people in their thousands.

I was made secretary-general of the new party and, as I obviously couldn't organize things from Mito, I moved down to Tokyo, where I got another 2D-K flat in the Musashino district.

Our sense of timing was right because, just a few months after we founded the new party, the upsurge which we expected took place.

By the beginning of 1968, the mass of small protests against separate issues were beginning to form themselves into a wider rebellion whose object was not merely peace in Vietnam, or a reduction of university fees, but the overthrow of existing authority. At Tokyo University, a long-running dispute over the intern system for medical students developed into a confrontation which challenged the entire relationship between the teachers and the taught. After the academic authorities had unwisely called in the police to evict a group of protesting students from the University Hall – a move which violated the traditional autonomy of universities and provoked comparisons with the activities of the wartime Political Police – a Students' Strike Coalition Committee was formed, and the entire university occupied. Professors and other symbols of reaction, such as the right-wing novelist Mishima Yukio, were summoned to face questioning by mass assemblies of students. The head of the University's Literary Faculty, Hayashi Kentarō, was released only after continuous questioning for one hundred and seventy-three hours.

The pattern of escalation from specific, often minor, grievances to general revolt was followed at campus after campus. By the end of 1968 one hundred and sixteen Japanese universities and colleges had been occupied by their students. Throughout Japan, lectures and enrolments ceased. Tokyo University, the core of the academic establishment, remained closed until 18–19 January 1969, when it was stormed and recaptured by the riot police.

On the streets of Japan's cities the scale and violence of confrontations between police and demonstrators also spiralled upwards. On 8 October 1967 Prime Minister Satō, who had just announced his support for American bombing raids on North Vietnam, left for an official visit to Saigon, and thousands of demonstrators besieged Haneda Airport in an attempt to stop him. The airport, which is built on reclaimed land, is connected to the Tokyo road system by a series of bridges. The aim of the demonstrators was to break through the police cordons which blocked these bridges, to occupy the airport and physically prevent the prime minister from embarking on the plane which was to carry him to South Vietnam.

The first Haneda demonstration was the beginning of the armed struggle. We were divided up into groups to fight for different bridges. *Chūkaku* was trying to break through one bridge, *Kakumaru* was trying for another and the smaller groups, including our party, were fighting for a third. But then the news came through that Yamazaki, a student from Kyoto University, had been killed by the police at Benten Bridge, so we all abandoned our separate targets and converged on Benten Bridge in a great single mass. First we gathered in front of the lines of police who were blocking the bridge, and began to hold an assembly to mourn our dead comrade. But before we had even finished the assembly the police started to fire tear-gas canisters at us, and we scattered.

It was from then that everyone started going to demonstrations armed. Mostly they carried heavy poles, because if you tie a flag or a placard on the end of the pole it becomes a political emblem, and the police cannot then arrest you for possessing an offensive weapon.

In September, when the police had entered Nihon University to arrest protesting students, one policeman had been struck on the head by a stone and killed. The government was rapidly reinforcing the weaponry and protective clothing of the riot police. In January 1968, when students gathered to protest at the arrival of the US aircraft carrier *Enterprise* in the port of Sasebo, even the onlookers who invariably crowded around the scene of any demonstration began to pelt the police with missiles. In March daily protests began outside a hospital used for treating US casualties from Vietnam, and the police adopted the simple expedient of arresting everyone on the scene. After massive nation-wide demonstrations on International Anti-War Day (21 October) the authorities, for the first time since the Korean War, used Japan's riot act, which was normally reserved for dealing with cases of gang warfare, to break up political protest.

We knew that what was happening was a revolt and not a revolution. But it was a revolt which was in no way comparable with the protests of 1960. This was something which went way beyond the comprehension of the established parties of the Old Left.

Our aim in the New Left was to lead the revolts forward into full-scale revolution. Everyone had their hopes fixed on 1970, the year when the Mutual Security Treaty with the United States would come up for renewal. If we could keep the momentum going until 1970, we believed that this would be the decisive point of the struggle.

Afterwards, Momo would look back on 1968 as the happiest year of his life. It was a time of endless activity: taking part in hundreds of demonstrations – at American bases, at universities, at the Japanese Self-Defence Force Headquarters – organizing other protests; writing articles and pamphlets; making speeches. For his small Communist Workers' Party a crucial source of finance came from their control of the Students' Committees at two of the occupied campuses: Osaka City University and Okayama University. Students' Union funds were channelled into whichever New Left group currently dominated the Committees, and Momo made frequent journeys to these Universities, not only to raise money for political agitation, but also to help organize the students, both those who belonged to his own Party and those of other, currently allied, groupings. It was here that Momo met two students whose names were later to become well-known in Japan: Tamiya Takamaro and Mori Tsuneo.

But, by the end of the year, the impetus of rebellion was beginning to weaken. The fissions within the movement were again deepening, and groups such as *Kakumaru* and *Chūkaku* were spending as much time fighting one another as fighting the police. Above all, despite a rebellion whose scale would previously have been unimaginable, the machinery of the Japanese establishment continued to function; industry went on turning out goods unchecked. Indeed, between 1967 and 1971 economic growth attained a new peak of 12.7 per cent a year. The flourishing economy was nourished in part by the detritus of the Vietnam War: in 1967 goods and services provided by Japanese companies to the US forces in Vietnam amounted to $55.8 million.

In 1969 the authorities launched their counter-offensive. The student-controlled campuses were recaptured, one by one. The first major stronghold to fall was Tokyo University, though here the students did not give up without a struggle. In the fight for the barricaded college buildings 8500 riot police, 700 armoured cars, three helicopters, four bulldozers and 4000 rounds of tear-gas were used and 631 students arrested. The Asahi newspaper described the scene in the University after the eviction of the students who had for the past half-year used it as their home and their political headquarters.

It looked like an empty building in the process of demolition . . . every room was filled with helmets, wooden poles, iron bars, mattresses, blankets, pots and pans, tins of food and packets of instant noodles.

On the second floor the rooms were full of milk bottles filled with petrol and with cotton-wool stoppers, all lined up ready to serve as petrol-bombs . . .[1]

On 13 November 1969, Prime Minister Satō left on a visit to the United States. There were widespread protests strikes, and we staged a big demonstration at Haneda Airport. As far as I was concerned that was the decisive battle, which would determine whether we could build up a successful movement to prevent the renewal of the Mutual Security Treaty. But we lost. The power of the police was simply too great, and we were militarily defeated. Something like two thousand people were arrested at that demonstration.

The following year a number of protests against the renewal of the Treaty were staged, but the energy of rebellion had already burnt itself out. The demonstrations were only a shadow of the great upsurges of 1960 and of the previous two years, and since neither the Japanese nor the American government raised any objections, the Treaty was automatically renewed for a further ten years.

Although in the end we failed, I felt that I was very lucky to have participated in the struggles of 1968.

Until that time it had seemed that, whether I was in the Communist Party or out of it, my views were always in the minority. In the early 1960s I had started on my own, working and working for what I believed, and I was just in time to see the realization of my theories in 1968. Of course the radical upsurge was mainly organized not by our Communist Workers' Party but by larger organizations like *Kakukyōdō* and *Bundo*. But still, it seems to me that many people work for the revolution for their whole lives without ever seeing any result. I was lucky enough to see, not the final harvest, but at least some kind of fruit of my labours. Once we accepted that the 1970 anti-Treaty movement had failed, we knew that there would be hard times ahead. But even though things were difficult, we had to go on organizing and preparing for the next struggle, which we believed might come in 1972, when American control of Okinawa was due to end, and the island was to be returned to Japan.

On 25 November 1970, we were holding a meeting of the Central Committee of the Communist Workers' Party in my flat in Musashino. A High-School student who belonged to our Party was supposed to be coming to the meeting, but he arrived rather late, and when he came in he said:

'Comrade Iida, Mishima Yukio and his followers have seized

control of the Japanese Self-Defence Headquarters, and they're trying to stage a *coup d'état*!'

I said: 'You must be joking!'

But when we turned on the television, sure enough, there were pictures of Mishima making some sort of speech to a crowd of soldiers. I could hardly believe my eyes.

Hiraoka Kimitake, alias Mishima Yukio, Momo's contemporary at Tokyo University, who had, like him, escaped conscription in the last years of the war, was by 1970 probably the most internationally famous of all Japanese novelists. His works such as *Confessions of a Mask, The Golden Pavilion* and *The Sailor Who Fell From Grace With The Sea* had received world-wide acclaim, and in 1968 he had been considered a serious candidate for the Nobel Prize for Literature. Mishima's writings had from the beginning contained a strongly nationalist flavour, but his nationalism remained at an essentially romantic and literary level until the 1960s, when he became increasingly obsessed with the fear of revolution and with the need to protect what he saw as the 'essence' of Japanese culture from the corruption of modern society. In the late 1960s the Japanese press gave widespread coverage to Mishima's political posturing: his impassioned debates with the left-wing students of Tokyo University, his cult of physical fitness, his hand-picked entourage of right-wing extremists, whom he named 'The Shield Society'. All of this, however, was generally laughed off as the harmless eccentricity of a man who, as a romantic nationalist in the predominantly left-wing environment of Japanese literary life, was in any case something of an oddity.

This attitude only heightened the impact of Mishima's action on that November day when, accompanied by four members of his 'Shield Society' and armed with a traditional Japanese sword, he went to the Self-Defence Force Headquarters, seized the commander-in-chief and demanded the right to address the troops. For several hours he harangued the soldiers, telling them that they must rise up and seize control of the government in order to protect the emperor and the nation from the menace of communism. Meanwhile, the television cameras which had quickly arrived on the scene relayed pictures of the spectacle to millions of incredulous viewers throughout the country.

Mishima was consciously trying to re-create the events of the

'February 26th Incident' of 1936, which he had sympathetically described in a short story entitled 'Patriotism'. But the men of the 1970s Self-Defence Force were very far removed from the peasant recruits who had formed the backbone of the pre-war imperial army. The young men whom Mishima now addressed were volunteers to a scientific military career. They responded to his appeals for a return of the *Samurai* tradition of their ancestors with alternating laughter and jeers.

Mishima's writings reveal a neurotic interest in the subject of suicide, and it is improbable that he expected his political adventure to end in any other way. After realizing the hopelessness of raising the Self-Defence Force to a nationalist rebellion, Mishima stepped back from the balcony where he had been standing during his speech into the room behind, and here he and one of his followers, in the traditional manner of dishonoured *Samurai*, disembowelled themselves with their swords.

As soon as the news of Mishima's suicide was broadcast, the phone in my flat started to ring and ring. It was people from the newspapers and magazines and television stations wanting me to comment on what had happened.

My immediate reaction was that it was quite bizarre that he should have chosen to do something like that in the autumn of 1970. If it had been two years earlier, at the height of the demonstrations, it would have been more comprehensible. But now, at the very moment when we had admitted defeat and everything was quiet, he had to go and launch a crusade to save the nation from communism. I thought the man must be a complete political idiot.

But all the same, I was very strongly aware of the fact that he was my exact contemporary. My friend Ishimoto at Tokyo University had known him well, and had kept in touch with him even after graduation. From Ishimoto I had heard how Mishima, like me, had avoided labour service during the war. And I knew, too, how he had avoided recruitment to the army. Later on he pretended that he had always wanted to serve in the army, and that they had sent him home because he was in poor health. But I think that was all nonsense. According to my experience no one who had received the Red Paper was ever sent home from the recruitment centres unless they specially claimed to be unfit for service. So I think that, like me and my friends, Mishima had taken that 'One Step Forward'.

Only there was one big difference between Mishima and me. I knew that I wanted to run away from the war, and I made that knowledge the basis on which I built my ideology. Because all true ideology must accept such facts, and not try to evade them.

But Mishima never accepted his fear of war and of death. Although his feet kept trying to run away, his head kept telling him that he *ought* to be brave, he *ought* to be patriotic. If you look at it in that way, it is quite easy to understand why he later went in for body-building and all kinds of masochistic physical activities, and why he came to believe in a form of right-wing stoicism. All of that was a way of punishing his body for its refusal to do what his ideology said it ought to do.

Mishima became rich and famous and successful, while I was poor and struggling. But in a way I still think that he had a harder life than me. At least my body and my mind were not divided, as his were. My head and my feet moved in the same direction.

So when the people from the media asked me for my reaction to Mishima's suicide, what I said was this – it's down in the record, and I wouldn't change it even if I could – I quoted the poem of Natsume Sōseki:

> Aru bakari
> Kiku nagerireyo
> Kan no naka

'As many chrysanthemums as you may have, lay them in his coffin.'

In 1968 Iida Toshifumi had suffered a stroke, and after the battles of the late 1960s were over Momo moved back to the house in Fujisawa to care for his helpless and bedridden father. By now Momo and Reiko had a second son, Kei, who was already a toddler. From 1971, the Iida family lived together in Fujisawa, while Momo continued his political work and his writing.

Those who had fought together in the uprisings of 1968 now took different paths. Many of the students went back to university and graduated, only a couple of years late, and still in time to find good posts in management or the civil service. Some drifted for a while before returning, by circuitous routes, to the bosom of the establishment. Just a few looked for new and still more defiant means to promote the revolution.

On 31 March 1970 a Japan Air Lines jet on an internal flight was seized by nine hijackers armed with an assortment of weapons ranging from dynamite to *Samurai* swords. After releasing passengers at Fukuoka and Seoul airports, the hijackers forced the crew to take them to Pyongyang in North Korea. The leader of the nine was Tamiya Takamaro, Momo's acquaintance from Osaka City University. The '*Samurai*-jack', as it became nicknamed, was the first occasion that the name of the Japanese Red Army hit the world headlines.

The International Section of the Japanese Red Army, whose aim was to create an overseas base for revolution, was responsible for the shooting of twenty-six people at Lod Airport in Israel in 1972, the raid on the French Embassy in the Hague in 1974, and the seizing of the US and Swedish Embassies in Kuala Lumpur in 1975.

Mori Tsuneo, whom Momo had known as a student at Okayama University, became a leading member of the Japan-based section, which had adopted the name of the United Red Army. Their strategy was to withdraw into the mountains, where they would establish guerrilla bases in preparation for a 'war' with the authorities, formally declared in January 1971. On 28 February 1972, after several arrests, police besieged the mountain chalet in which five members of the United Red Army had barricaded themselves. The ensuing gun-battle was televised live by most Japanese TV stations, which cancelled all other programmes apart from news bulletins until the siege ended with the arrest of the five Red Army members. At first, the guerrillas received considerable sympathy from many sections of the Japanese Left. But the sympathy rapidly turned to revulsion. For, holed up in their hideouts in the winter snows of 1971–72, the United Red Army leaders had become prey to some terrible paranoia. Of twenty-nine young men and women who had joined their ranks in December 1971, it was found that twelve had been 'executed' by their comrades for lack of revolutionary spirit. Mori, who was among those arrested, committed suicide soon after. The trial of the remainder of United Red Army was still continuing, ten years after the event.

The people who joined the United Red Army were making the same mistake as the Mountain Village Guerrillas of the 1950s. They thought they could copy the Chinese Revolution. But Japan is not like that. It is a little island country. There is no room in Japan for Long Marches.

As for the International Section of the Japanese Red Army, I can understand why they have chosen their path. Sometimes it is hard to build a revolutionary movement at home, and it is tempting to look for bases in other parts of the world. But in the end I think that their activities are just escapism. However difficult it may be to make a revolution in Japan, you still have to stay here and try, because once you leave Japan you become cut off from the Japanese masses, just as the communist leaders did in their exile before the war.

To continue the struggle within Japan was indeed hard. The reversion of Okinawa in 1972 did not provide the spark for any repeat of the events of 1967–68. Momo, however, neither abandoned the struggle nor looked for a new strategy, but went on as before writing, organizing the activities of the Communist Workers' Party, editing radical publications, entertaining visitors from left-wing organization overseas, and always looking out for signs of a new stirring of revolutionary currents in Japanese society.

Momo's two sons are growing up: one now at Middle School, the other at High School. Although he abhors the Japanese school system, and fears a rightward trend in educational values, Momo nevertheless sends his boys to ordinary state schools, believing that their education should be no different from that of other children.

I never discuss politics with my sons. As far as I am concerned, once they are grown up they may believe whatever they like and choose whatever career they like. At the moment, they don't seem to be greatly interested in politics. My elder boy likes mountaineering, and the little one likes soccer and has just started learning tennis. I don't have very much time to spend with my family, really. I've never taken a holiday in my life, and I don't suppose I ever will.

Mostly, my wife looks after the children and deals with their education. I suppose you could say that it contradicts my revolutionary views to leave my wife to do the housework. But the fact is that in practice it is just impossible to be a professional revolutionary and look after a household as well. It may be hypocritical, but that's just the way things work.

In 1980, Iida Toshifumi died. On the day of a death in Japan all the relatives and friends gather in the house to comfort the bereaved and to recall the life and the achievements of the person who has died. So Momo heard again many half-forgotten stories from his childhood, and revived the memories of his father's ascent from poverty to wealth.

1980 also was the twentieth anniversary of the signing of the Mutual Security Treaty between the United States and Japan, and the year in which the Treaty was renewed for the second time. In 1960, hundreds of thousands had marched through Tokyo to oppose the signing of the Treaty. By 1970, the number had fallen to a few thousand. In 1980, the demonstrators against the second renewal were numbered only in hundreds.

Once upon a time, in a certain village (runs the best-loved of Japanese fairy stories) there lived an old man and an old woman. One day the old man had gone to the mountain to gather firewood, and the old woman had gone to the stream to wash the clothes. While she was washing, tumbling down in the current of water came the biggest peach she had ever seen in her life. The woman caught the peach and took it home to her husband for their supper, but when they cut the peach open, instead of a stone, they found a baby boy curled up inside. The old man and the old woman were filled with joy, because they had no children. They named the child Momotarō (Peach Boy) because he was born from a peach, and they brought him up like their own son.

Now it happened that, in the region where the old couple lived, there was an island inhabited by marauding ogres, who often used to come to the shore and ravage the countryside round about. When Momotarō had grown into a sturdy young man, one day he said to the old man and the old woman: 'I thank you for taking care of me so well, but now I must leave you, for I am going to destroy the wicked ogres of Ogre Island'.

His foster-parents pleaded with Momotarō not to go on this dangerous journey, but his mind was made up. So the old man gave him a shining sword, and the old woman gave him a bag of dumplings, and he set off on the road towards Ogre Island.

On the way, Momotarō saw a monkey picking fruit in a tree. 'Come with me,' said Momotarō, 'for I am going to fight the wicked ogres of Ogre Island.' And he threw the monkey one of his dumplings, and the monkey followed him.

A little further along the road they met a wild goose.

'Come with us,' said Momotarō 'for we are going to fight the wicked ogres of Ogre Island.' He gave the goose a dumpling, and the goose also went with them.

They had not gone many miles more when they met a dog.

'Come with us,' said Momotarō, 'for we are going to fight the wicked ogres of Ogre Island.' He gave a dumpling to the dog too, and the dog also followed him.

The four friends went together along the road towards Ogre Island. After many hardships and adventures they found a boat and sailed to the island. The ogres were taken by surprise. Momotarō fell upon them with his sword, the monkey pulled their hair, the wild goose pecked their eyes and the dog bit their shins. Soon all the wicked ogres were killed. On the island Momotarō found hoards of treasure which the ogres had accumulated by plundering the people of that district. He took the treasure back to the old man and the old woman, and they all lived happily ever after.

A little while ago I read a book of reminiscences, in which the author described how she first told the story of Momotarō to her younger sister. When she reached the end of the story, her sister suddenly burst into tears.

'What's wrong?' asked the author.

'Oh, the poor ogres, the poor ogres!' sobbed the little girl.

That story impressed me very deeply. I felt that it is wonderful for a child to have such sensitivity that she could feel sorry for the ogres. But at the same time I also felt that someone as sensitive as that could never survive in the real, hard world. And when I read further in the book I found that, in fact, the little sister had died young.

When I think about my sons and how I should like them to grow up, in a way I feel that I should like them to have that sort of perceptiveness and feeling, so that they too would be able to weep for the ogres. But then when I think about the realities of the world, and the struggles which will come when they are older, I think, if they have such sensitivity, how will they manage, how will they survive?

15

Epilogue

By the late fifties of the Shōwa Age Japan had at last attained the goal whose pursuit ran like a theme through the policies of all her governments from the Meiji Restoration onwards: the goal of an assured place in the ranks of the richest and most advanced industrialized nations. By 1980 Japan's Gross National Product was second only to that of the United States. In areas of advanced technology such as the production of industrial robots, Japan led the world – it is forecast that by the end of the century the country will have one robot for every ten human beings.

From the early 1970s onwards, Japan has begun to receive a constant stream of Western visitors – businessmen, bureaucrats, academics – all seeking the elusive formula of industrial success, just as Japan's leaders had sought it in the West during the last decades of the nineteenth century: and all confronted, just as Japan's leaders had once been, with the difficulty of distinguishing the cultural icing from the economic cake.

Those whose lives have spanned the Shōwa Age can perceive the benefits of economic success, visible and tangible in every aspect of their lives: even in the physical stature of their own children. Fourteen-year-old Japanese schoolboys in the late 1970s were on average nine centimetres taller than their counterparts twenty years earlier. The three people whose experiences we have followed in this book were born at a time when the average life expectancy of a Japanese child at birth was less than forty-five years. Japanese girl-children born in the year Shōwa fifty have an average life expectancy of seventy-seven.

Not one of these three people would question the fact that the life of today's children is happier than the childhood of their own generation. As Saitō Mutsuo put it:

317

Some things I think have been lost, above all the sense of lasting human relationships which used to be so strong when I was young. Nowadays friendships seem to be more shallow – they are strong while there is some mutual benefit involved, but after that they just dissolve.

But of course on the whole young people are happier now, not only because they are materially better off, but in other ways too. They have more freedom. They can do what they like. Most important of all, they are growing up in a country which is at peace. When I was young, there was always war going on. We were constantly aware in the back of our minds of the atmosphere of war. It must be a great thing to grow up in peacetime.

But as Iida Momo's comments suggest, a certain unease underlies the awareness of greater prosperity.

In my lifetime we have change from being a society where most people didn't get enough to eat to being one where many people have *too* much to eat. Moralists may say that it's a bad thing to have too much, but, in the end, it's surely better than having too little.

At the same time, I still feel that there is something phoney about this prosperity. For people of my generation, it's impossible to forget the cost at which it has been achieved.

A couple of weeks before Prince Hiro's graduation, two plane-loads of people arrived in Japan from the People's Republic of China. These people – sixty in all – were just a small fraction of the thousand or more children, remnants of the once large and powerful Japanese communities in mainland Asia, who were orphaned or left behind by their parents in the massive and chaotic exodus which came with the end of the Pacific War.

After thirty-five years of separation these children, grown to middle age, are beginning to return, looking for lost families and for a home – an imaginary Japan which they have created from half-remembered fairy tales and patriotic boasts of homesick adults. Most now speak no Japanese at all, and it is perhaps surprising that, after so long an interval, forty-two of the sixty succeeded in tracing surviving relatives, and chose to remain with them in Japan. Now, with difficulty, they must begin the gradual adaptation to a life utterly remote both from their adult experiences in China and from their fractured child-

hood images of Japan. Many, no doubt, will achieve a momentary
fame and prosperity by selling their stories to the press and
television.

The other eighteen members of the group, having found no
families, nor anything to persuade them to remain, returned to
China to continue their existence in the shadows of history: forgotten
fragments left behind by the political cataclysms of the Shōwa Age.

As one of them waited to board his flight at Tokyo International
Airport he was approached by a journalist and asked for his
impressions of his visit.

Since I could not find my relatives in Japan I have no special
impression about this country,' he said, 'I have nothing to talk
about further.'

Notes

Chapter 1

1 This description of the death and funeral of the Emperor Taishō is based on accounts published in the *Japan Weekly Chronicle*, 30 December 1926; 6, 13 and 27 January 1927; and 10 and 17 February 1927.
2 *Japan Weekly Chronicle*, 2 September 1926.
3 *Ibid.*, 6 January 1927.
4 *Ibid.*, 27 January 1927.
5 Saburo Ienaga, *Japan's Last War* (Oxford, Basil Blackwell).

PART I

Chapter 2

1 Otis Manchester Poole, *The Death of Old Yokohama* (London, Allen & Unwin, 1968), p.37.
2 The first twenty-eight emperors are now regarded as being mythical, and contemporary Japanese history books normally start from the Emperor Kimmei in the 6th century AD. Pre-war text-books, however, treated all 124 as real historical figures.
3 Report of the Lytton Commission, reprinted in *Documents on International Affairs*, 1932. (Royal Institute of International Affairs, London), p.321.
4 Elizabeth Green, 'Progress of the Manchurian Disease', *Pacific Affairs*, January 1932, pp. 53–54.
5 Memorandum by US Assistant Military Attaché in Japan, reprinted in *Foreign Relations of the United States 1932* (US Department of State 1948), p.713.

6 Quoted in L. Allen, *Japan: The Years of Triumph* (London, Macdonald, 1971), p. 92.
7 Released under the English title *One Hundred Men and a Girl*, and starring Deanna Durban, this film enjoyed immense popularity in Japan in the late 1930s.
8 *Japan Weekly Chronicle*, 16 December 1937.

Chapter 3

1 Quoted in Joseph C. Grew, *Ten Years in Japan* (London, Hammond, Hammond & Co., 1944), pp. 49–50.
2 Kita Ikki, quoted in George M. Wilson, *Radical Nationalist in Japan: Kita Ikki, 1883–1937* (Cambridge, Mass., Harvard University Press, 1969), p. 86.
3 Translated in Ryusaku Tsunoda, Wm. Theodore de Bary and Donald Keene (eds), *Sources of Japanese Tradition*, Vol. II, NY and London (Columbia University Press, 1958), pp. 139–40.
4 One sen = one hundredth of a yen. In the values of the mid-1930s there were about 4 yen to the US dollar.
5 *Nihon Shoki*, Tr. W. G. Aston, quoted in Tsunoda, de Bary and Keene, *op. cit.* Vol. I, pp. 27–28.
6 Grew, *op.cit.*, pp. 304–05.

Chapter 4

1 W. H. Chamberlin, *Japan Over Asia* (London, Duckworth, 1938), p.212.
2 Quoted in Chamberlin, *op.cit.*, pp. 212–13.
3 Grew, *op.cit.*, p.133.
4 Quoted in *ibid.*, p. 213.
5 *New York Times*, 31 July 1938.
6 *Asahi Shimbun*, 4 August 1940.
7 Asano Ryozo, quoted in *Japan Times Weekly*, 15 June 1939.
8 *Ibid.*, 29 May 1941.
9 Quoted in Grew, *op.cit.*, p. 415.

PART II

Chapter 5

1 The attack on Pearl Harbor took place on the morning of Monday, 8 December, Japanese time, but on Sunday, 7 December, US time.

2 Tsutsui Chihirō, 'Our Southern Reconstruction Policy', *Contemporary Japan*, December 1942, p. 1746.

3 Fukuzawa Yūkichi, *The Autobiography of Fukuzawa Yūkichi*, Tr. Kiyooka Eiichi (Tokyo, Hokusei-do, 1937).

4 Koizumi Shinzō, *Kaigun Shukei Tai-i Koizumi Shinkichi* (Tokyo, Bunshun Bunko, 1975), pp. 67–68.

5 *Yuima-Kyo* (Vimalakirti Sutra), quoted in Tsunoda, de Bary and Keene, *Sources of Japanese Tradition*, Vol. I, pp. 104–05.

6 Irokawa Daikichi, in Todai Juppachi-kai (ed.), *Gakuto Shutsujin no Kiroku* (Tokyo, Chukō Shinsho, 1978), pp. 71–77.

7 'Gendai-Shi o Tsukuru Hitobito: Niizeki Yasatarō', *Ekonomisuto*, 1 February 1972, p. 86.

8 Chie Nakane, *Japanese Society* (Penguin Books, 1973), p. 134.

9 'Tokkō Ikinokori 32-nen-me no Shōgen', *Bungei Shunjū*, September 1977, p. 308.

10 Quoted in Nihon Senbotsu Gakusei Kinen-Kai (ed.), *Kike Wadatsumi no Koe* (2nd edition) (Tokyo, Kappa Books, 1974), pp. 13–14.

Chapter 6

1 *Taishō Jūgo-nen Umare* (Tokyo, Kawade Shobō, 1980), p. 80.

2 *Asahi Shimbun*, 13 August 1941.

3 *Ibid.*, 9 July 1942.

4 Minobe Tatsukichi was a professor at Tokyo Imperial University who, in the late Meiji period, advanced the theory that the emperor is an organ of state whose role is to represent the unity of the nation and endorse the acts of government. This theory was the focus of bitter attacks by Japanese nationalists from 1935 onwards, and Minobe was forced into retirement and disgrace.

5 *Asahi Shimbun*, 5 December 1943.

6 *Ibid.*, 23 August 1944.

Chapter 7

1 The Red Cross ship *Awamaru* was sunk by American submarines off Taiwan on 1 April 1945, with the loss of 2003 lives.

2 Mishima Yukio, *Confessions of a Mask*, tr. Meredith Weatherby (London, Panther Books, 1972), p. 114.

3 *The Histories of Herodotus* (Vol. I), tr. G. Rawlinson (London and New York, Dent Dutton, 1964), pp. 15–16.

Chapter 8

1 Quoted in Leonard Mosley, *Hirohito: Emperor of Japan* (London, Weidenfeld & Nicolson), pp. 335–56.

PART III

1 Quoted in J. Nathan, *Mishima: A Biography* (London, Hamish Hamilton, 1975), p. 70.

Chapter 9

1 'Basic Initial Post-Surrender Directive', quoted in J. Livingston, J. Moore and F. Oldfather (eds), *The Japan Reader*, Vol. II (Penguin Books, 1976), p.9.
2 *Asahi Shimbun*, 23 July 1947.
3 Hirota Kōki (1876–1948) – a career diplomat who became Foreign Minister and briefly Prime Minister in the 1930s, and was Japanese Ambassador to Thailand during the war.
4 'National Security Council Memorandum', in Livingston, Moore and Oldfather, *op.cit.*, p. 224.
5 *Asahi Shimbun*, 25 May 1957.

Chapter 10

1 Fukuhara Rintarō, 'Women, Gods and Letters', *Japan Quarterly*, Vol. I, No. 1, October–December 1964, p. 88.
2 Quoted in Matsuoka Yoko, 'A Column for Women', *Japan Quarterly*, Vol. I, No. 1, October–December 1954, p. 117.
3 Romain Rolland, *Vie de Beethoven* (Paris, Librairie Hachette, 1944), p.14.
4 Dazai Osamu (1909–48) – one of the most influential figures in the literary life of Japan immediately after the Pacific War. Together with his mistress, he committed suicide by drowning.

Chapter 11

1 'Basic Initial Post-Surrender Directive', in Livingston, Moore and Oldfather (eds), *op.cit.*, p. 11.
2 Miriam Farley, *Aspects of Japan's Labor Problems* (New York, Institute of Pacific Relations, 1950), p. 66.
3 Arisawa Hiromi (ed.), *Shōwa Keizai-Shi* (Vol. II) (Tokyo, Nikkei Shinsho, 1980), p. 31.
4 *Nihon Kyōsantō no Gojū-nen* (Tokyo, Nihon Kyōsantō Chūō Iinkai Shuppankyoku, 1978), p. 146.
5 Hidaka Rokurō, quoted in George R. Packard III, *Protest in Tokyo* (Princeton, NJ, Princeton University Press, 1966), p. 237.

Chapter 12

1 M. Reich and N. Huddle, *Island of Dreams: Environmental Crisis in Japan* (New York and London, Autumn Press, 1975), p. 59.
2 *Japan Information Bulletin*, 1970, pp. 64–65.
3 *Ibid.*, pp. 159–61.
4 Uzawa Hirofumi, quoted in Miyoshi Shūichi, 'Dollar Crisis', *Japan Quarterly*, January–March 1972, p. 30.
5 *Nihon Keizai Shimbun*, 13 December 1973.
6 Imazu Hiroshi, 'Power Mosaic: Hotbed of the Lockheed Case', *Japan Quarterly*, July–September 1976, p. 2238.
7 *Asahi Shimbun*, 2 March 1976.

Chapter 13

1 S.A. Broadbridge, *Industrial Dualism in Japan* (London, Frank Cass, 1966), p. 50.
2 H. Hesse, *My Belief: Essays on Life and Art* (London, Jonathan Cape, 1976), pp. 63–64.

Chapter 14

1 *Asahi Shimbun*, 21 January 1969.

Glossary of Japanese Terms

Akatonbo (lit. 'Dragonfly')	light training aircraft used by wartime Japanese air forces
butsudan ('Buddha shelf')	small Buddhist altar commonly found in Japanese houses
burakumin	oppressed social minority descended from the 'outcasts' of pre-Meiji Japan
fundoshi	loin-cloth
furoshiki	large square of material used for carrying parcels
futon	sleeping mat
hikiagesha ('returnees')	i.e. Japanese emigrants to other parts of Asia who were repatriated at the end of the Pacific War
kabuki	form of Japanese theatrical performance which originated in the seventeenth century
kami	god
kamidana ('God shelf')	household Shintō altar
kamishibai ('paper play')	traditional form of entertainment in which a travelling storyteller illustrates his stories with a series of brightly coloured picture cards
kana	Japanese phonetic characters
kanji	Chinese/Japanese ideogram characters
keibōdan (abbr.)	Wartime Civil Defence force

kendō	form of martial art in which two contestants engage in combat armed with long bamboo poles
kokuminfuku	uniform-like costume widely worn by Japanese civilians during the Pacific War
kokutai (lit. 'national body').	a term commonly used by pre-war nationalists when referring to the Japanese nation
kombinato	an industrial estate containing a complex of interrelated heavy industries
koseki	family register
kuni	country, nation
mompe	loose trousers worn by women
nattō	fermented soy beans
nō	Japanese classical drama
omiai	arranged meeting of prospective marriage partners
sake	rice wine
Sanbetsu (abbr.)	left-wing national union movement, formed in 1946 and dissolved in 1958.
shōgi	Japanese chess
Sōhyō (abbr.)	national trade-union organization, formed in 1950
sumō	traditional form of Japanese wrestling
sushi	Japanese dish of vinegared rice with fish, egg or vegetables
Taisei Yokusankai ('Imperial Rule Assistance Association')	national organization formed to replace political parties in 1940
tanka	thirty-one-syllable poem
tatami	straw matting commonly used on the floor of Japanese houses

tokkōtai ('Special Attack Squad')	wartime suicide squadron
Tonarigumi ('neighbourhood groups')	local organizations created in pre-war Japan to circulate government directives and strengthen state control of society
utai	form of singing used to accompany *nō* theatre performances
yakuza	gangsters
yobikō	crammer school preparing students for High School or university entrance examinations
zaibatsu (lit. 'financial clique')	integrated, hierarchically structured industrial and financial combine
Zengakuren (abbr.)	Radical student organization formed in 1948

Index

Abe Sada, 83–4
Aikoku Fujinkai (Patriotic
  Women's League), 55, 63, 90
Akihito, Prince, 23, 46, 78, 201,
  213, 236, 283
Akutagawa Ryūnosuke, 87, 284
Ampo Treaty, 214, 239, 266–71,
  307, 309, 315
Axis Pact, 39–40

Baseball, 81–2, 103
Black market, 136, 161, 163, 200,
  203, 205, 241, 263
Burakumin, 64, 259

China, invasion of (*see also* Nanking,
  invasion of), 30–1, 51, 54, 58, 87,
  88–90, 92–4
Chūkaku Faction, 265, 306, 308
Communist Party, 6, 165–7, 244,
  251, 252, 254, 255–65, 269–70,
  271, 300–2, 309
Constitution, Maiji, 103; post-war,
  202–3, 219–20

Dazai Osamu, 232, 284
Democratic Party (*see also* Liberal
  Democratic Party), 257

Education, pre-war system, 17–18,
  24–5, 29, 31–2, 37–8, 40, 48–9,
  53–4, 58, 62, 73, 75, 84–5;
  post-war system, 201, 314;
  Imperial Rescript on, 18, 26,
  47–8, 75–6

February 26 Incident (1936), 28–9,
  77–9

Great Kantō Earthquake, 4, 15–16,
  70
Guadalcanal, Battle of, 106–7, 149

Hayashi Kentarō, 306
Hirohito, Emperor, 3, 7, 17, 84,
  112, 115, 133, 184–9, 197–9, 220,
  228, 240, 283
Hiroshima, atomic bombing of, 139,
  182
Hirota Kōki, 206

Ienaga Saburō, 9
Ikeda Hayato, 271
Imperial Rule Assistance
  Association, *see* Taisei
  Yokusankai
Indo-China, invasion of, 93

Japanese Red Army, 265–6, 313–14

Kakumaru Faction, 265, 306, 308
Kamishibai, 54, 246
Kishi Nobusuke, 206, 267, 268, 271
Konoe Fuminaro, 31, 94, 103
Korea, Japanese colonial rule of,
  42–3, 44–5, 46, 51, 57–8
Korean War, 153, 206–7, 208, 251,
  259, 262, 263, 286, 307

Liberal Democratic Party (*see also*
  Liberal Party, Democratic Party),
  261, 263, 267, 271, 288–9, 303

329